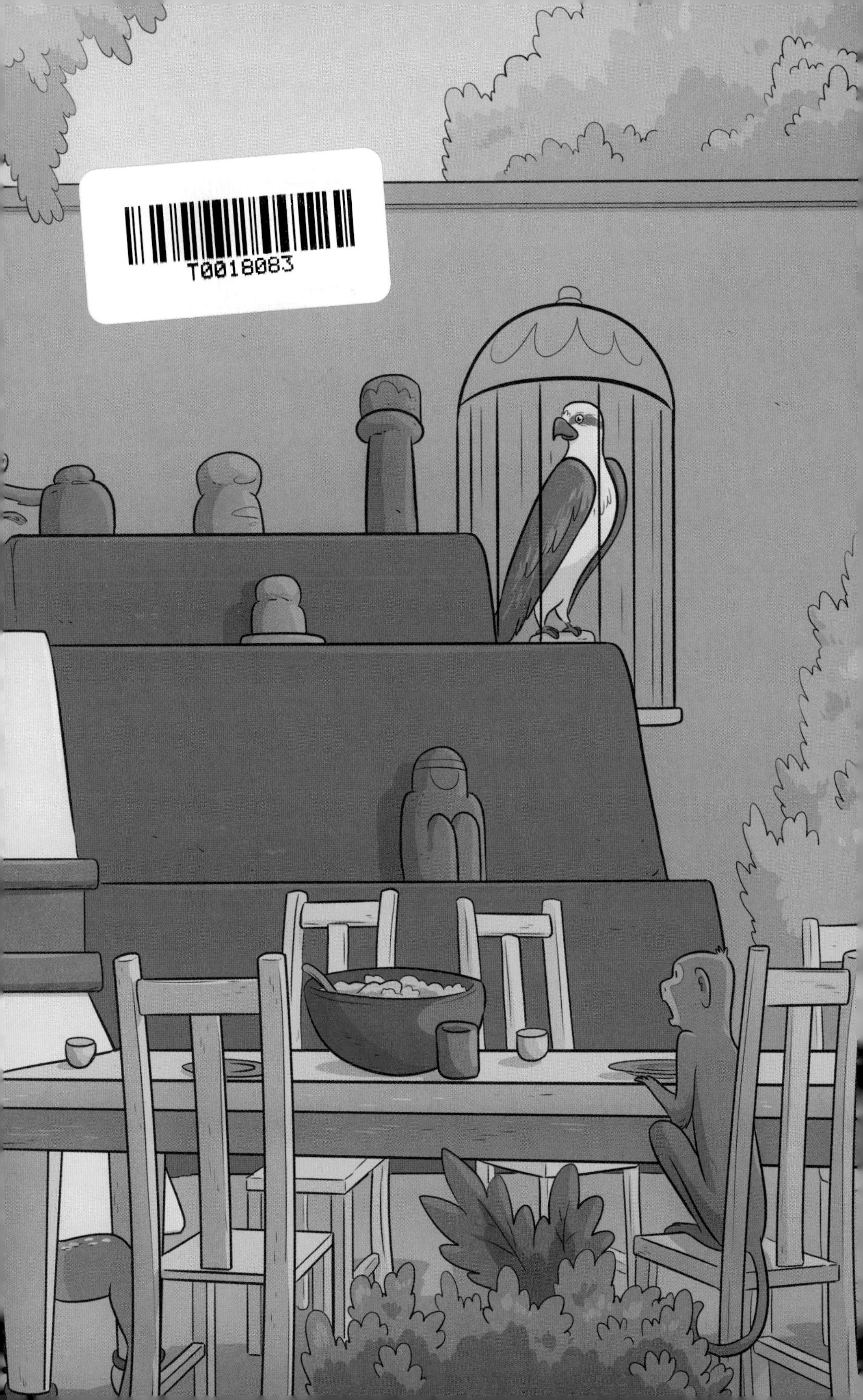

SHOW ME HISTORY! ™

FRIDA KAHLO

The REVOLUTIONARY PAINTER!

BY
JAMES BUCKLEY JR.

ILLUSTRATED BY
CASSIE ANDERSON

LETTERING & DESIGN BY
SWELL TYPE

COVER ART BY
IAN CHURCHILL

PORTABLE
PRESS

SAN DIEGO, CALIFORNIA

Portable Press
An imprint of Printers Row Publishing Group
9717 Pacific Heights Blvd, San Diego, CA 92121
www.portablepress.com • mail@portablepress.com

Printers Row Publishing Group is a division of Readerlink Distribution Services, LLC. Portable Press is a registered trademark of Readerlink Distribution Services, LLC.

Correspondence regarding the content of this book should be sent to Portable Press, Editorial Department, at the above address. Author and illustrator inquiries should be sent to Oomf, Inc., www.oomf.com.

Portable Press
Publisher: Peter Norton • Associate Publisher: Ana Parker
Art Director: Charles McStravick
Senior Developmental Editor: April Graham Farr
Editor: Angela Garcia
Production Team: Julie Greene, Rusty von Dyl

Produced by Oomf, Inc., www.Oomf.com
Director: Mark Shulman
Producer: James Buckley Jr.

Author: James Buckley Jr.
Illustrator: Cassie Anderson
Assistant Editor: Michael Centore
Lettering & design by Swell Type: John Roshell, Forest Dempsey, Sarah Jacobs, Drewes McFarling, Miles Gaushell
Cover illustrator: Ian Churchill

Library of Congress Control Number: 2021932484

ISBN: 978-1-64517-433-2

Printed in China

25 24 23 22 21   1 2 3 4 5

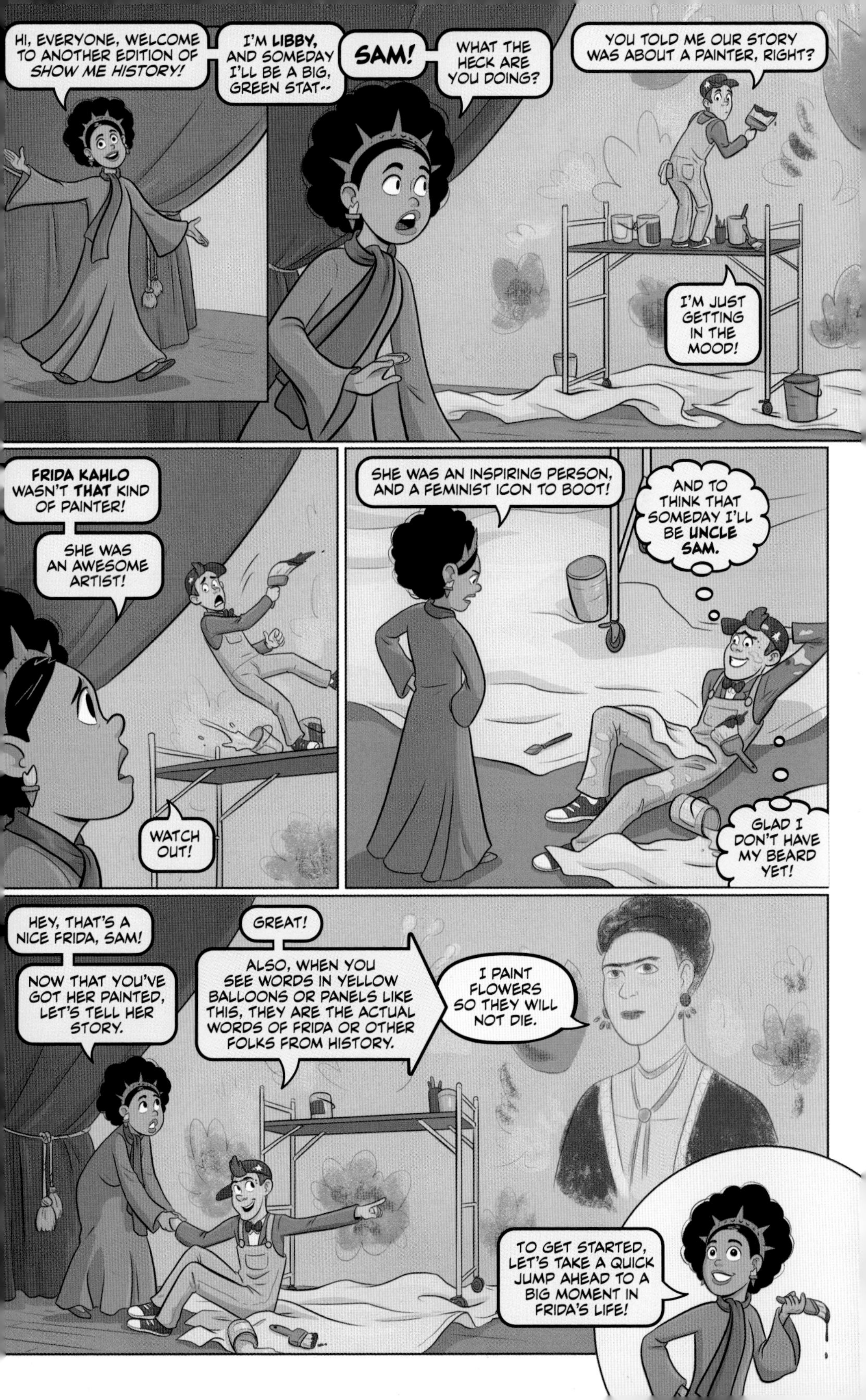

HI, EVERYONE, WELCOME TO ANOTHER EDITION OF *SHOW ME HISTORY!*
I'M **LIBBY,** AND SOMEDAY I'LL BE A BIG, GREEN STAT--
SAM!
WHAT THE HECK ARE YOU DOING?
YOU TOLD ME OUR STORY WAS ABOUT A PAINTER, RIGHT?
I'M JUST GETTING IN THE MOOD!
FRIDA KAHLO WASN'T **THAT** KIND OF PAINTER!
SHE WAS AN AWESOME ARTIST!
WATCH OUT!
SHE WAS AN INSPIRING PERSON, AND A FEMINIST ICON TO BOOT!
AND TO THINK THAT SOMEDAY I'LL BE **UNCLE SAM.**
GLAD I DON'T HAVE MY BEARD YET!
HEY, THAT'S A NICE FRIDA, SAM!
NOW THAT YOU'VE GOT HER PAINTED, LET'S TELL HER STORY.
GREAT!
ALSO, WHEN YOU SEE WORDS IN YELLOW BALLOONS OR PANELS LIKE THIS, THEY ARE THE ACTUAL WORDS OF FRIDA OR OTHER FOLKS FROM HISTORY.
I PAINT FLOWERS SO THEY WILL NOT DIE.
TO GET STARTED, LET'S TAKE A QUICK JUMP AHEAD TO A BIG MOMENT IN FRIDA'S LIFE!

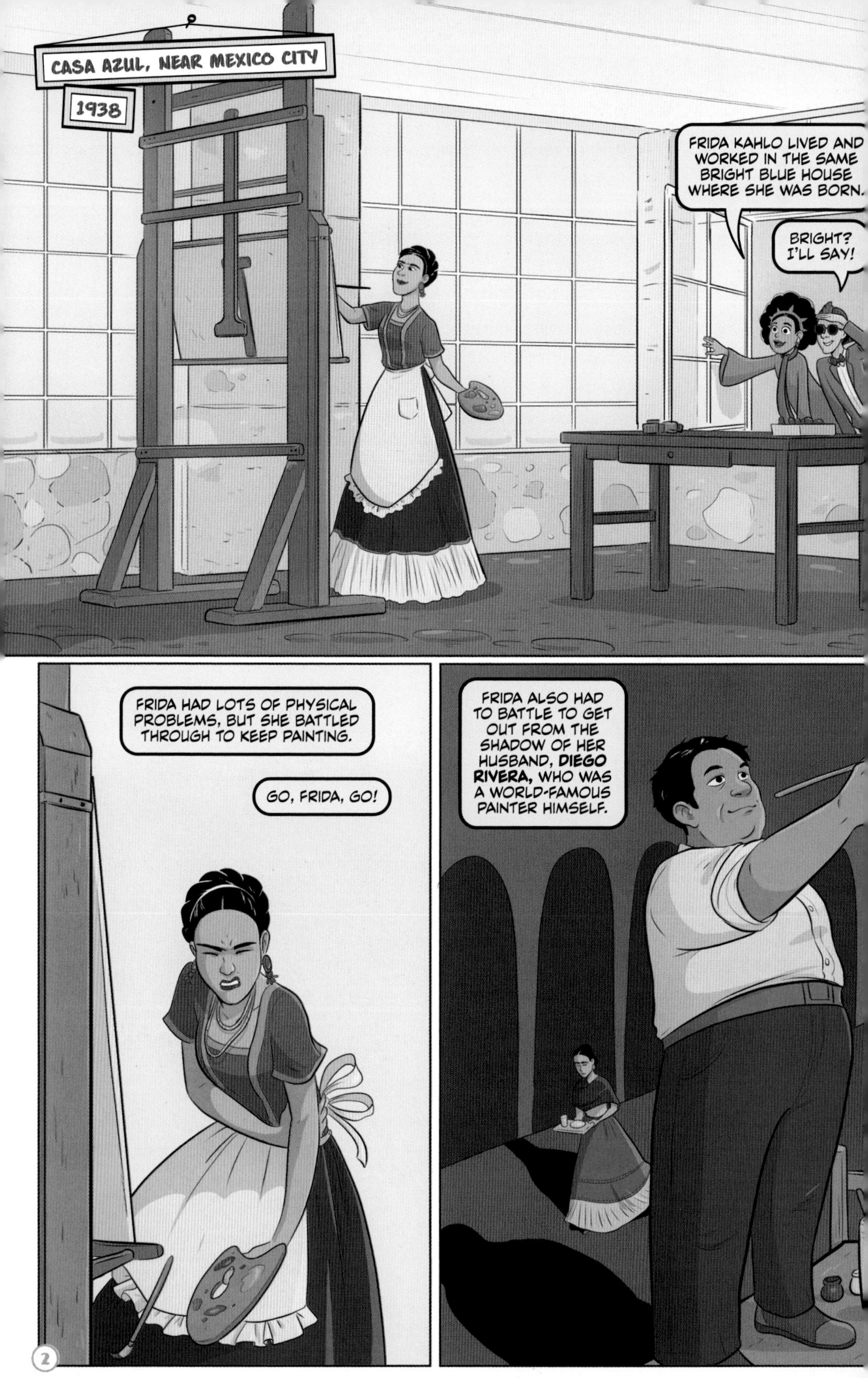

CASA AZUL, NEAR MEXICO CITY
1938
FRIDA KAHLO LIVED AND WORKED IN THE SAME BRIGHT BLUE HOUSE WHERE SHE WAS BORN.
BRIGHT? I'LL SAY!
FRIDA HAD LOTS OF PHYSICAL PROBLEMS, BUT SHE BATTLED THROUGH TO KEEP PAINTING.
GO, FRIDA, GO!
FRIDA ALSO HAD TO BATTLE TO GET OUT FROM THE SHADOW OF HER HUSBAND, **DIEGO RIVERA,** WHO WAS A WORLD-FAMOUS PAINTER HIMSELF.

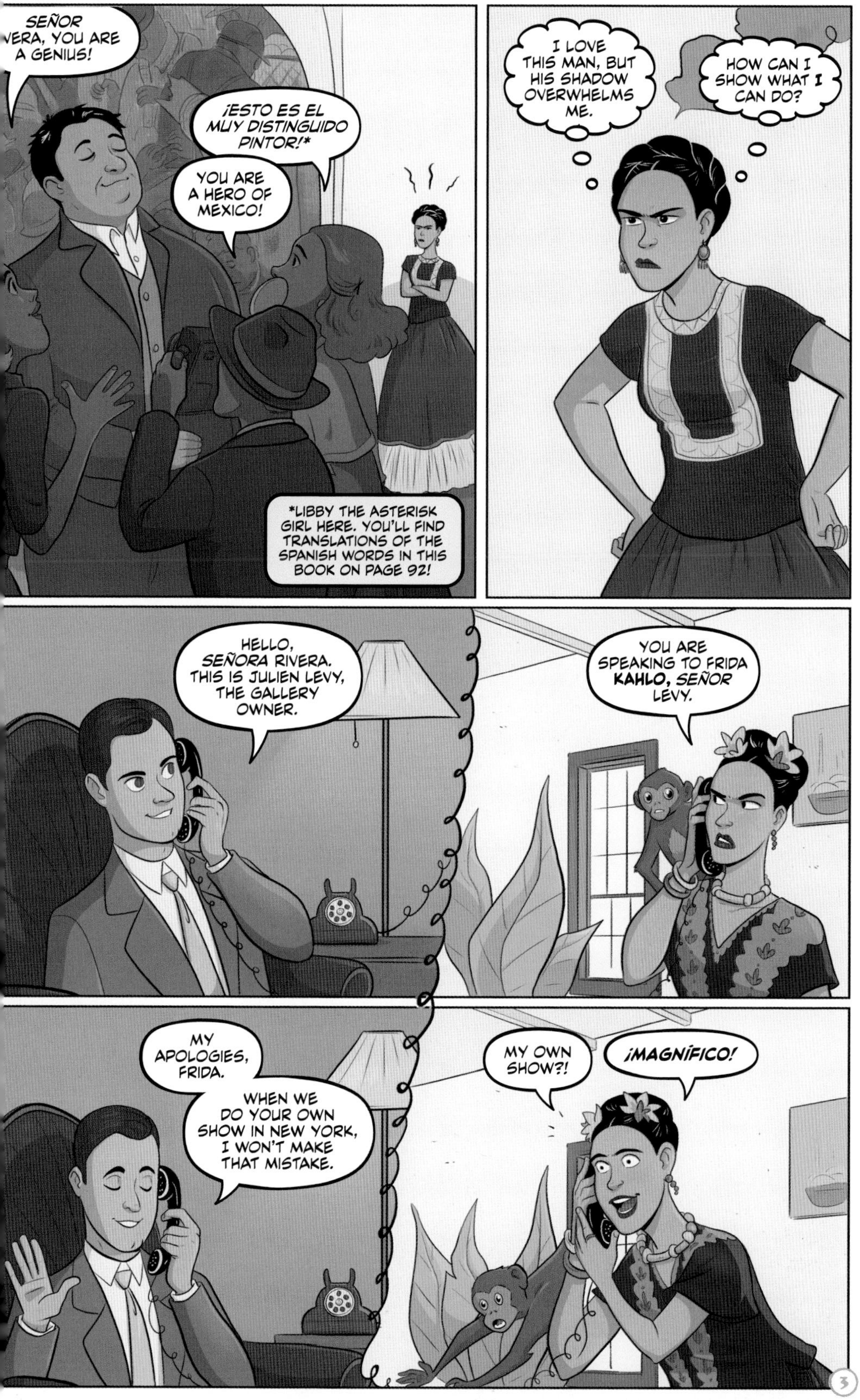
SEÑOR
VERA, YOU ARE A GENIUS!
¡ESTO ES EL MUY DISTINGUIDO PINTOR!*
YOU ARE A HERO OF MEXICO!
*LIBBY THE ASTERISK GIRL HERE. YOU'LL FIND TRANSLATIONS OF THE SPANISH WORDS IN THIS BOOK ON PAGE 92!
I LOVE THIS MAN, BUT HIS SHADOW OVERWHELMS ME.
HOW CAN I SHOW WHAT I CAN DO?
HELLO, SEÑORA RIVERA. THIS IS JULIEN LEVY, THE GALLERY OWNER.
YOU ARE SPEAKING TO FRIDA KAHLO, SEÑOR LEVY.
MY APOLOGIES, FRIDA.
WHEN WE DO YOUR OWN SHOW IN NEW YORK, I WON'T MAKE THAT MISTAKE.
MY OWN SHOW?!
¡MAGNÍFICO!

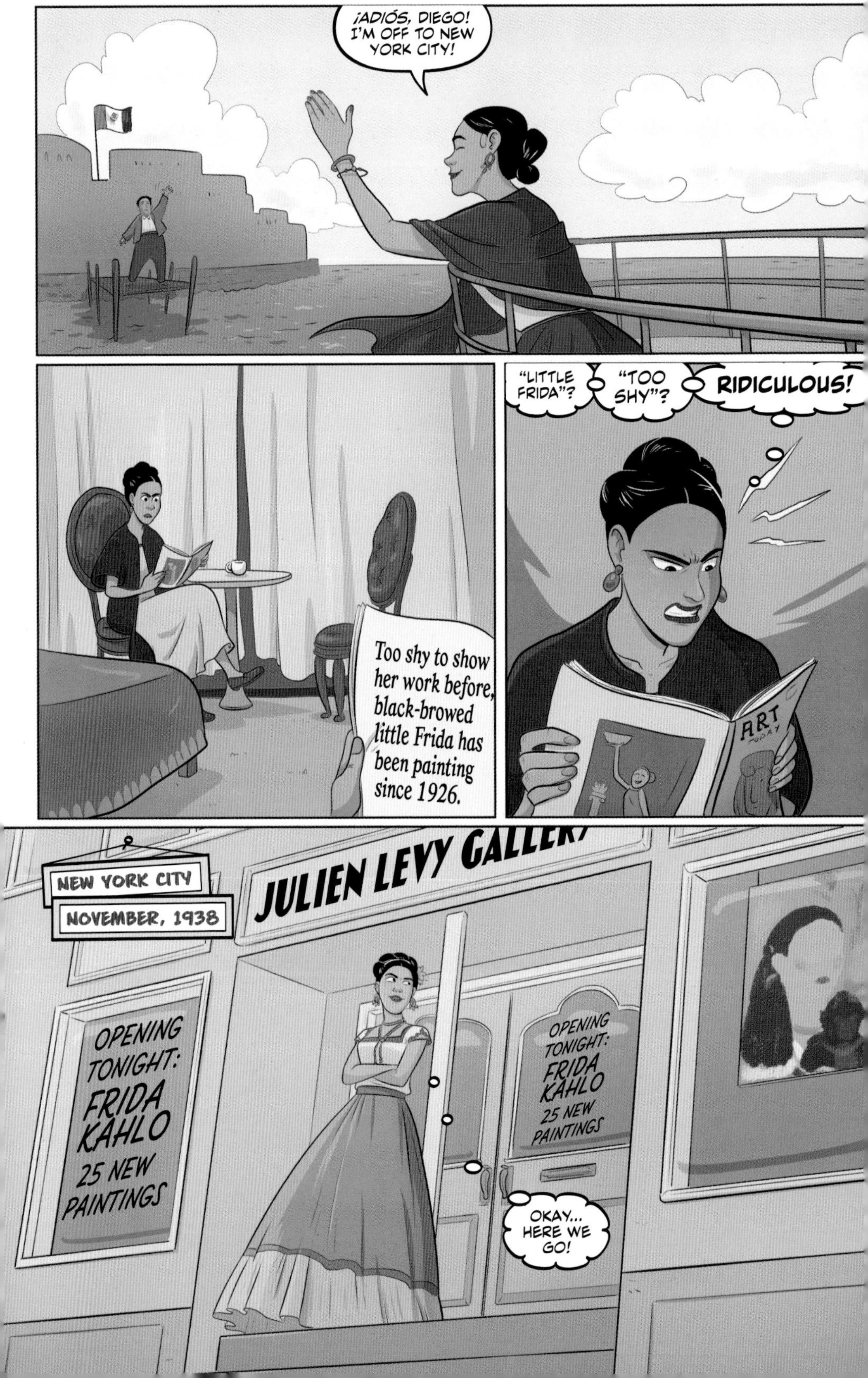
¡ADIÓS, DIEGO! I'M OFF TO NEW YORK CITY!
Too shy to show her work before, black-browed little Frida has been painting since 1926.
"LITTLE FRIDA"?
"TOO SHY"?
RIDICULOUS!
ART TODAY
NEW YORK CITY
NOVEMBER, 1938
JULIEN LEVY GALLER
OPENING TONIGHT: FRIDA KAHLO 25 NEW PAINTINGS
OPENING TONIGHT: FRIDA KAHLO 25 NEW PAINTINGS
OKAY... HERE WE GO!

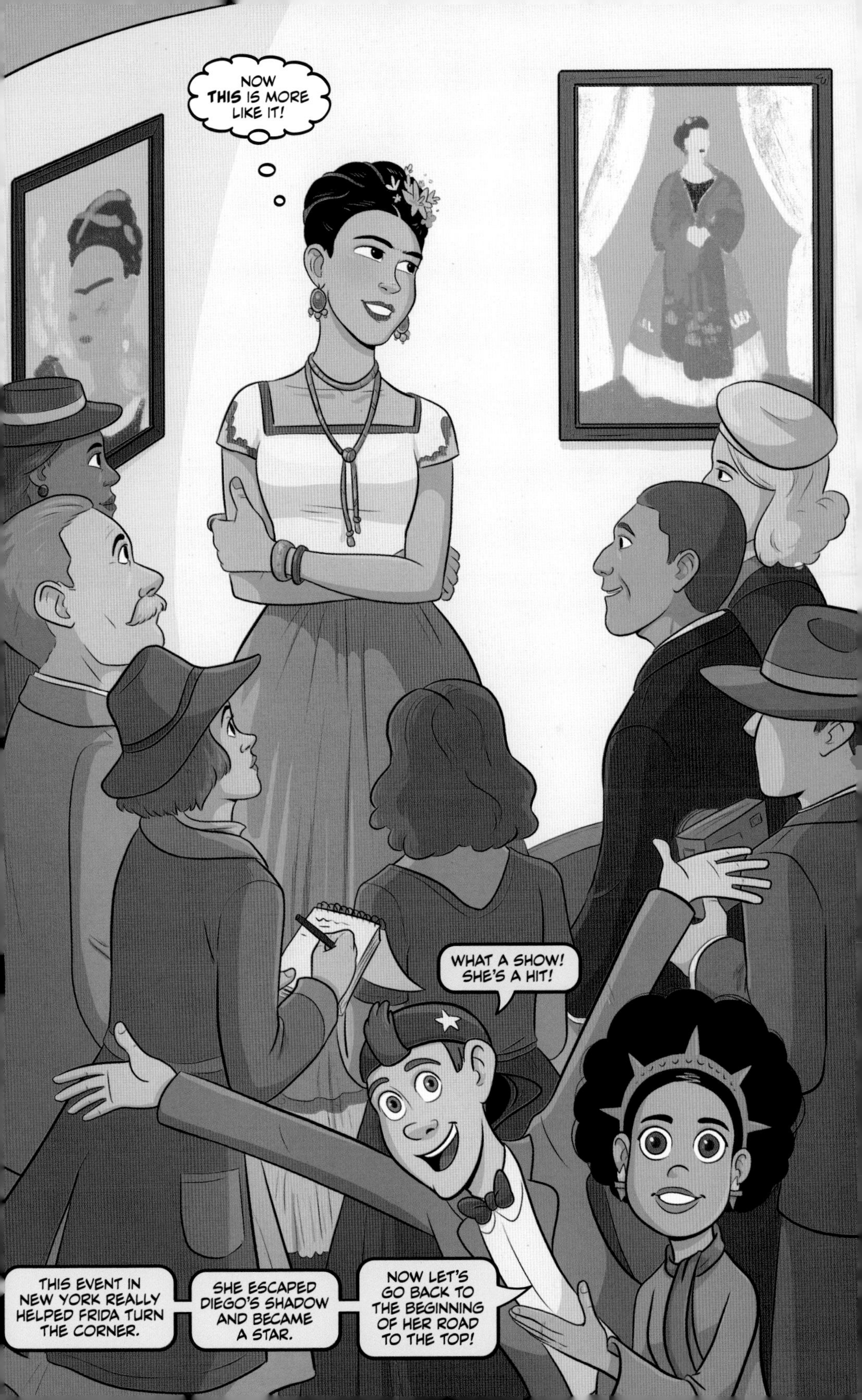
NOW THIS IS MORE LIKE IT!
WHAT A SHOW! SHE'S A HIT!
THIS EVENT IN NEW YORK REALLY HELPED FRIDA TURN THE CORNER.
SHE ESCAPED DIEGO'S SHADOW AND BECAME A STAR.
NOW LET'S GO BACK TO THE BEGINNING OF HER ROAD TO THE TOP!

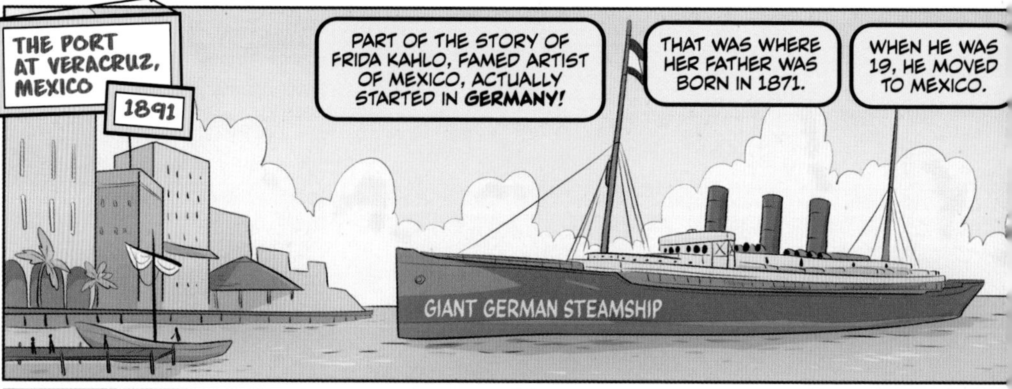
THE PORT AT VERACRUZ, MEXICO
1891
PART OF THE STORY OF FRIDA KAHLO, FAMED ARTIST OF MEXICO, ACTUALLY STARTED IN GERMANY!
THAT WAS WHERE HER FATHER WAS BORN IN 1871.
WHEN HE WAS 19, HE MOVED TO MEXICO.
GIANT GERMAN STEAMSHIP

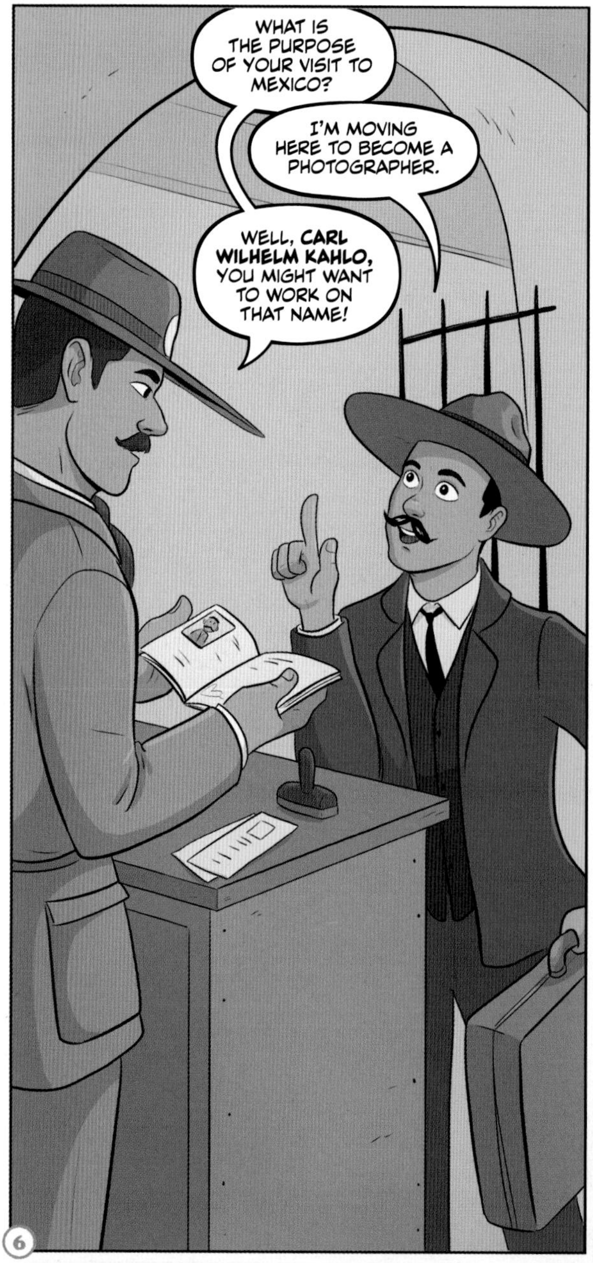
WHAT IS THE PURPOSE OF YOUR VISIT TO MEXICO?
I'M MOVING HERE TO BECOME A PHOTOGRAPHER.
WELL, CARL WILHELM KAHLO, YOU MIGHT WANT TO WORK ON THAT NAME!

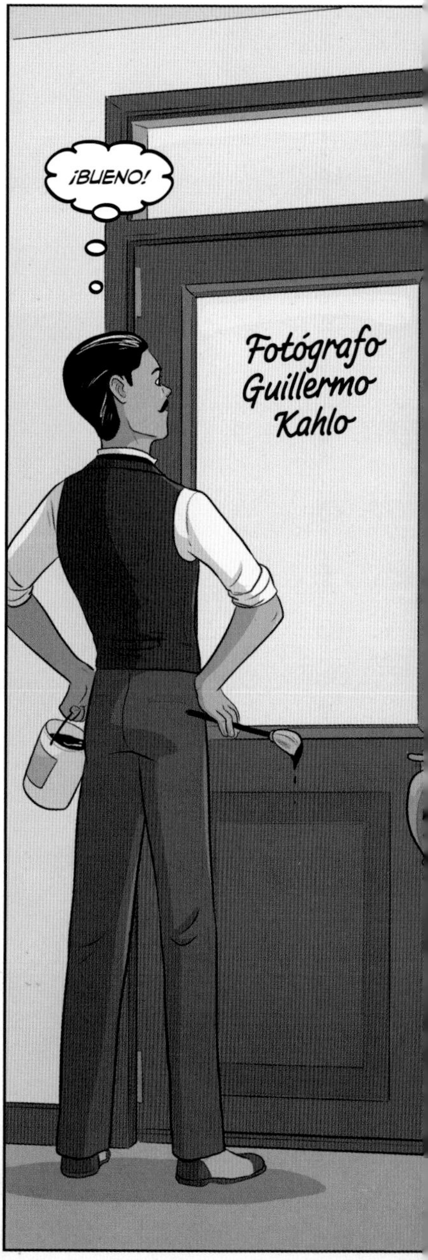
¡BUENO!
Fotógrafo Guillermo Kahlo

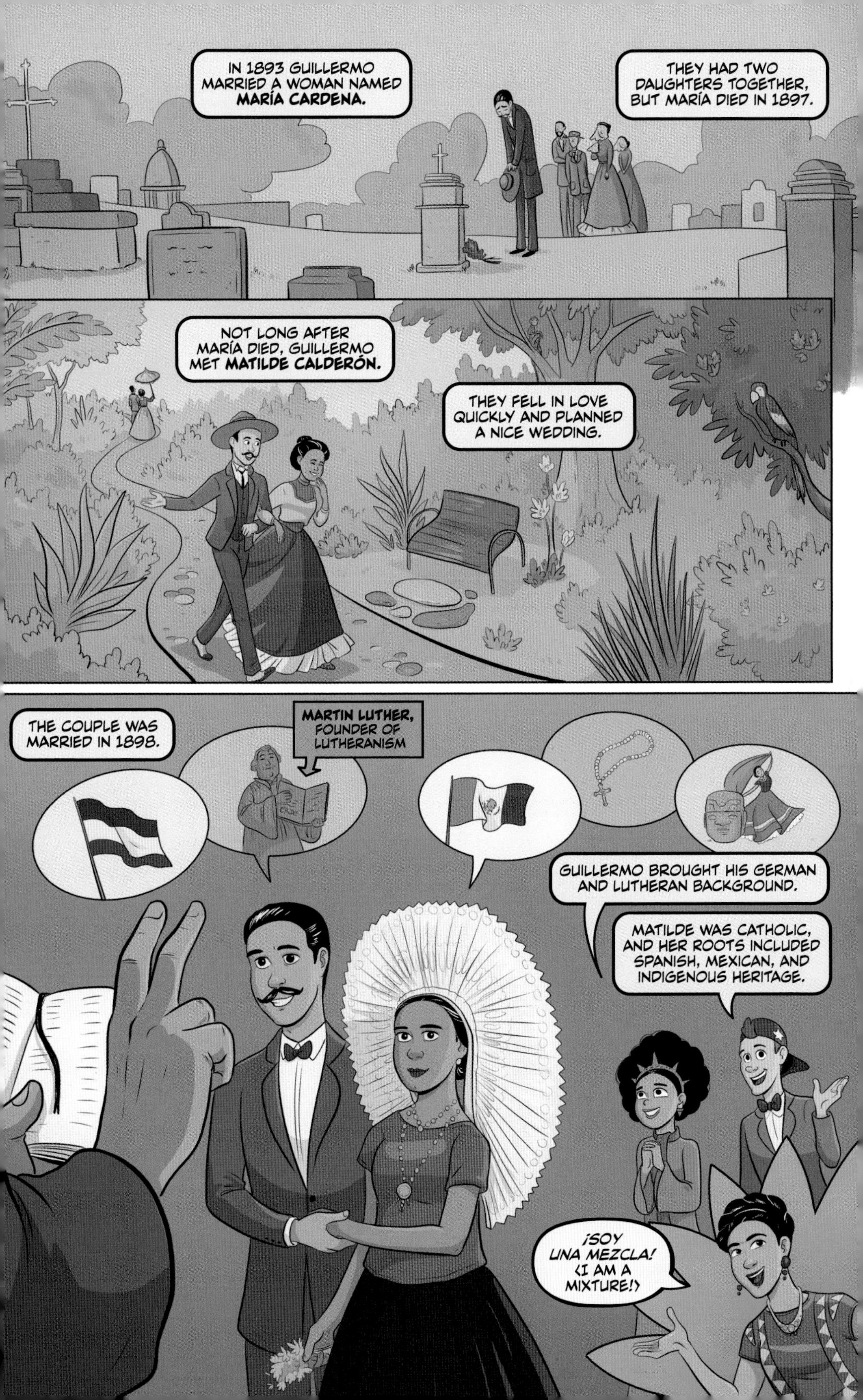
IN 1893 GUILLERMO MARRIED A WOMAN NAMED **MARÍA CARDENA.**
THEY HAD TWO DAUGHTERS TOGETHER, BUT MARÍA DIED IN 1897.
NOT LONG AFTER MARÍA DIED, GUILLERMO MET **MATILDE CALDERÓN.**
THEY FELL IN LOVE QUICKLY AND PLANNED A NICE WEDDING.
THE COUPLE WAS MARRIED IN 1898.
MARTIN LUTHER, FOUNDER OF LUTHERANISM
GUILLERMO BROUGHT HIS GERMAN AND LUTHERAN BACKGROUND.
MATILDE WAS CATHOLIC, AND HER ROOTS INCLUDED SPANISH, MEXICAN, AND INDIGENOUS HERITAGE.
¡SOY UNA MEZCLA! ‹I AM A MIXTURE!›

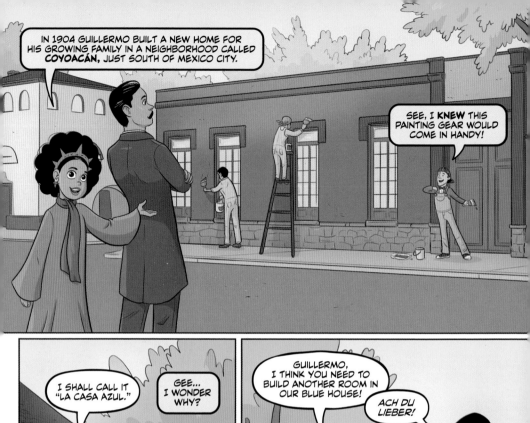

IN 1904 GUILLERMO BUILT A NEW HOME FOR HIS GROWING FAMILY IN A NEIGHBORHOOD CALLED **COYOACÁN,** JUST SOUTH OF MEXICO CITY.

SEE, I **KNEW** THIS PAINTING GEAR WOULD COME IN HANDY!

I SHALL CALL IT "LA CASA AZUL."

GEE... I WONDER WHY?

GUILLERMO, I THINK YOU NEED TO BUILD ANOTHER ROOM IN OUR BLUE HOUSE!

ACH DU LIEBER!

MATILDE, BORN 1898

ADRIANA, BORN 1902

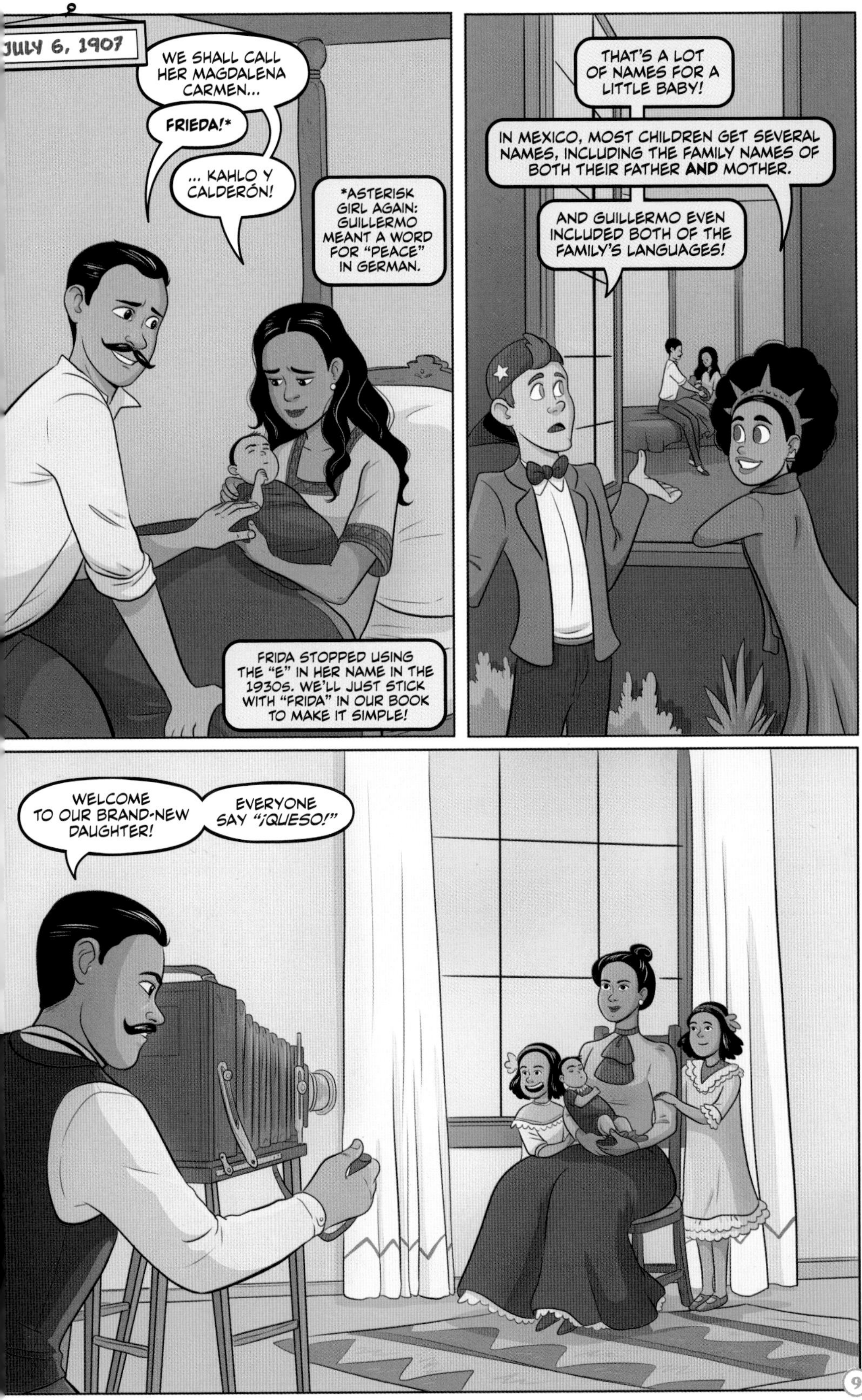
JULY 6, 1907
WE SHALL CALL HER MAGDALENA CARMEN...
FRIEDA!*
... KAHLO Y CALDERÓN!
*ASTERISK GIRL AGAIN: GUILLERMO MEANT A WORD FOR "PEACE" IN GERMAN.
FRIDA STOPPED USING THE "E" IN HER NAME IN THE 1930s. WE'LL JUST STICK WITH "FRIDA" IN OUR BOOK TO MAKE IT SIMPLE!
THAT'S A LOT OF NAMES FOR A LITTLE BABY!
IN MEXICO, MOST CHILDREN GET SEVERAL NAMES, INCLUDING THE FAMILY NAMES OF BOTH THEIR FATHER AND MOTHER.
AND GUILLERMO EVEN INCLUDED BOTH OF THE FAMILY'S LANGUAGES!
WELCOME TO OUR BRAND-NEW DAUGHTER!
EVERYONE SAY "¡QUESO!"

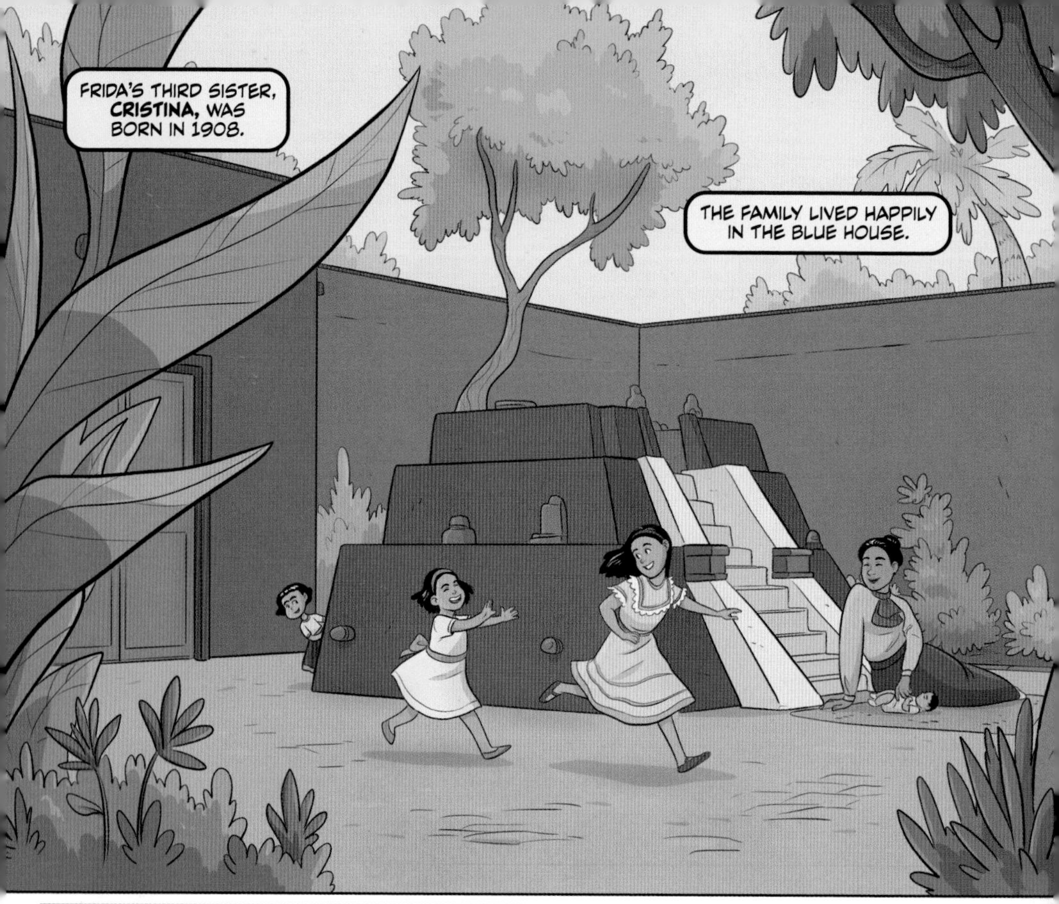
FRIDA'S THIRD SISTER, **CRISTINA,** WAS BORN IN 1908.
THE FAMILY LIVED HAPPILY IN THE BLUE HOUSE.

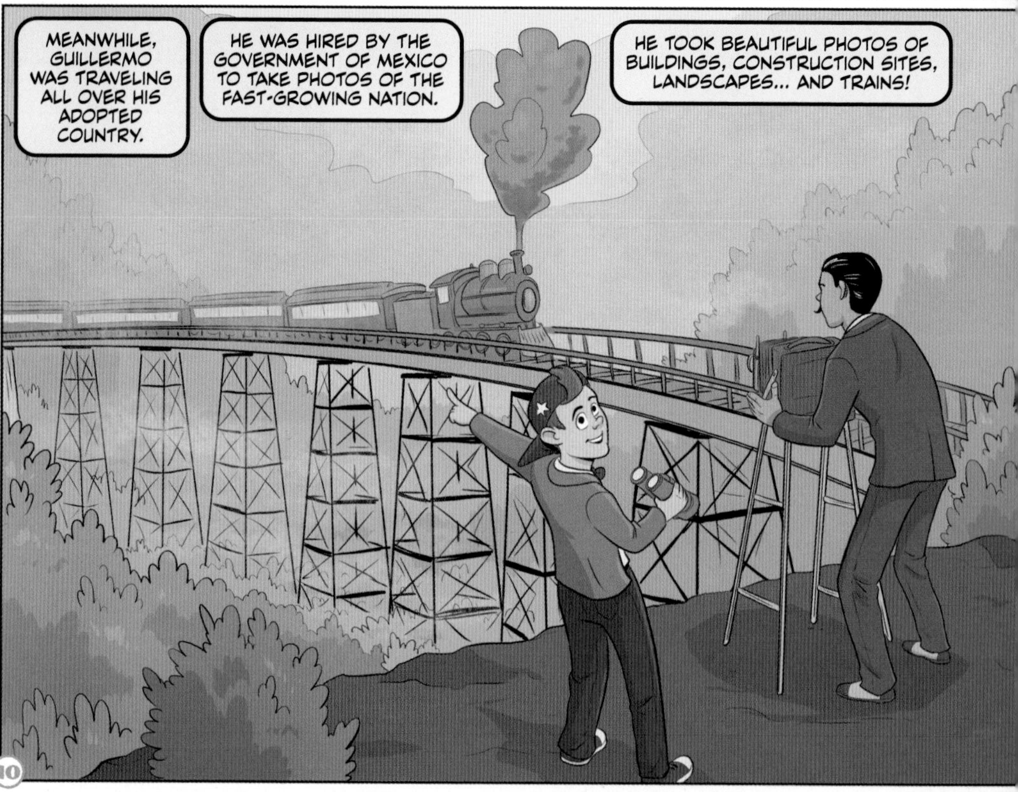
MEANWHILE, GUILLERMO WAS TRAVELING ALL OVER HIS ADOPTED COUNTRY.
HE WAS HIRED BY THE GOVERNMENT OF MEXICO TO TAKE PHOTOS OF THE FAST-GROWING NATION.
HE TOOK BEAUTIFUL PHOTOS OF BUILDINGS, CONSTRUCTION SITES, LANDSCAPES... AND TRAINS!

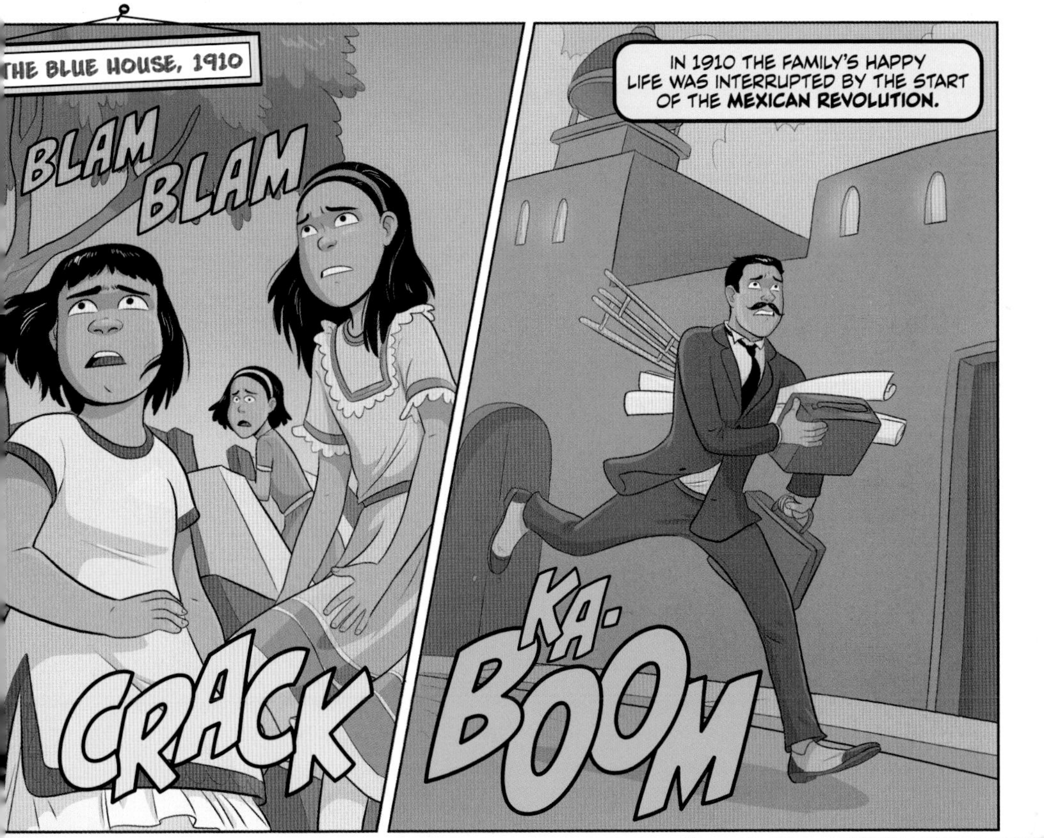
THE BLUE HOUSE, 1910
BLAM
BLAM
CRACK
IN 1910 THE FAMILY'S HAPPY LIFE WAS INTERRUPTED BY THE START OF THE **MEXICAN REVOLUTION.**
KA-BOOM

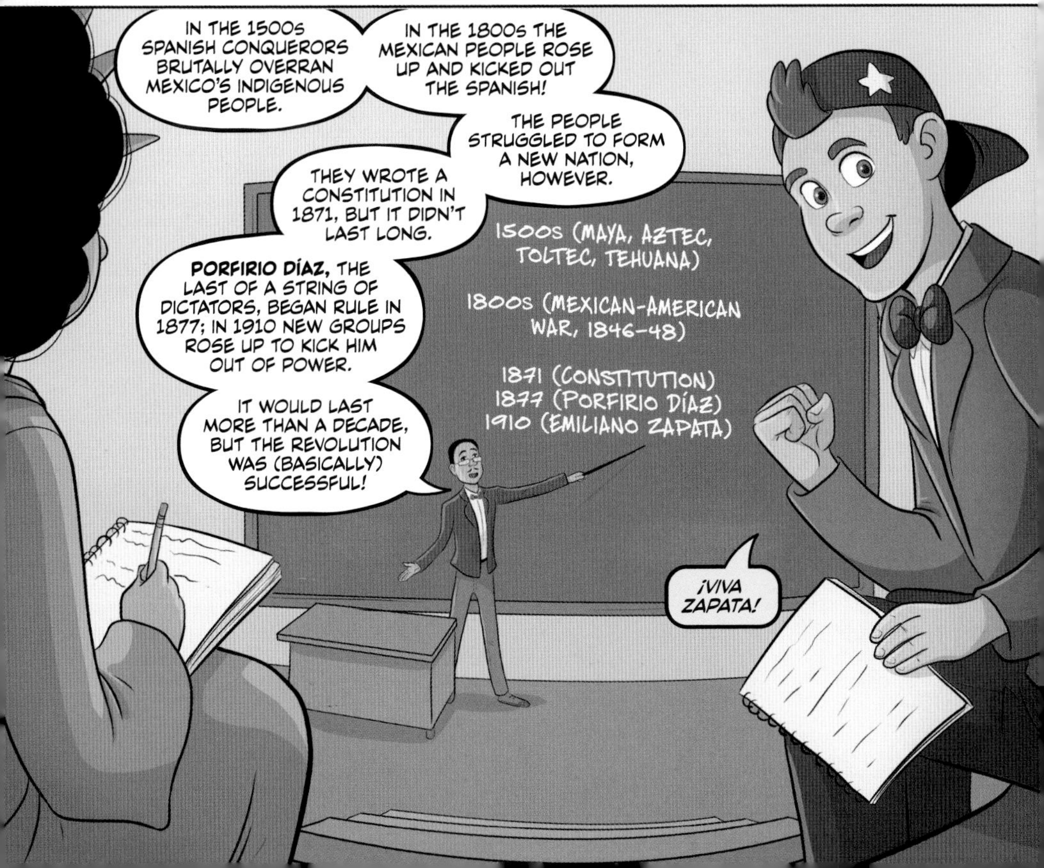
IN THE 1500s SPANISH CONQUERORS BRUTALLY OVERRAN MEXICO'S INDIGENOUS PEOPLE.
IN THE 1800s THE MEXICAN PEOPLE ROSE UP AND KICKED OUT THE SPANISH!
THE PEOPLE STRUGGLED TO FORM A NEW NATION, HOWEVER.
THEY WROTE A CONSTITUTION IN 1871, BUT IT DIDN'T LAST LONG.
PORFIRIO DÍAZ, THE LAST OF A STRING OF DICTATORS, BEGAN RULE IN 1877; IN 1910 NEW GROUPS ROSE UP TO KICK HIM OUT OF POWER.
IT WOULD LAST MORE THAN A DECADE, BUT THE REVOLUTION WAS (BASICALLY) SUCCESSFUL!
1500s (MAYA, AZTEC, TOLTEC, TEHUANA)
1800s (MEXICAN-AMERICAN WAR, 1846–48)
1871 (CONSTITUTION)
1877 (PORFIRIO DÍAZ)
1910 (EMILIANO ZAPATA)
¡VIVA ZAPATA!

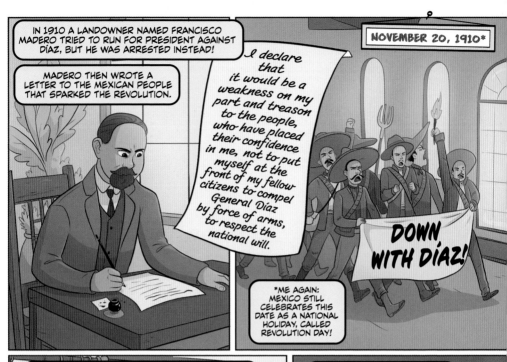

IN 1910 A LANDOWNER NAMED FRANCISCO MADERO TRIED TO RUN FOR PRESIDENT AGAINST DÍAZ, BUT HE WAS ARRESTED INSTEAD!

MADERO THEN WROTE A LETTER TO THE MEXICAN PEOPLE THAT SPARKED THE REVOLUTION.

I declare that it would be a weakness on my part and treason to the people, who have placed their confidence in me, not to put myself at the front of my fellow citizens to compel General Díaz by force of arms, to respect the national will.

NOVEMBER 20, 1910*

DOWN WITH DÍAZ!

*ME AGAIN: MEXICO STILL CELEBRATES THIS DATE AS A NATIONAL HOLIDAY, CALLED REVOLUTION DAY!

AS THE FIGHTING WENT ON, MATILDE OFTEN HAD TO QUICKLY GET HER DAUGHTERS INDOORS WHEN THE DANGER GOT TOO NEAR THE HOUSE.

DON'T WORRY, MI HIJAS, NOTHING BAD CAN HAPPEN IN THE BLUE HOUSE!

BLAM BLAM

BANG

THE FIGHTING SOMETIMES GOT CLOSE TO FRIDA'S HOME.

SOMETIMES THE REBELS FOUND A SAFE PLACE TO HIDE IN THE BLUE HOUSE GARDEN.

THE KAHLO FAMILY SUPPORTED THE IDEA OF A FREE MEXICO!

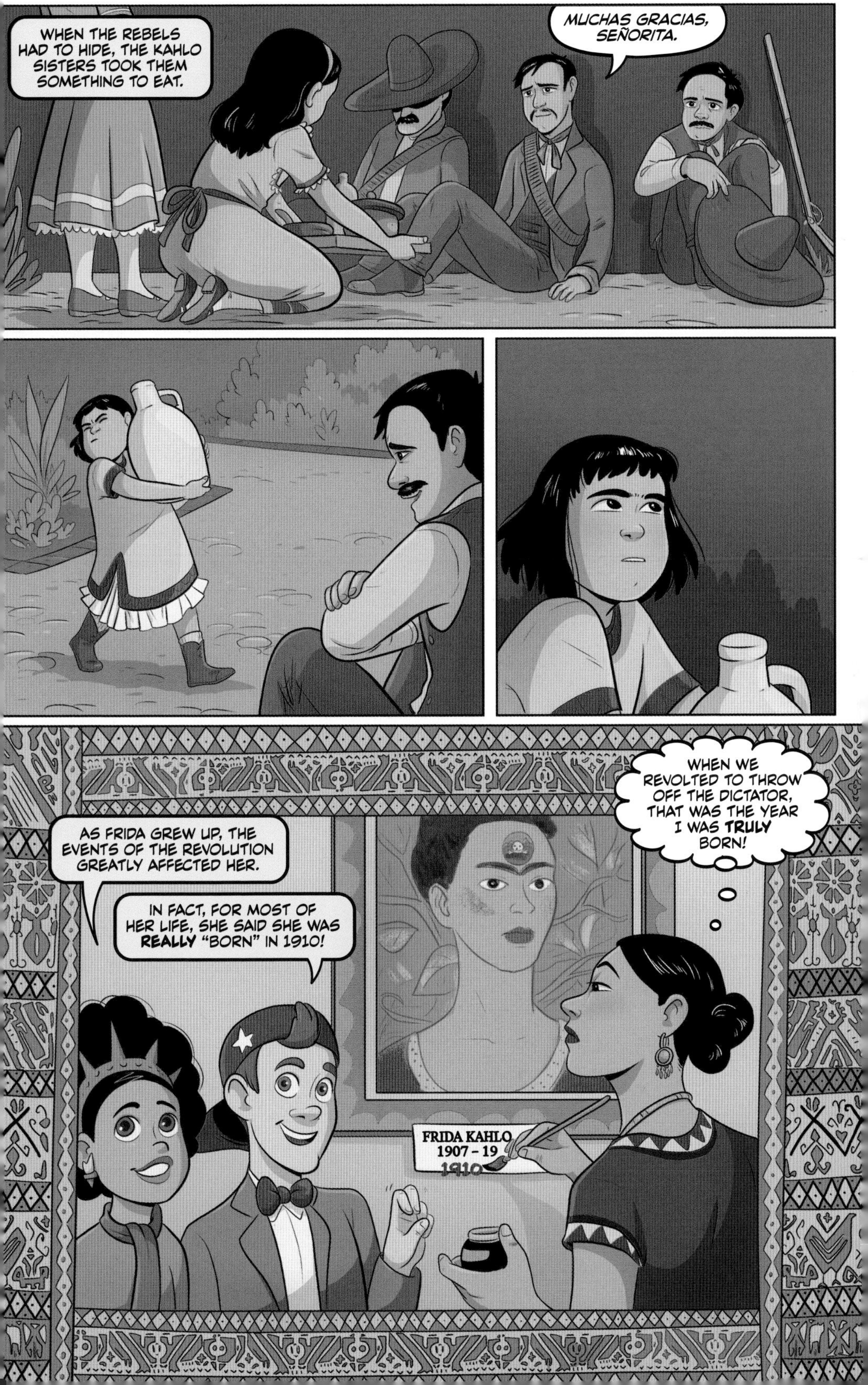
WHEN THE REBELS HAD TO HIDE, THE KAHLO SISTERS TOOK THEM SOMETHING TO EAT.
MUCHAS GRACIAS, SEÑORITA.
AS FRIDA GREW UP, THE EVENTS OF THE REVOLUTION GREATLY AFFECTED HER.
IN FACT, FOR MOST OF HER LIFE, SHE SAID SHE WAS **REALLY** "BORN" IN 1910!
WHEN WE REVOLTED TO THROW OFF THE DICTATOR, THAT WAS THE YEAR I WAS **TRULY** BORN!
FRIDA KAHLO
1907 – 19
1910

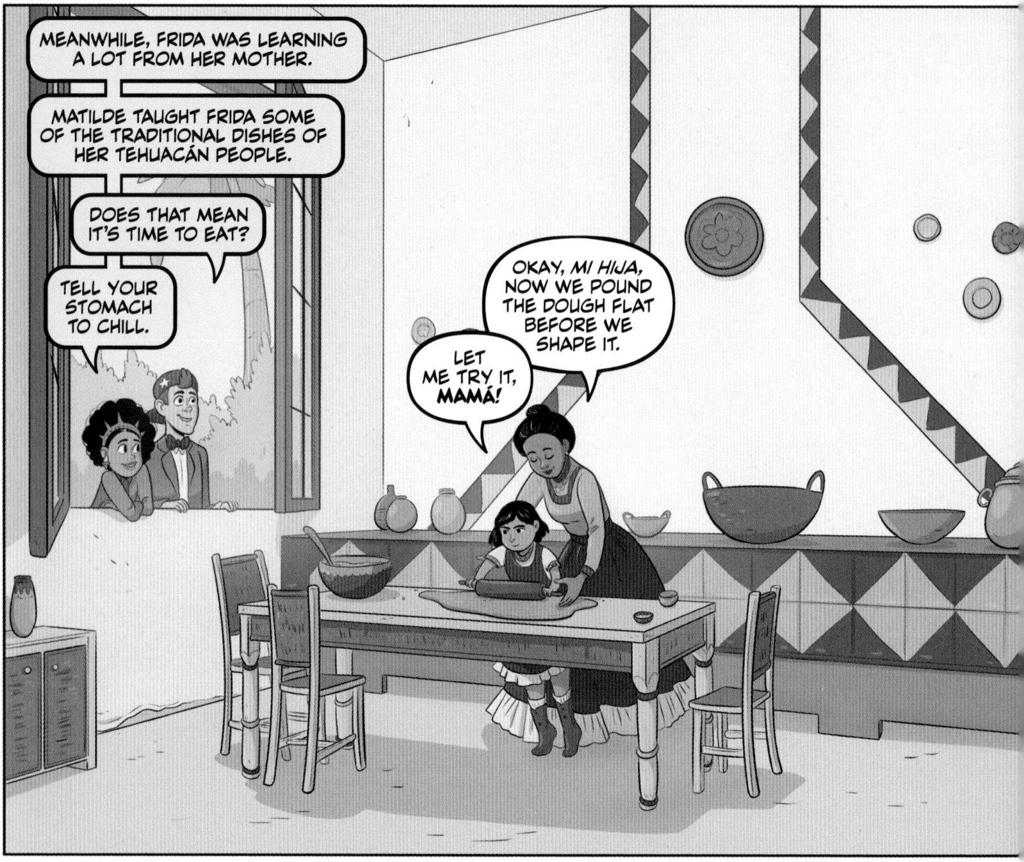
MEANWHILE, FRIDA WAS LEARNING A LOT FROM HER MOTHER.
MATILDE TAUGHT FRIDA SOME OF THE TRADITIONAL DISHES OF HER TEHUACÁN PEOPLE.
DOES THAT MEAN IT'S TIME TO EAT?
TELL YOUR STOMACH TO CHILL.
OKAY, *MI HIJA*, NOW WE POUND THE DOUGH FLAT BEFORE WE SHAPE IT.
LET ME TRY IT, **MAMÁ!**

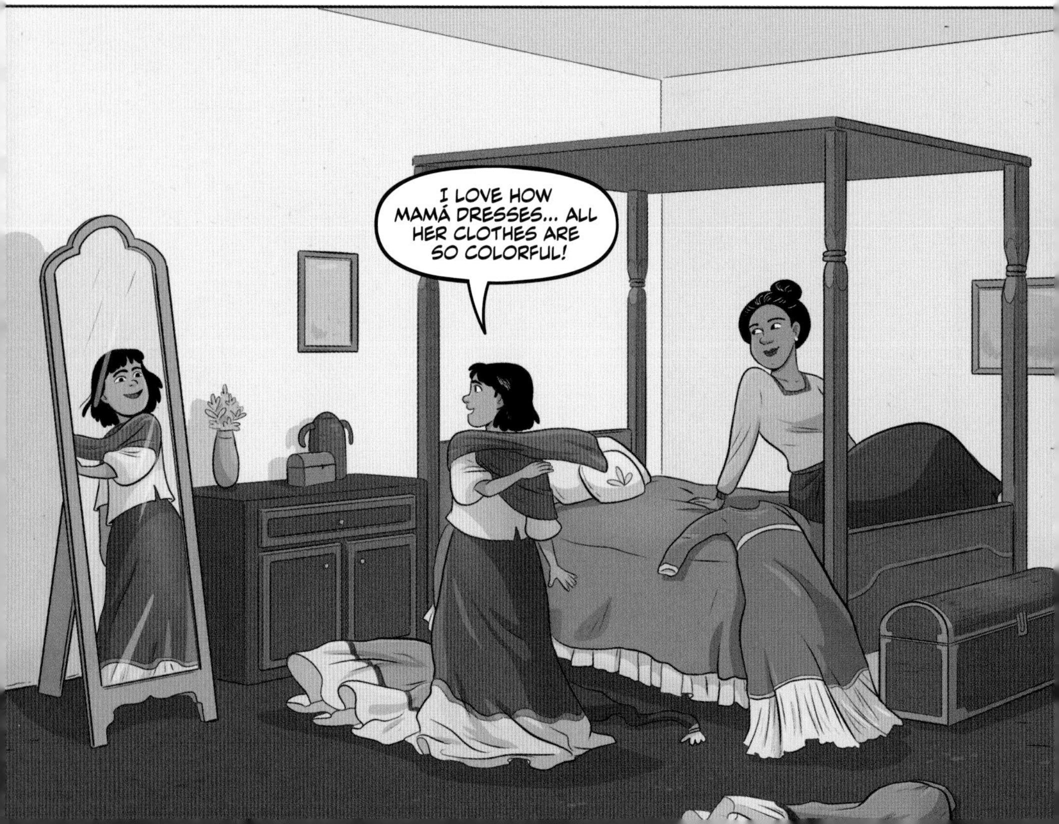
I LOVE HOW MAMÁ DRESSES... ALL HER CLOTHES ARE SO COLORFUL!

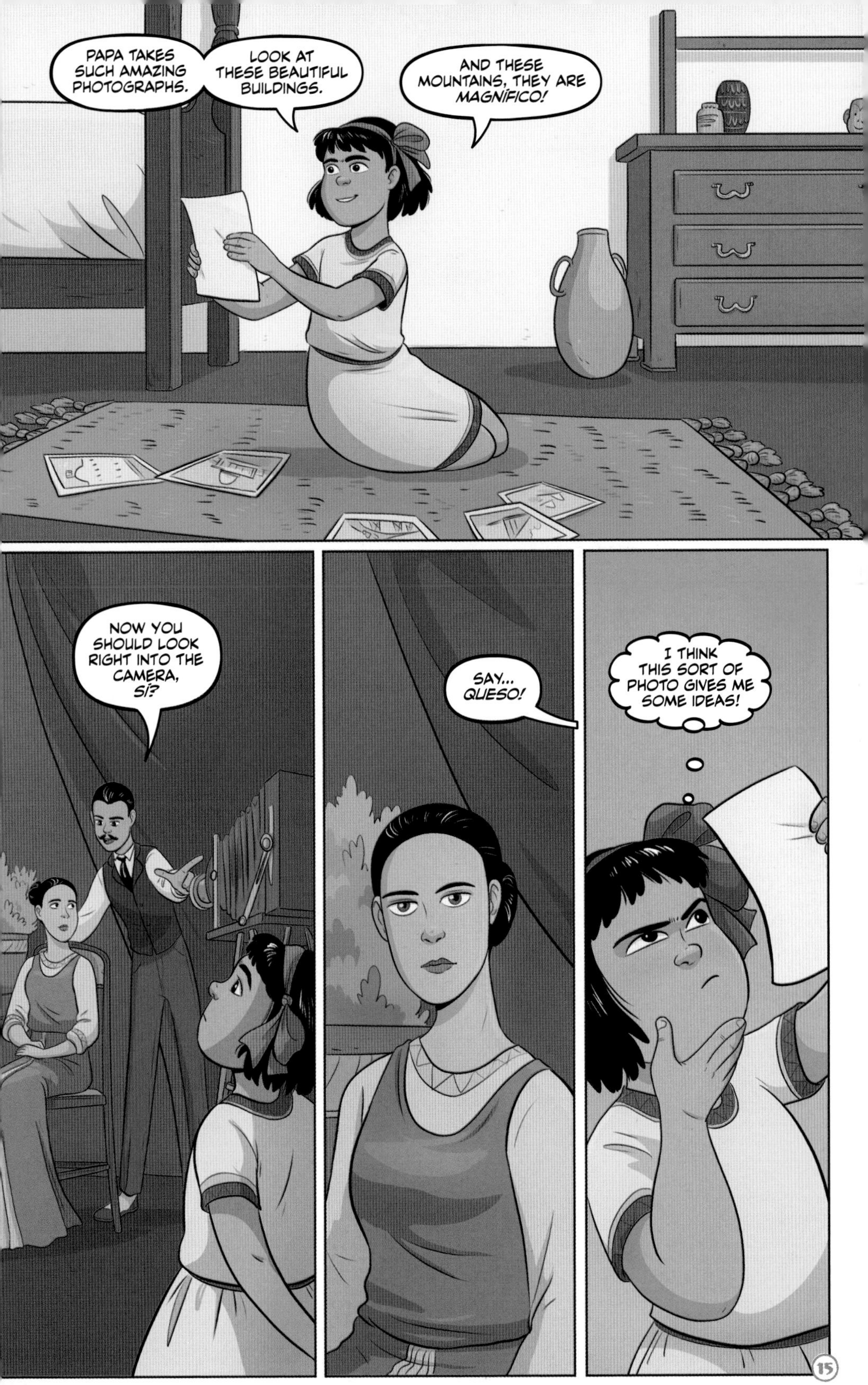
PAPA TAKES SUCH AMAZING PHOTOGRAPHS.
LOOK AT THESE BEAUTIFUL BUILDINGS.
AND THESE MOUNTAINS, THEY ARE *MAGNÍFICO!*
NOW YOU SHOULD LOOK RIGHT INTO THE CAMERA, *SÍ?*
SAY... *QUESO!*
I THINK THIS SORT OF PHOTO GIVES ME SOME IDEAS!

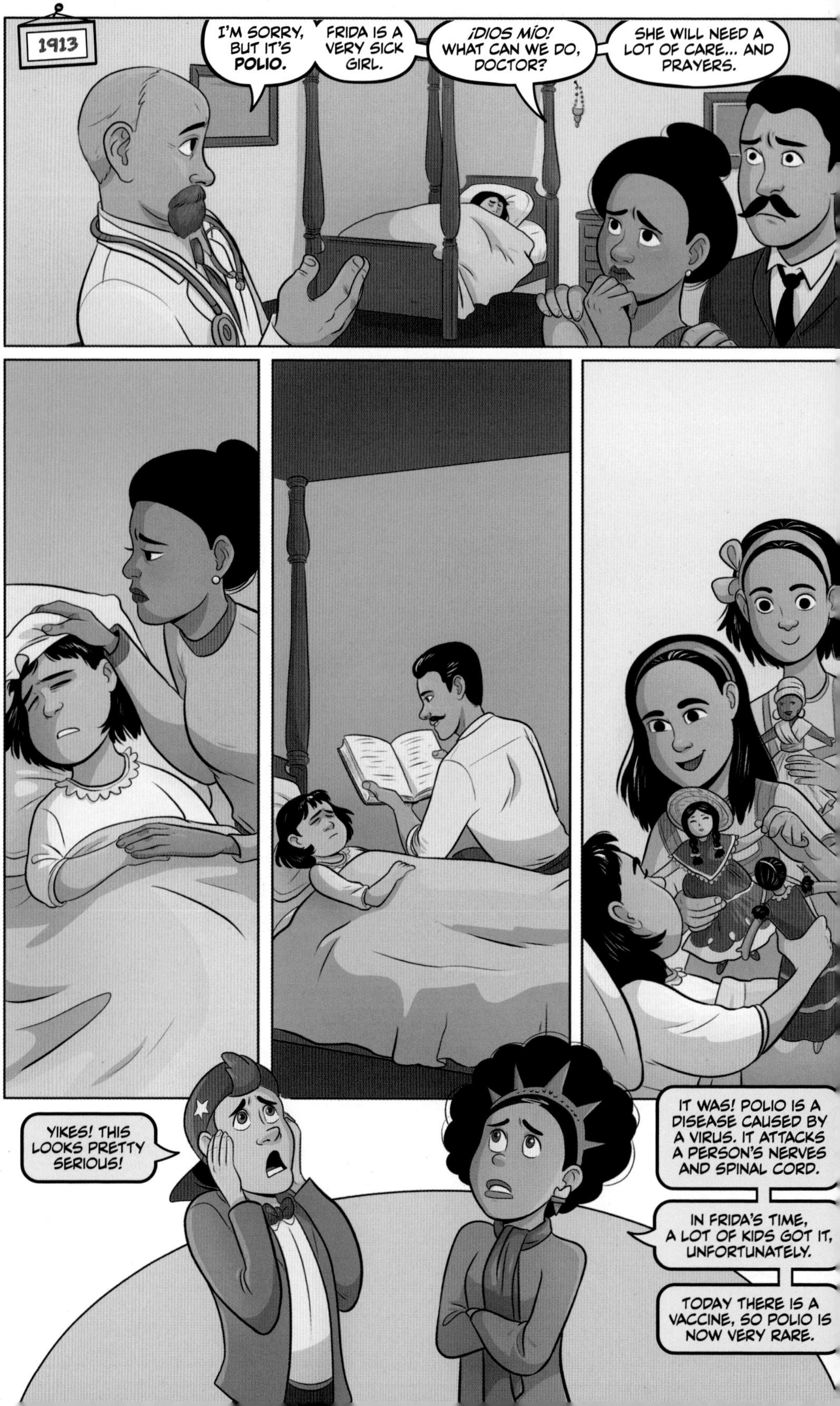
1913
I'M SORRY, BUT IT'S **POLIO.**
FRIDA IS A VERY SICK GIRL.
¡DIOS MÍO! WHAT CAN WE DO, DOCTOR?
SHE WILL NEED A LOT OF CARE... AND PRAYERS.
YIKES! THIS LOOKS PRETTY SERIOUS!
IT WAS! POLIO IS A DISEASE CAUSED BY A VIRUS. IT ATTACKS A PERSON'S NERVES AND SPINAL CORD.
IN FRIDA'S TIME, A LOT OF KIDS GOT IT, UNFORTUNATELY.
TODAY THERE IS A VACCINE, SO POLIO IS NOW VERY RARE.

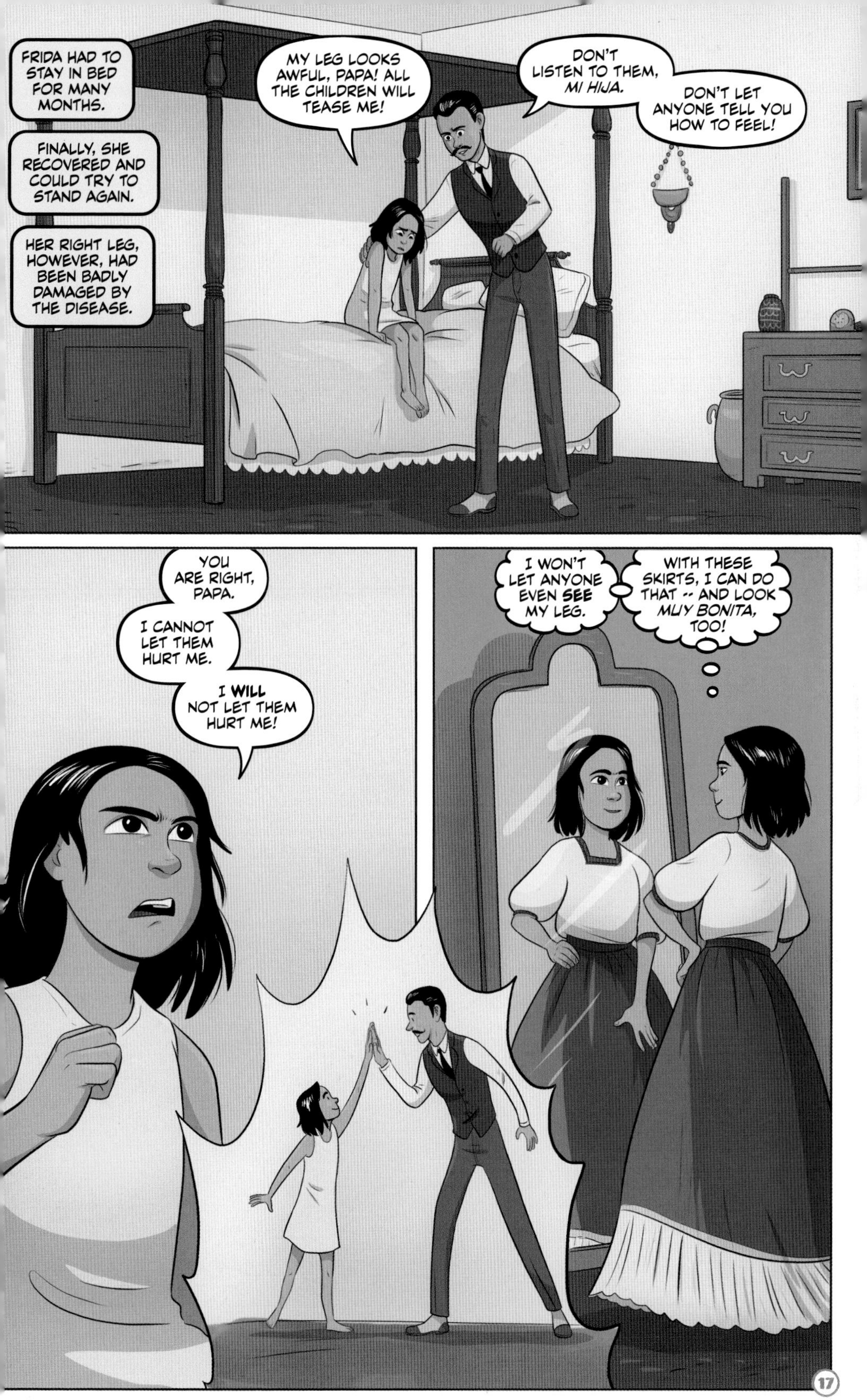
FRIDA HAD TO STAY IN BED FOR MANY MONTHS.
FINALLY, SHE RECOVERED AND COULD TRY TO STAND AGAIN.
HER RIGHT LEG, HOWEVER, HAD BEEN BADLY DAMAGED BY THE DISEASE.
MY LEG LOOKS AWFUL, PAPA! ALL THE CHILDREN WILL TEASE ME!
DON'T LISTEN TO THEM, *MI HIJA.*
DON'T LET ANYONE TELL YOU HOW TO FEEL!
YOU ARE RIGHT, PAPA.
I CANNOT LET THEM HURT ME.
I **WILL** NOT LET THEM HURT ME!
I WON'T LET ANYONE EVEN **SEE** MY LEG.
WITH THESE SKIRTS, I CAN DO THAT -- AND LOOK *MUY BONITA,* TOO!

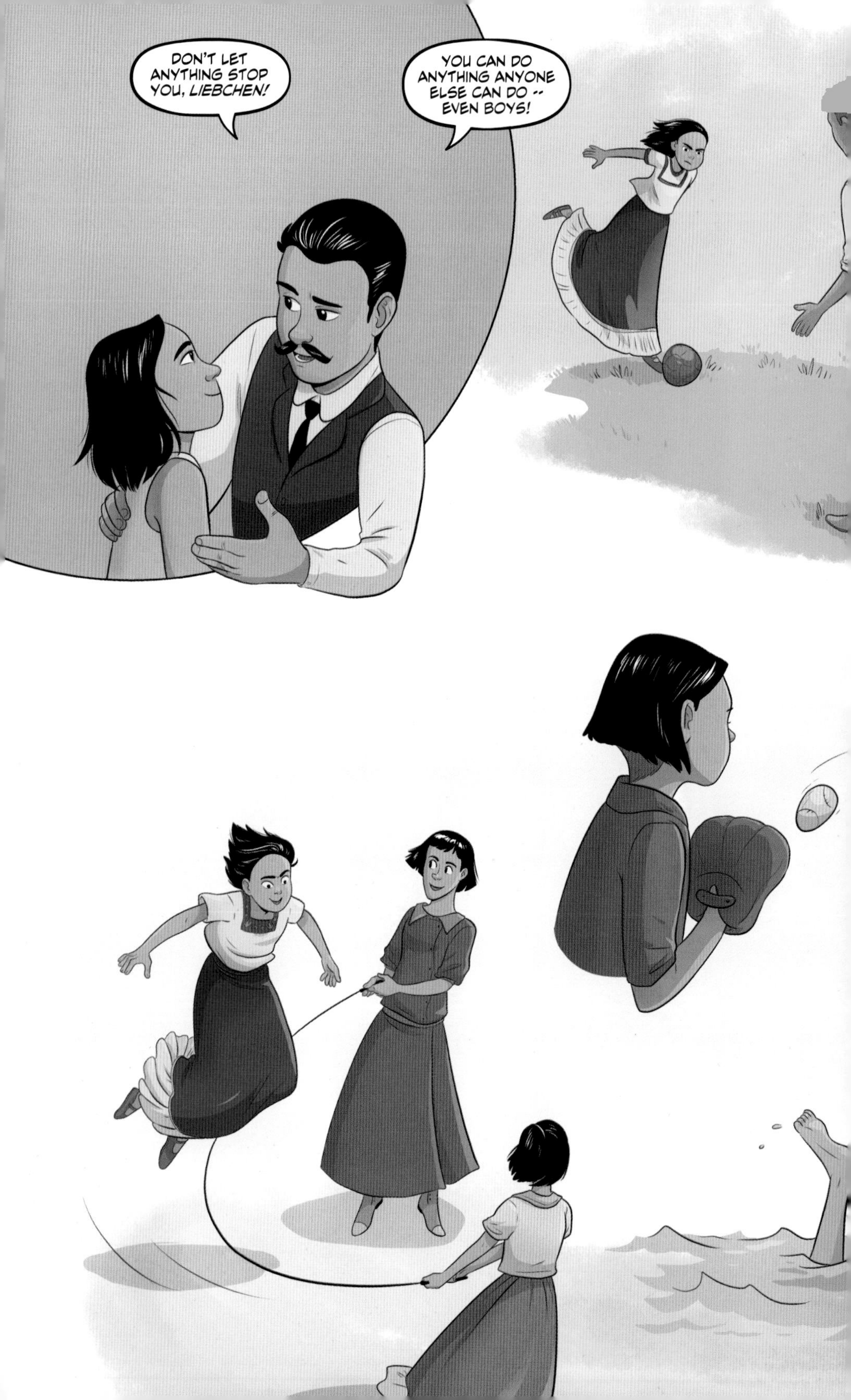
DON'T LET ANYTHING STOP YOU, *LIEBCHEN!*
YOU CAN DO ANYTHING ANYONE ELSE CAN DO -- EVEN BOYS!

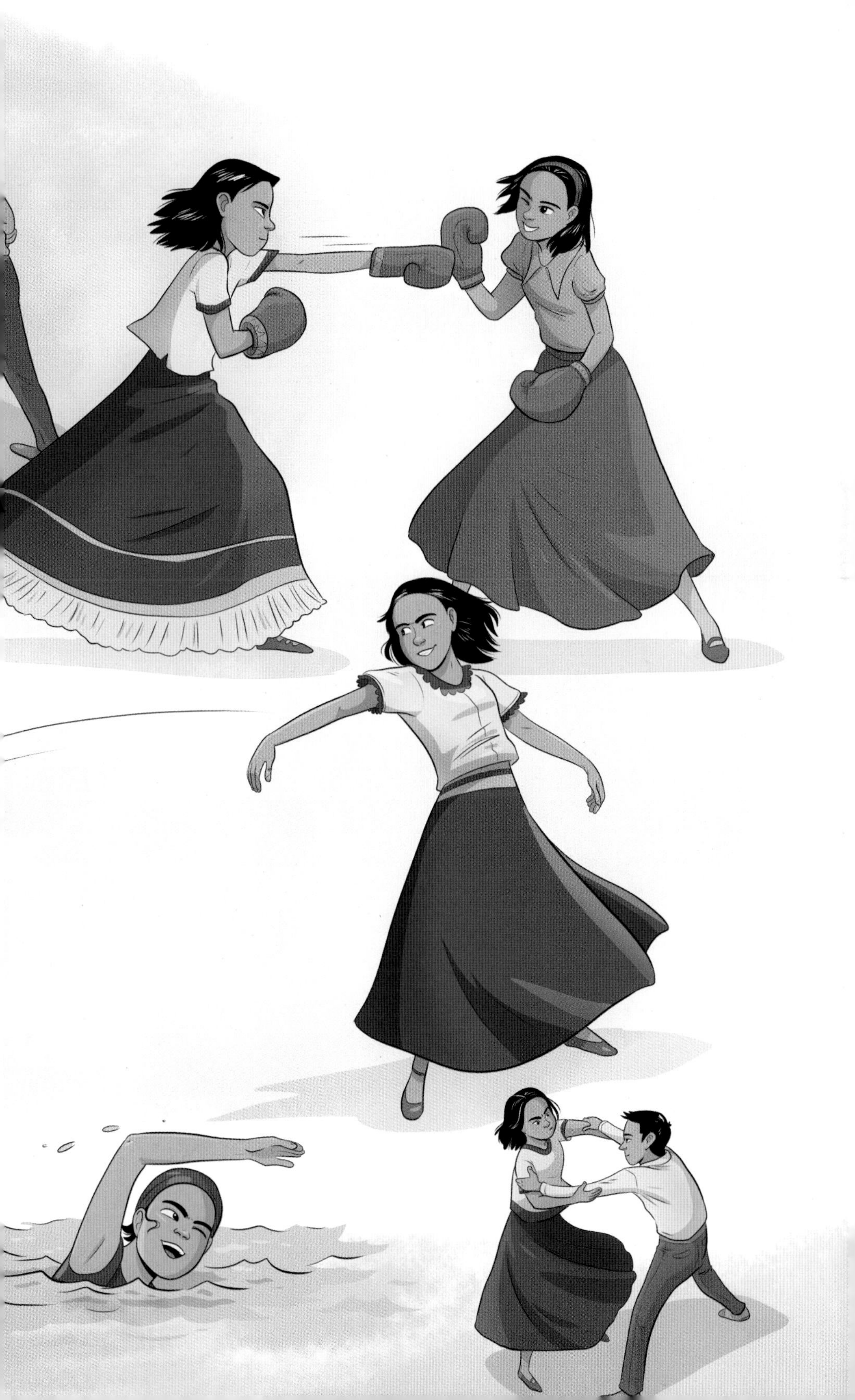

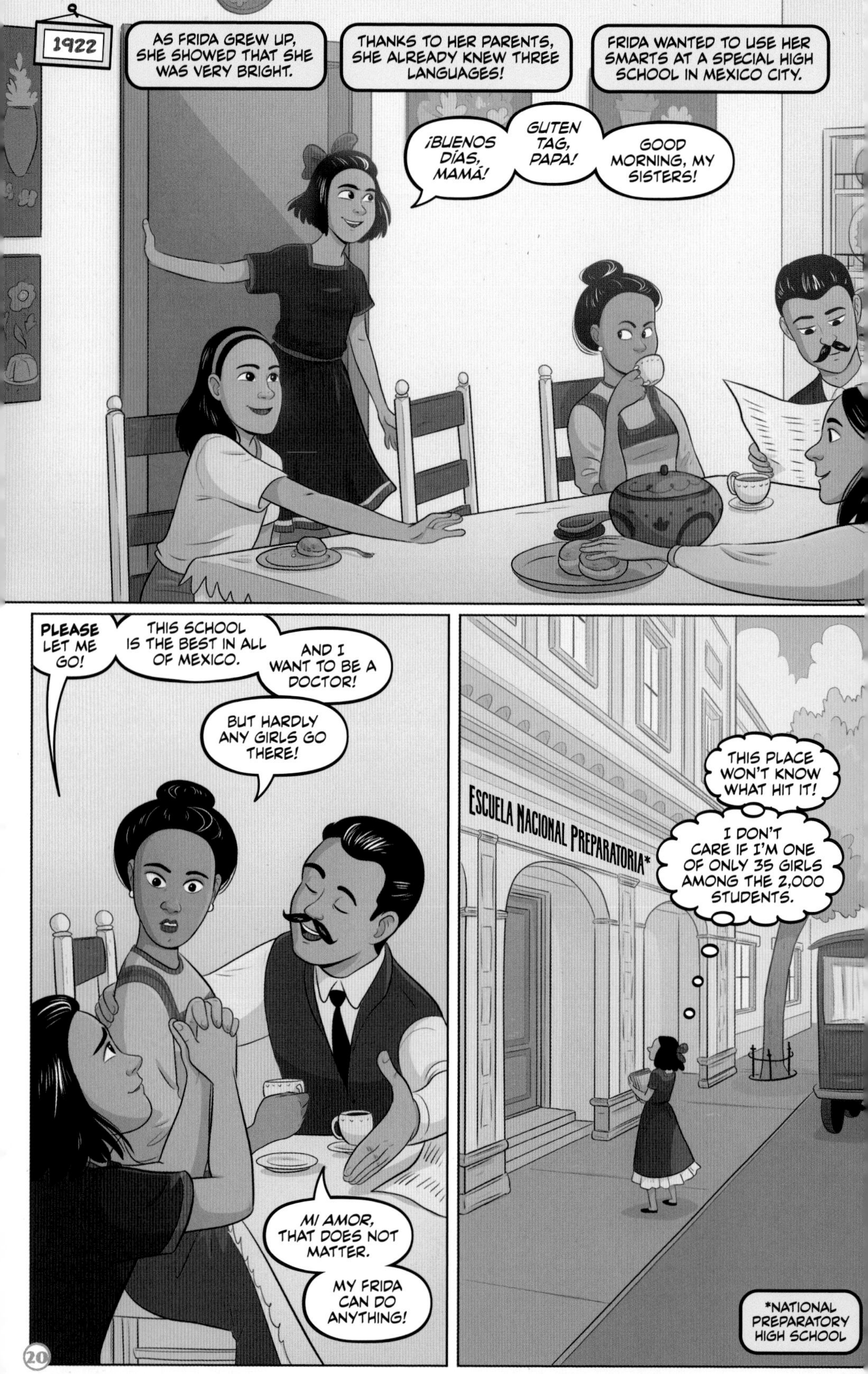
1922
AS FRIDA GREW UP, SHE SHOWED THAT SHE WAS VERY BRIGHT.
THANKS TO HER PARENTS, SHE ALREADY KNEW THREE LANGUAGES!
FRIDA WANTED TO USE HER SMARTS AT A SPECIAL HIGH SCHOOL IN MEXICO CITY.
¡BUENOS DÍAS, MAMÁ!
GUTEN TAG, PAPA!
GOOD MORNING, MY SISTERS!
PLEASE LET ME GO!
THIS SCHOOL IS THE BEST IN ALL OF MEXICO.
AND I WANT TO BE A DOCTOR!
BUT HARDLY ANY GIRLS GO THERE!
MI AMOR, THAT DOES NOT MATTER.
MY FRIDA CAN DO ANYTHING!
ESCUELA NACIONAL PREPARATORIA*
THIS PLACE WON'T KNOW WHAT HIT IT!
I DON'T CARE IF I'M ONE OF ONLY 35 GIRLS AMONG THE 2,000 STUDENTS.
*NATIONAL PREPARATORY HIGH SCHOOL

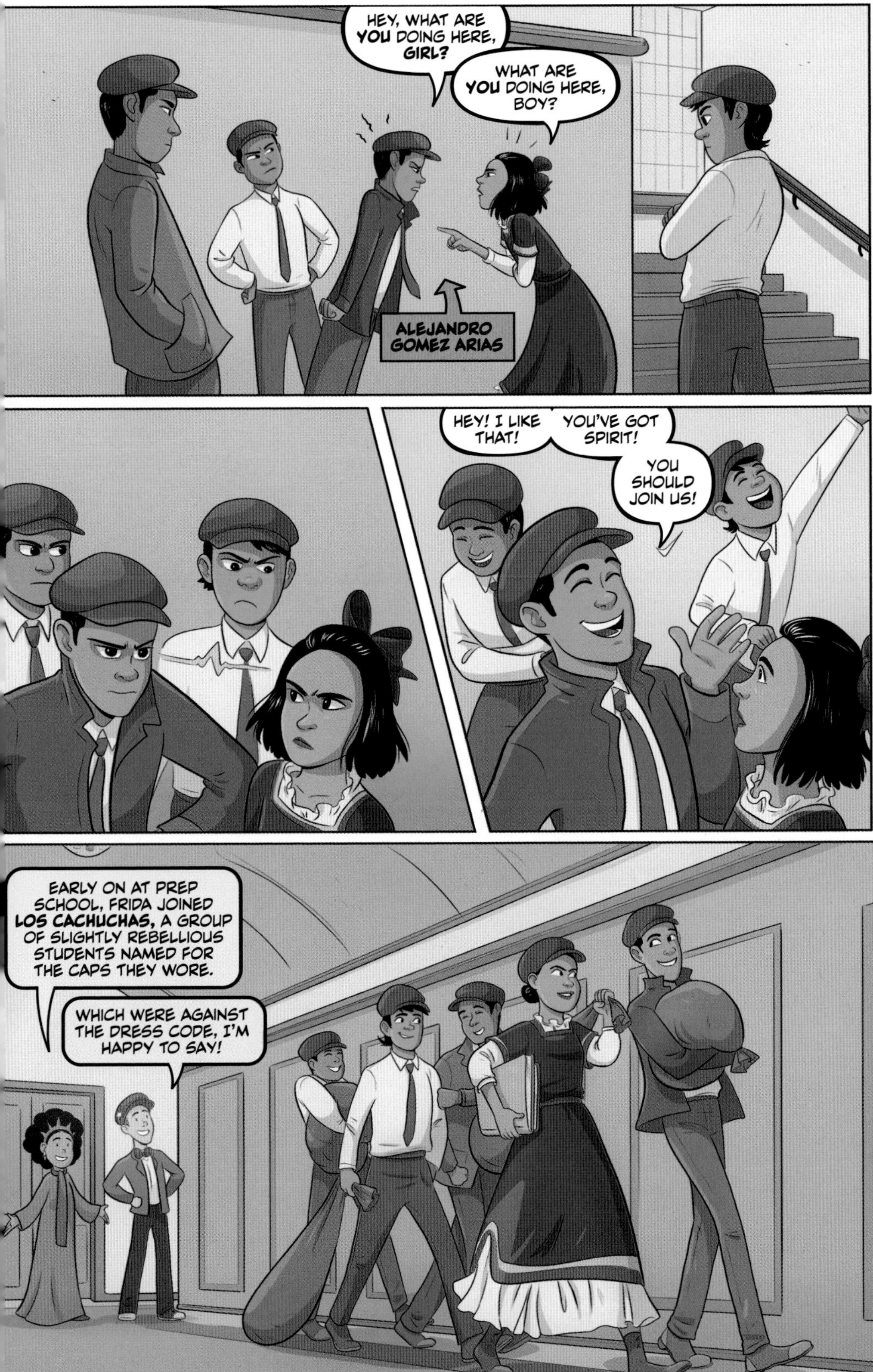
HEY, WHAT ARE YOU DOING HERE, GIRL?
WHAT ARE YOU DOING HERE, BOY?
ALEJANDRO GOMEZ ARIAS
HEY! I LIKE THAT!
YOU'VE GOT SPIRIT!
YOU SHOULD JOIN US!
EARLY ON AT PREP SCHOOL, FRIDA JOINED LOS CACHUCHAS, A GROUP OF SLIGHTLY REBELLIOUS STUDENTS NAMED FOR THE CAPS THEY WORE.
WHICH WERE AGAINST THE DRESS CODE, I'M HAPPY TO SAY!

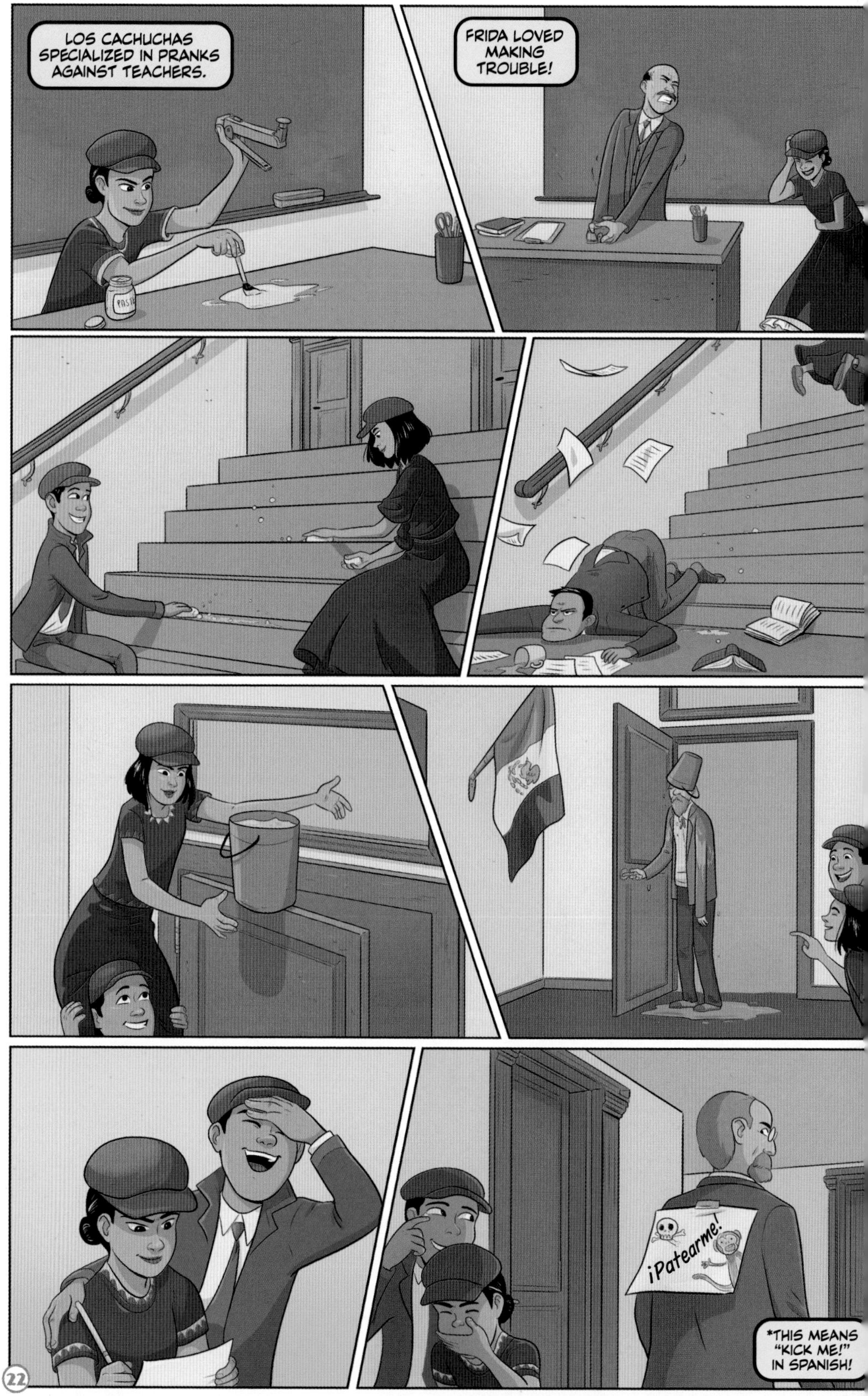
LOS CACHUCHAS SPECIALIZED IN PRANKS AGAINST TEACHERS.
PASTE
FRIDA LOVED MAKING TROUBLE!
¡Patearme!
*THIS MEANS "KICK ME!" IN SPANISH!

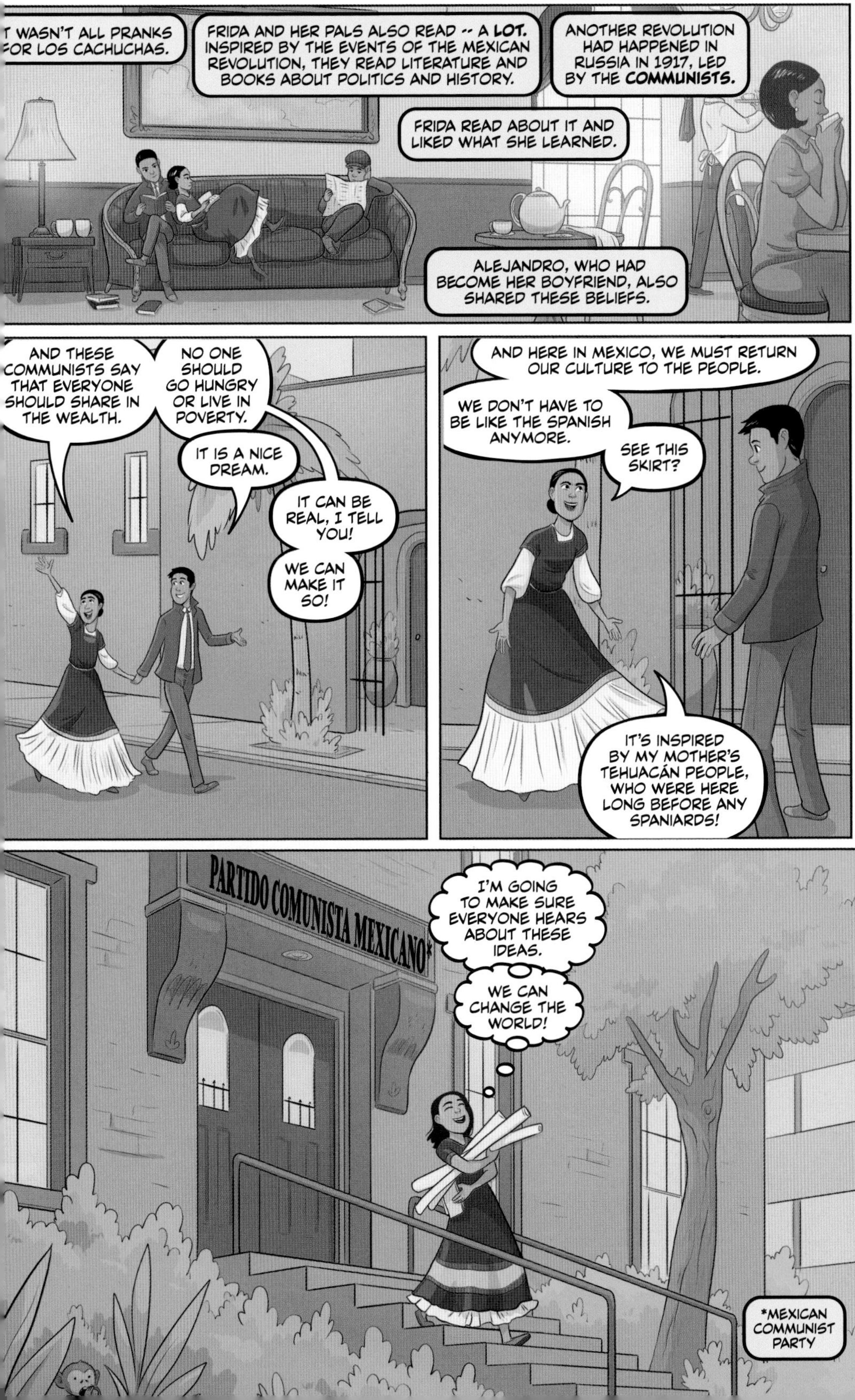
T WASN'T ALL PRANKS FOR LOS CACHUCHAS.
FRIDA AND HER PALS ALSO READ -- A **LOT.** INSPIRED BY THE EVENTS OF THE MEXICAN REVOLUTION, THEY READ LITERATURE AND BOOKS ABOUT POLITICS AND HISTORY.
ANOTHER REVOLUTION HAD HAPPENED IN RUSSIA IN 1917, LED BY THE **COMMUNISTS.**
FRIDA READ ABOUT IT AND LIKED WHAT SHE LEARNED.
ALEJANDRO, WHO HAD BECOME HER BOYFRIEND, ALSO SHARED THESE BELIEFS.
AND THESE COMMUNISTS SAY THAT EVERYONE SHOULD SHARE IN THE WEALTH.
NO ONE SHOULD GO HUNGRY OR LIVE IN POVERTY.
IT IS A NICE DREAM.
IT CAN BE REAL, I TELL YOU!
WE CAN MAKE IT SO!
AND HERE IN MEXICO, WE MUST RETURN OUR CULTURE TO THE PEOPLE.
WE DON'T HAVE TO BE LIKE THE SPANISH ANYMORE.
SEE THIS SKIRT?
IT'S INSPIRED BY MY MOTHER'S TEHUACÁN PEOPLE, WHO WERE HERE LONG BEFORE ANY SPANIARDS!
PARTIDO COMUNISTA MEXICANO*
I'M GOING TO MAKE SURE EVERYONE HEARS ABOUT THESE IDEAS.
WE CAN CHANGE THE WORLD!
*MEXICAN COMMUNIST PARTY

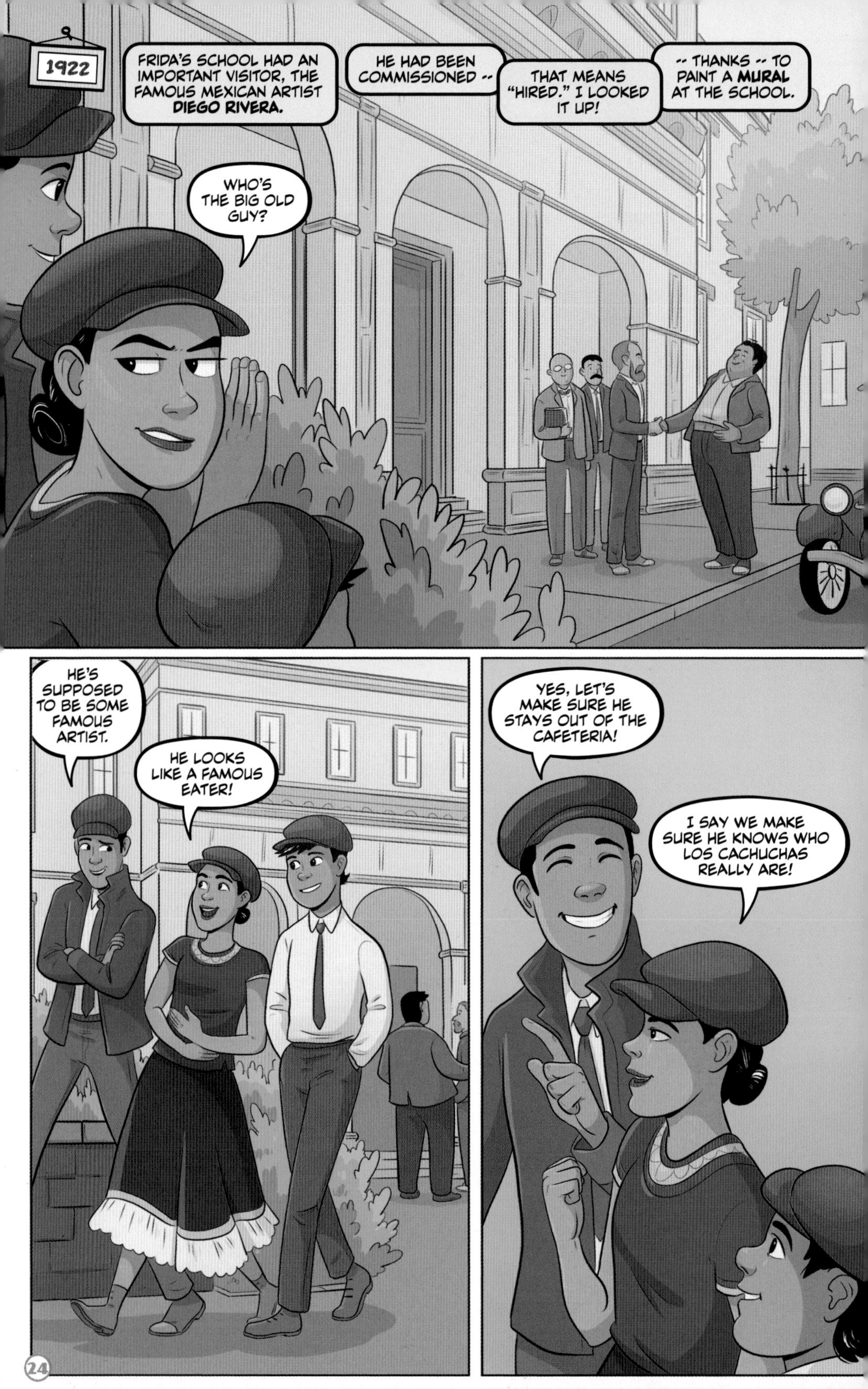
1922
FRIDA'S SCHOOL HAD AN IMPORTANT VISITOR, THE FAMOUS MEXICAN ARTIST **DIEGO RIVERA.**
HE HAD BEEN COMMISSIONED --
THAT MEANS "HIRED." I LOOKED IT UP!
-- THANKS -- TO PAINT A **MURAL** AT THE SCHOOL.
WHO'S THE BIG OLD GUY?
HE'S SUPPOSED TO BE SOME FAMOUS ARTIST.
HE LOOKS LIKE A FAMOUS EATER!
YES, LET'S MAKE SURE HE STAYS OUT OF THE CAFETERIA!
I SAY WE MAKE SURE HE KNOWS WHO LOS CACHUCHAS REALLY ARE!

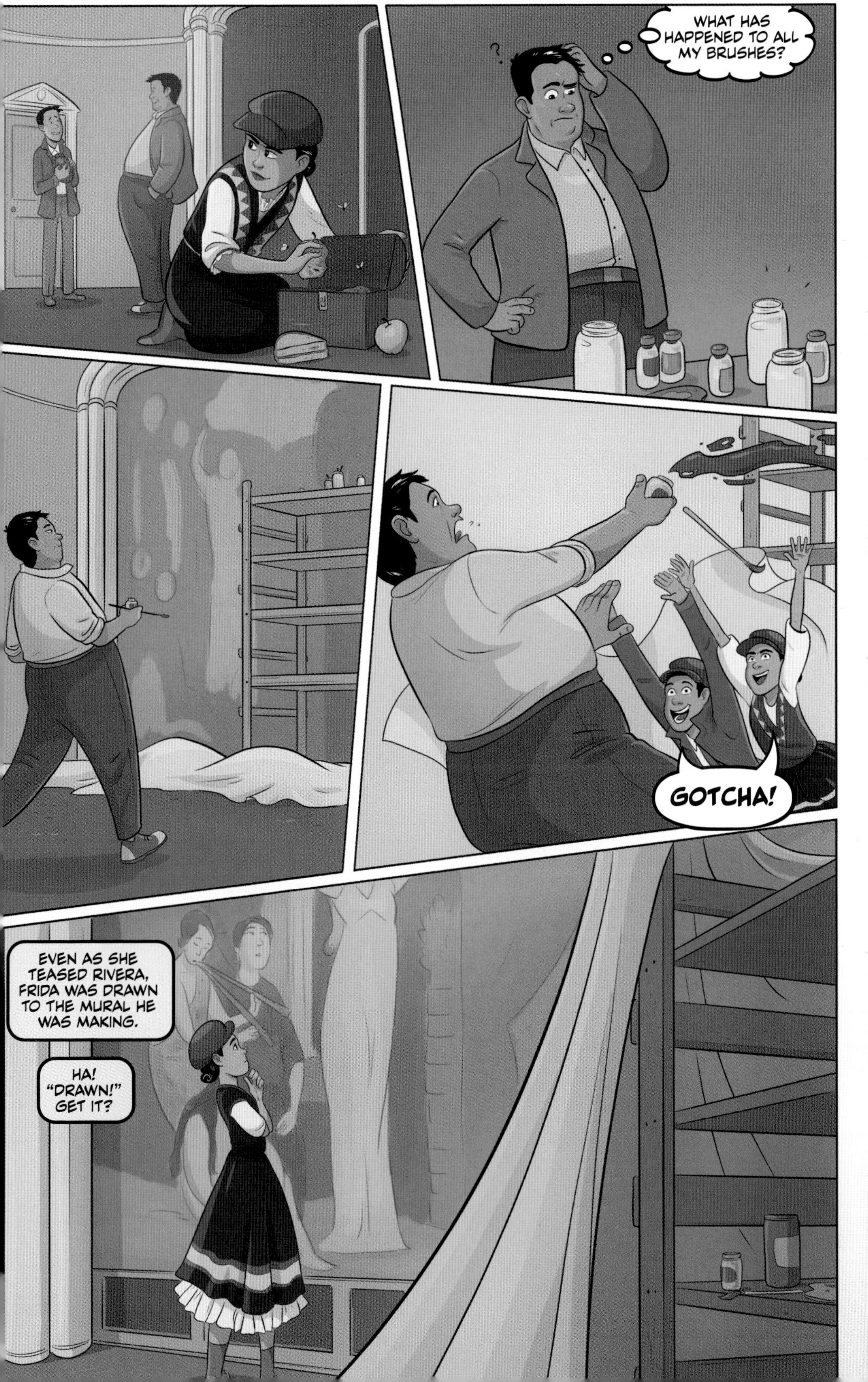
WHAT HAS HAPPENED TO ALL MY BRUSHES?
GOTCHA!
EVEN AS SHE TEASED RIVERA, FRIDA WAS DRAWN TO THE MURAL HE WAS MAKING.
HA! "DRAWN!" GET IT?

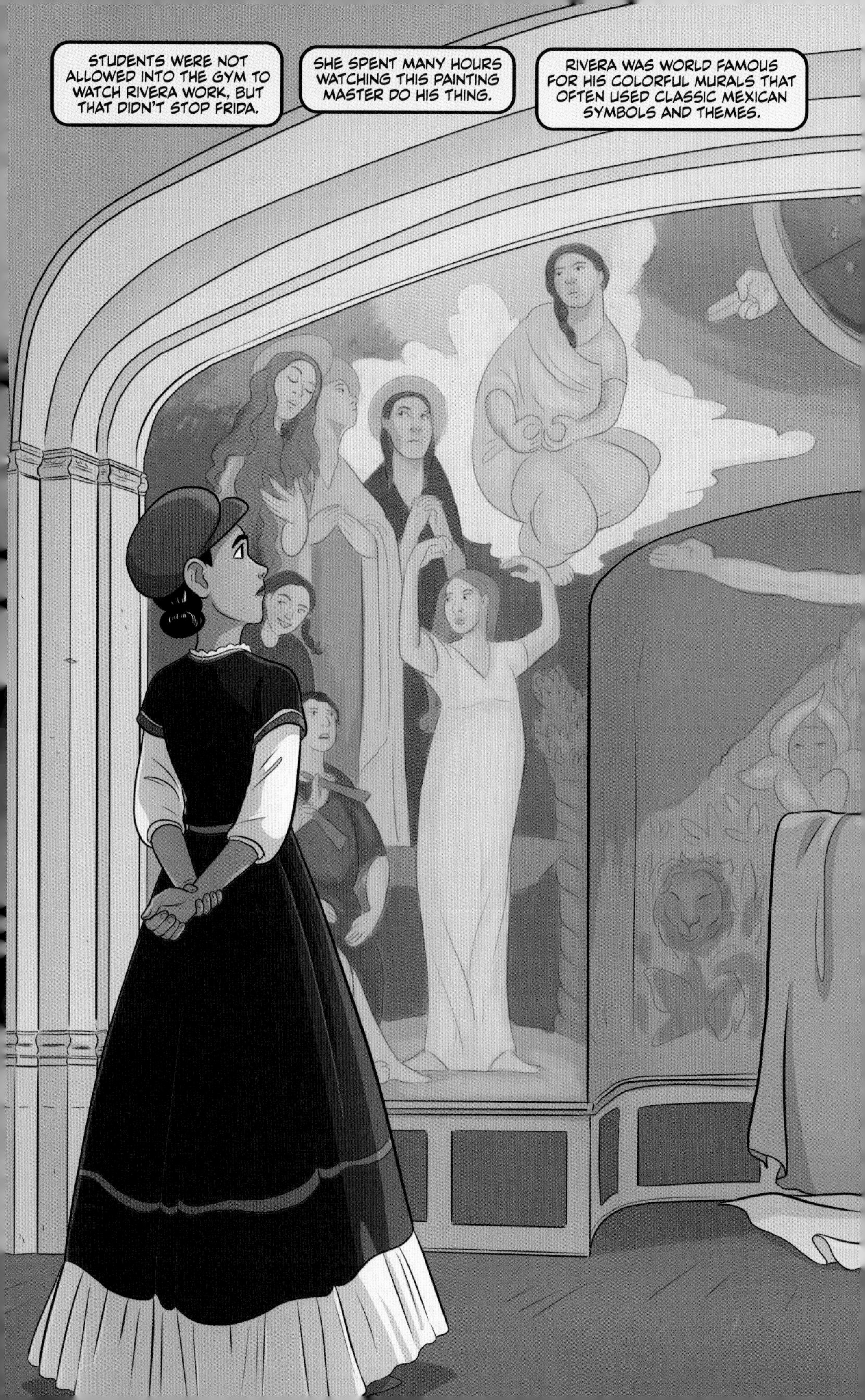
STUDENTS WERE NOT ALLOWED INTO THE GYM TO WATCH RIVERA WORK, BUT THAT DIDN'T STOP FRIDA.
SHE SPENT MANY HOURS WATCHING THIS PAINTING MASTER DO HIS THING.
RIVERA WAS WORLD FAMOUS FOR HIS COLORFUL MURALS THAT OFTEN USED CLASSIC MEXICAN SYMBOLS AND THEMES.

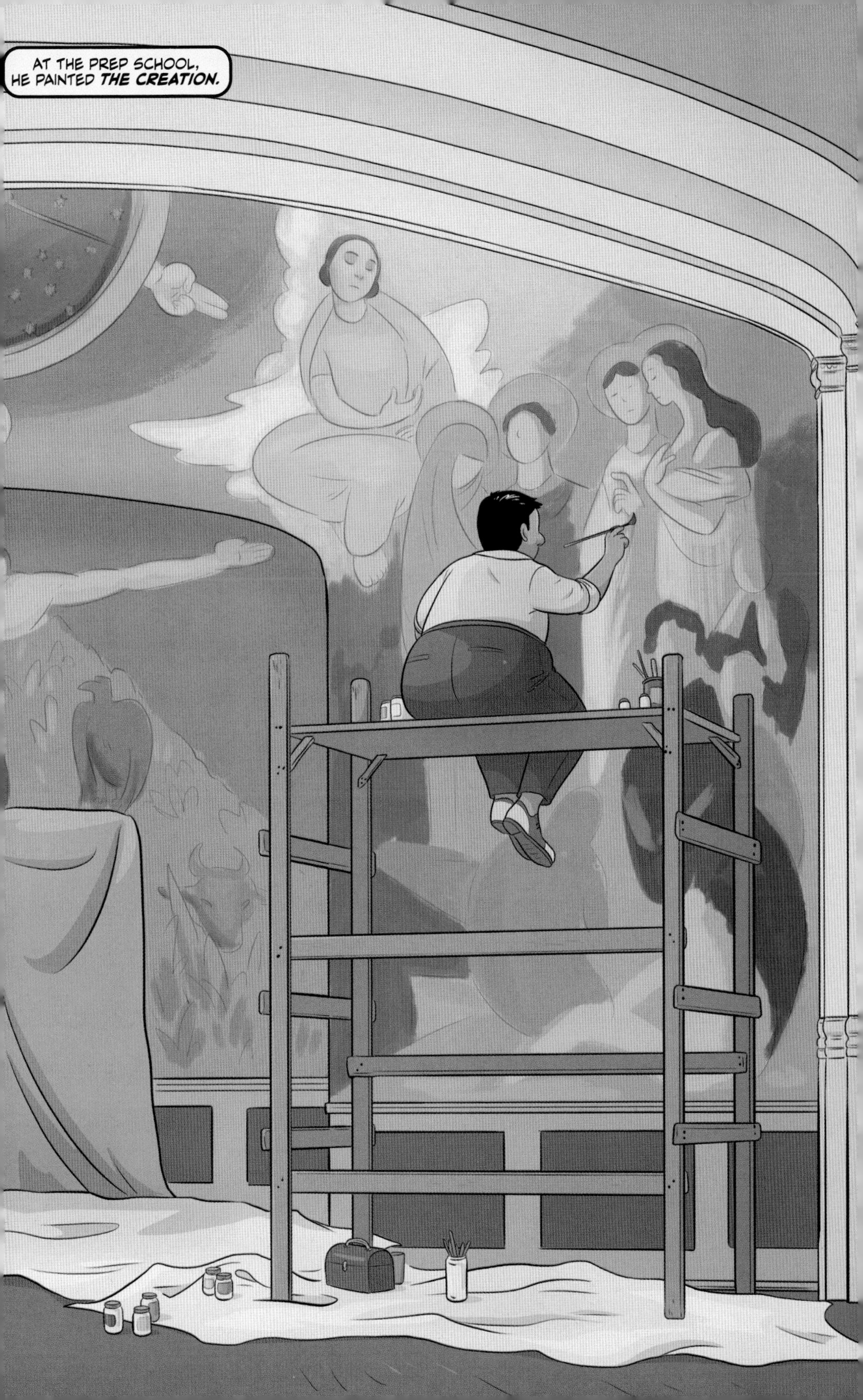
AT THE PREP SCHOOL, HE PAINTED *THE CREATION.*

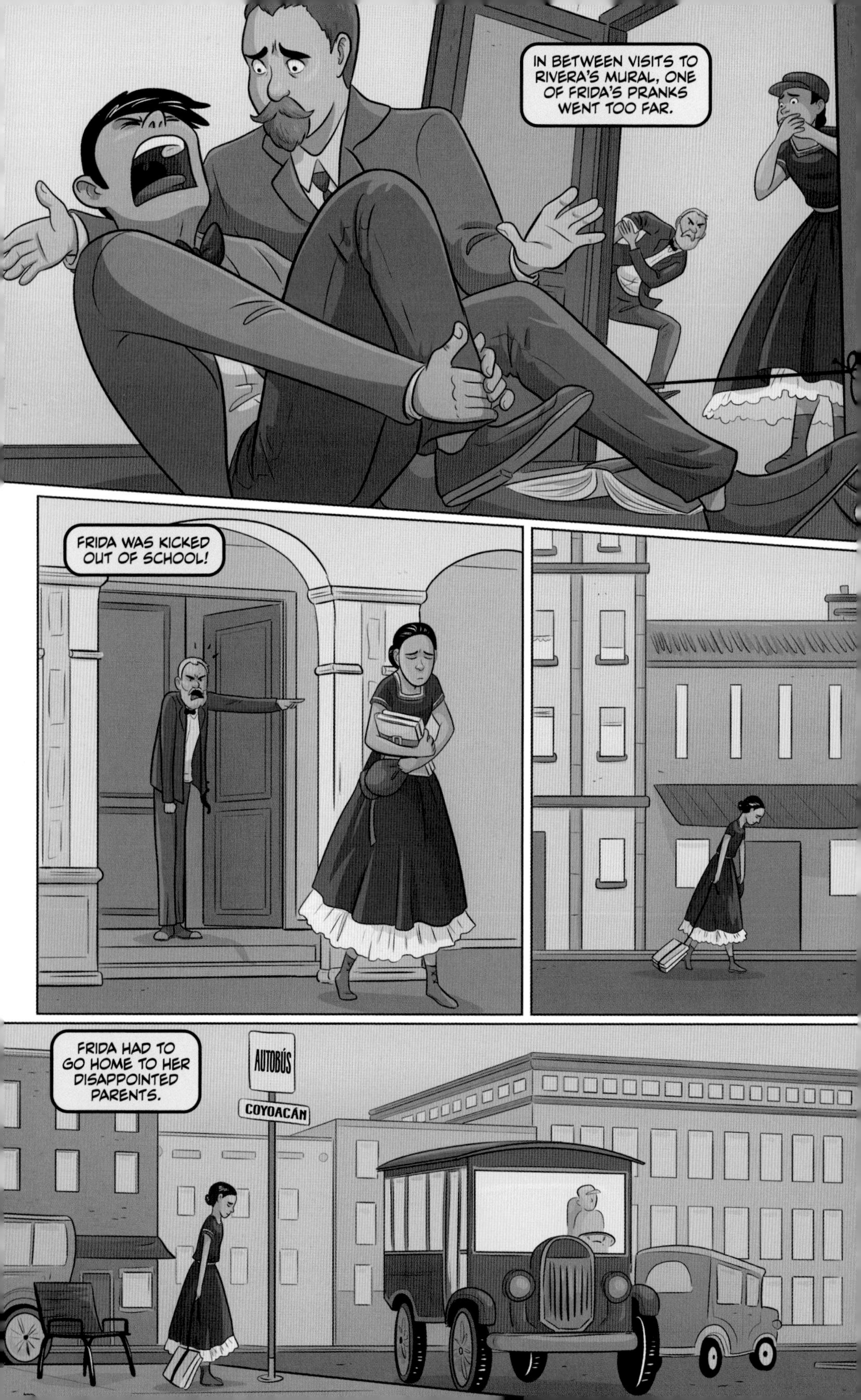
IN BETWEEN VISITS TO RIVERA'S MURAL, ONE OF FRIDA'S PRANKS WENT TOO FAR.
FRIDA WAS KICKED OUT OF SCHOOL!
FRIDA HAD TO GO HOME TO HER DISAPPOINTED PARENTS.
AUTOBÚS
COYOACÁN

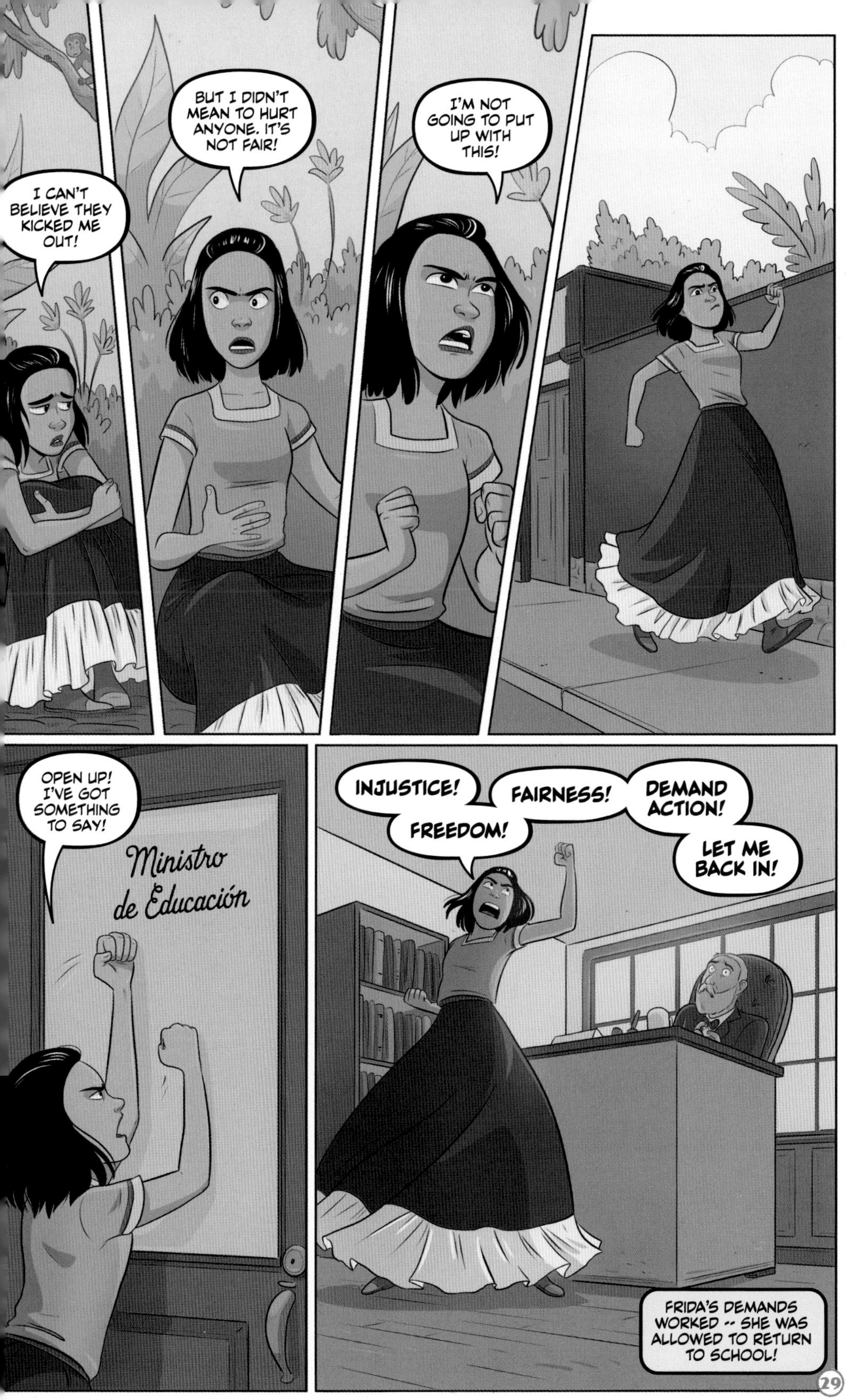
I CAN'T BELIEVE THEY KICKED ME OUT!
BUT I DIDN'T MEAN TO HURT ANYONE. IT'S NOT FAIR!
I'M NOT GOING TO PUT UP WITH THIS!
OPEN UP! I'VE GOT SOMETHING TO SAY!
Ministro de Educación
INJUSTICE!
FREEDOM!
FAIRNESS!
DEMAND ACTION!
LET ME BACK IN!
FRIDA'S DEMANDS WORKED -- SHE WAS ALLOWED TO RETURN TO SCHOOL!

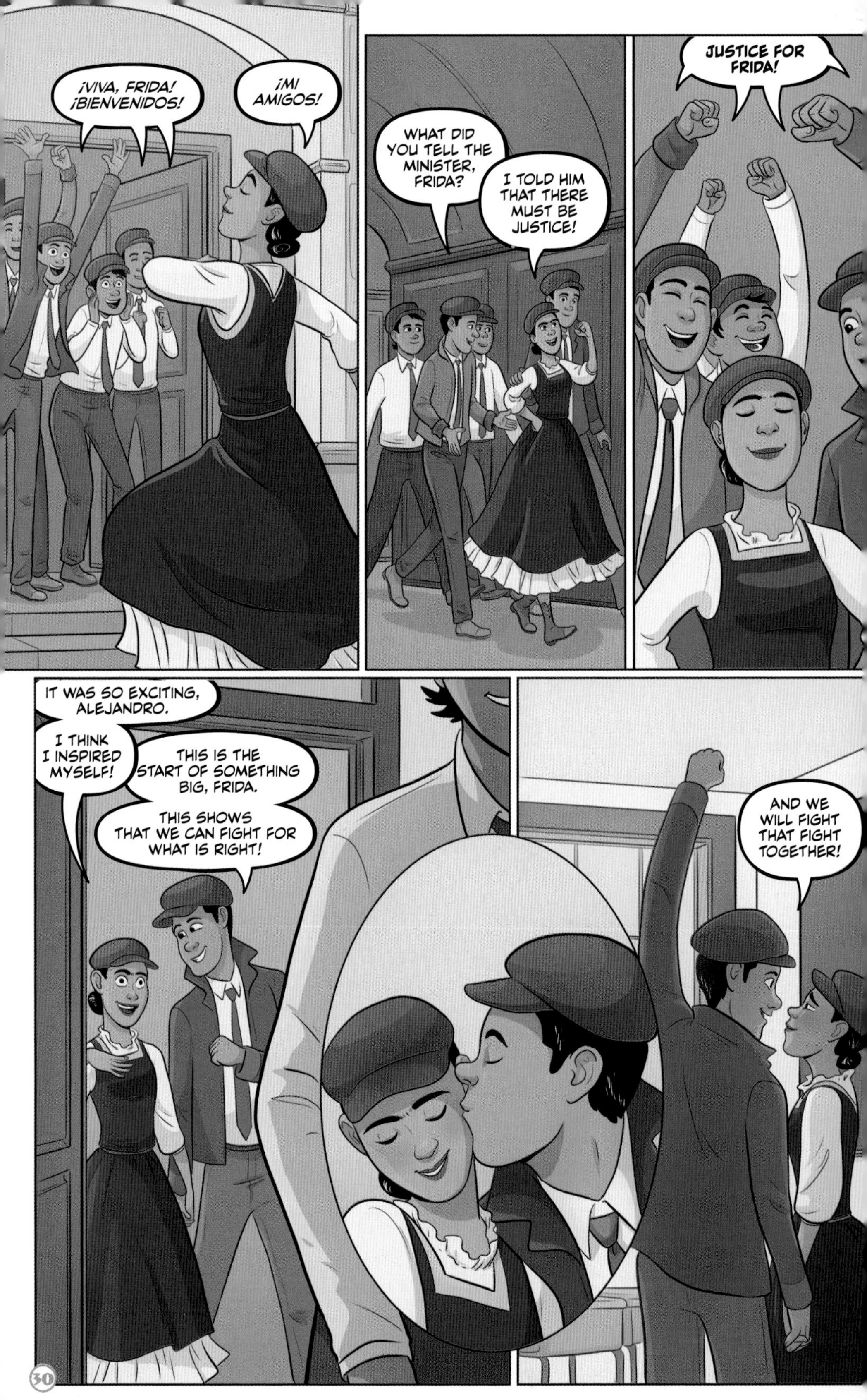

¡VIVA, FRIDA! ¡BIENVENIDOS!
¡MI AMIGOS!
WHAT DID YOU TELL THE MINISTER, FRIDA?
I TOLD HIM THAT THERE MUST BE JUSTICE!
JUSTICE FOR FRIDA!
IT WAS SO EXCITING, ALEJANDRO.
I THINK I INSPIRED MYSELF!
THIS IS THE START OF SOMETHING BIG, FRIDA.
THIS SHOWS THAT WE CAN FIGHT FOR WHAT IS RIGHT!
AND WE WILL FIGHT THAT FIGHT TOGETHER!

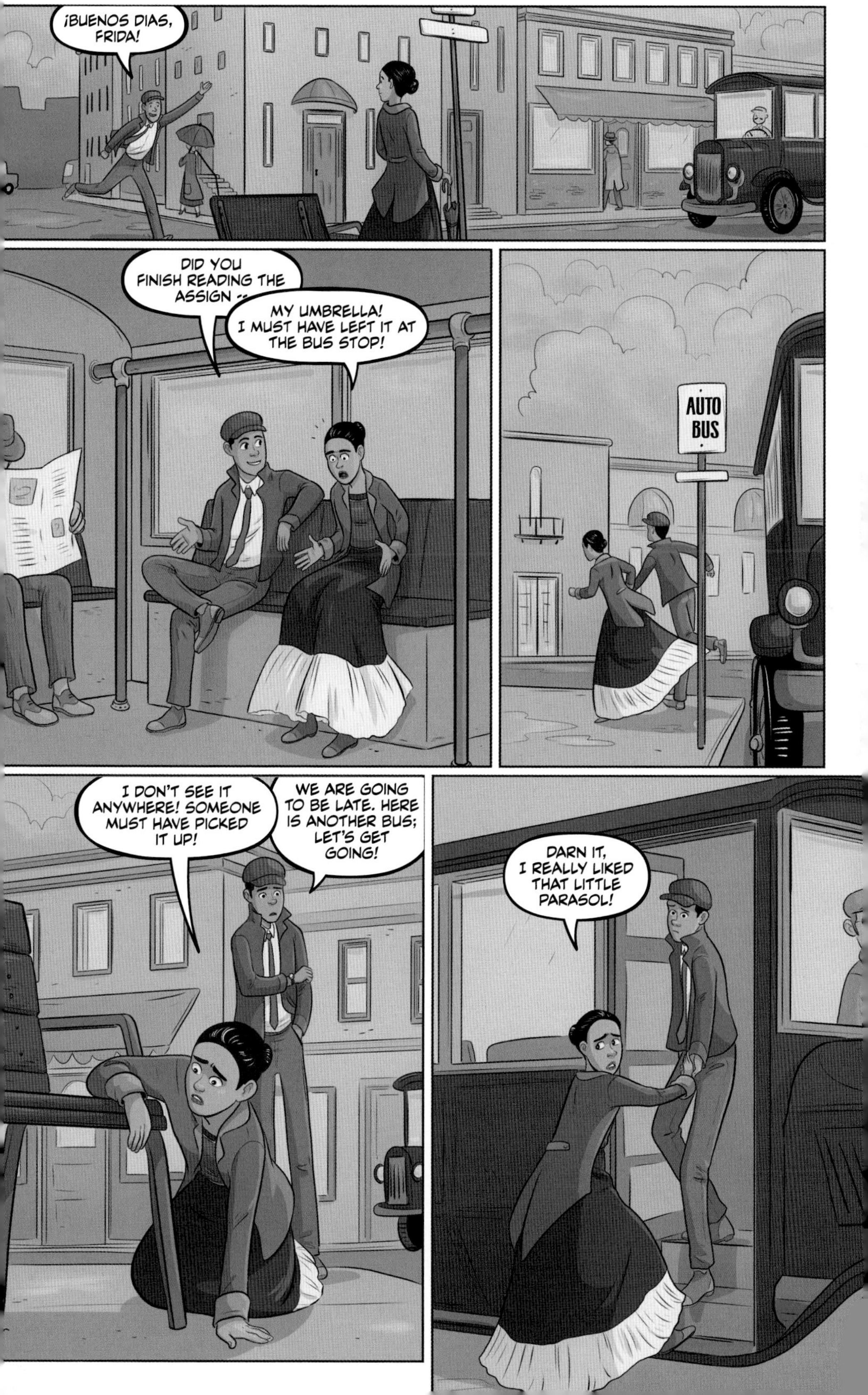

¡BUENOS DIAS, FRIDA!
DID YOU FINISH READING THE ASSIGN --
MY UMBRELLA! I MUST HAVE LEFT IT AT THE BUS STOP!
AUTO BUS
I DON'T SEE IT ANYWHERE! SOMEONE MUST HAVE PICKED IT UP!
WE ARE GOING TO BE LATE. HERE IS ANOTHER BUS; LET'S GET GOING!
DARN IT, I REALLY LIKED THAT LITTLE PARASOL!

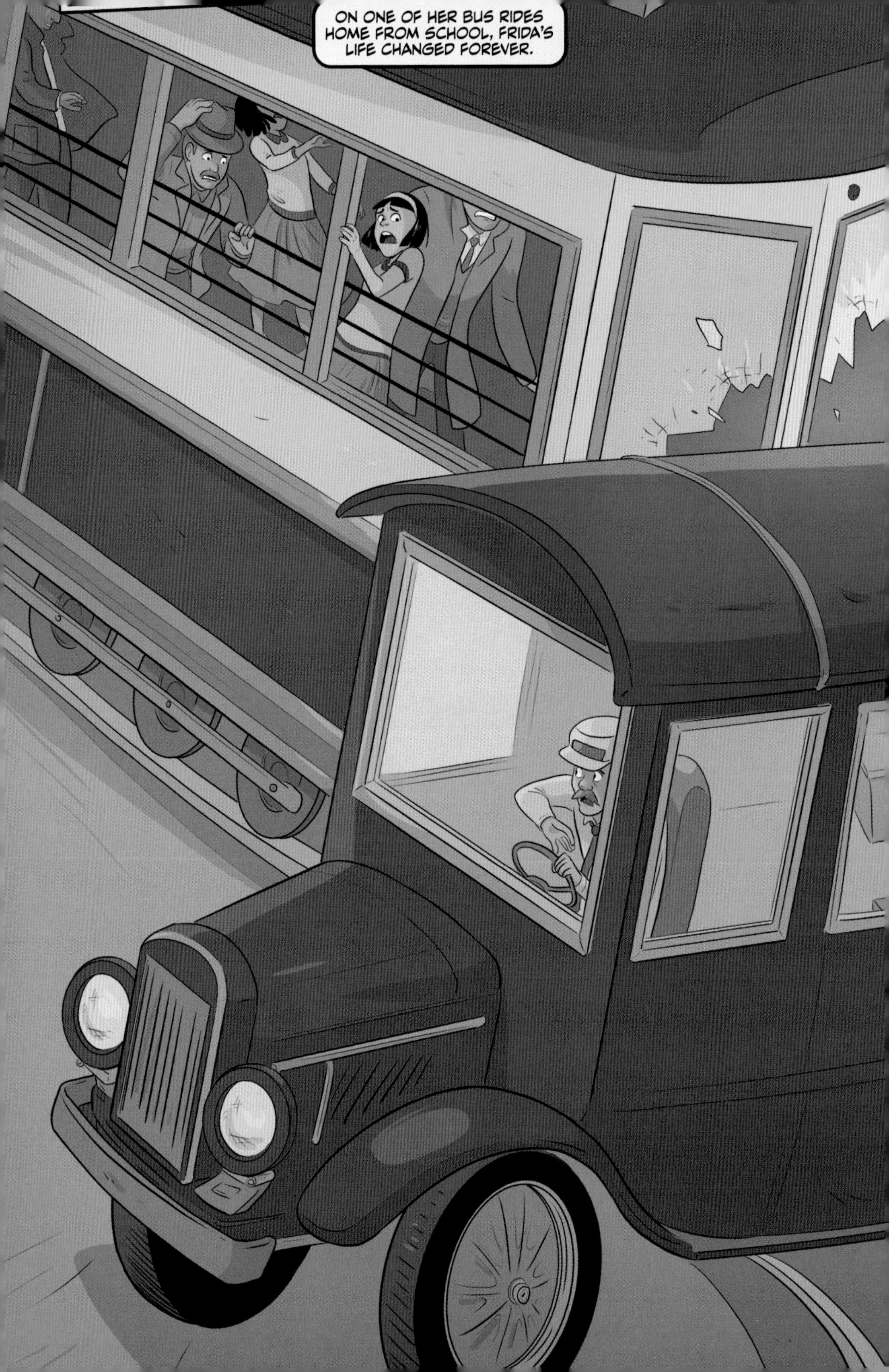
ON ONE OF HER BUS RIDES HOME FROM SCHOOL, FRIDA'S LIFE CHANGED FOREVER.

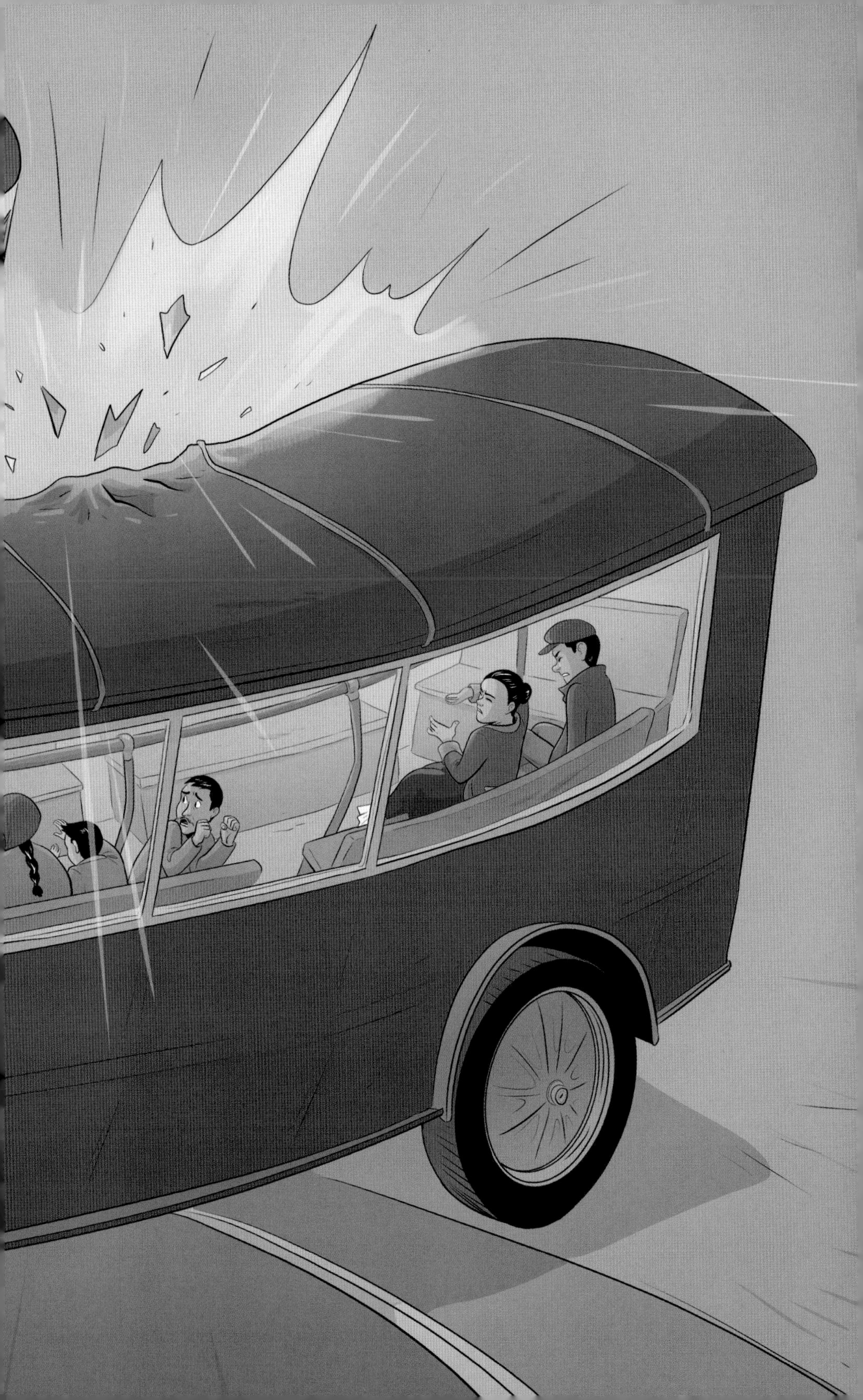

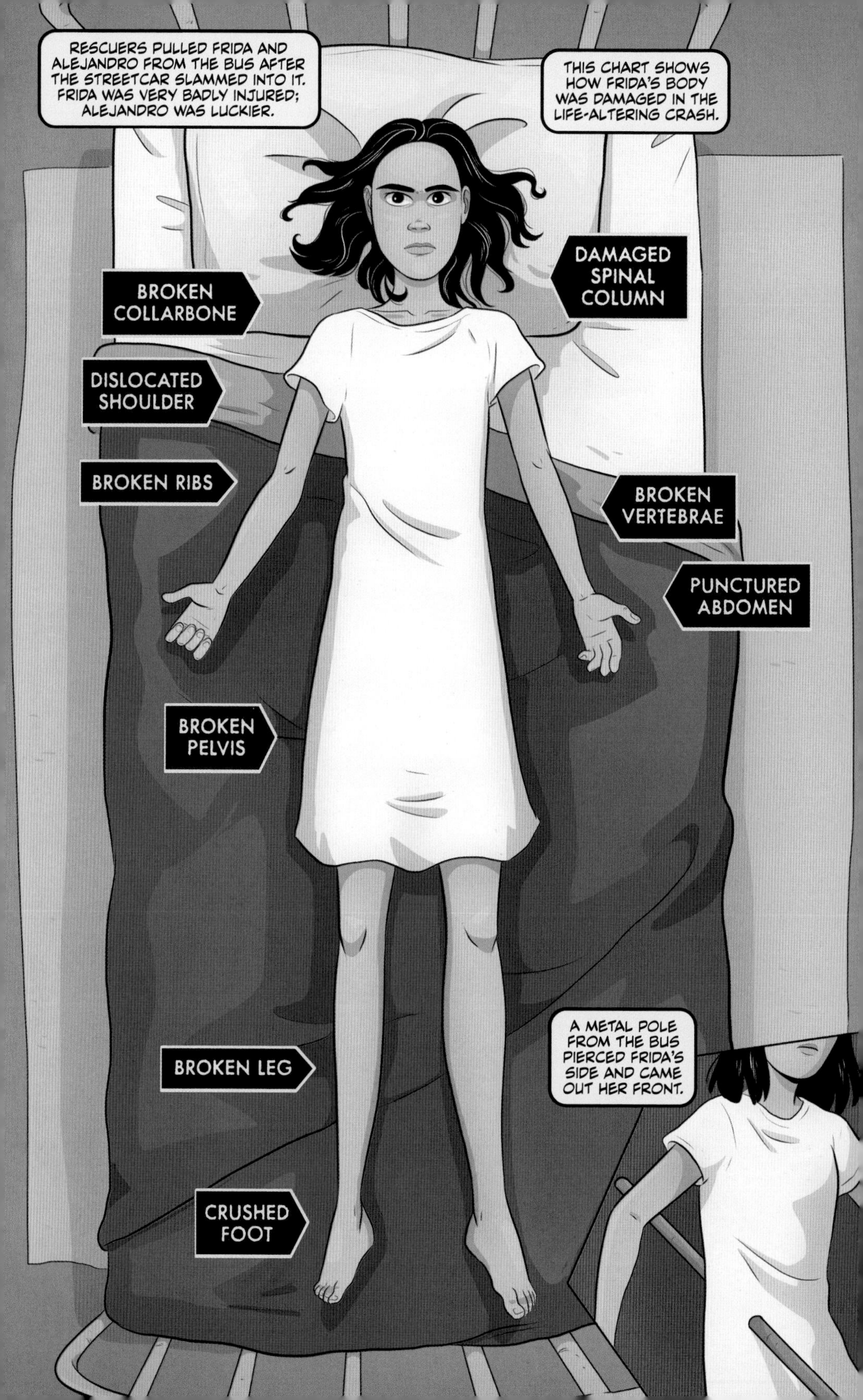
RESCUERS PULLED FRIDA AND ALEJANDRO FROM THE BUS AFTER THE STREETCAR SLAMMED INTO IT. FRIDA WAS VERY BADLY INJURED; ALEJANDRO WAS LUCKIER.
THIS CHART SHOWS HOW FRIDA'S BODY WAS DAMAGED IN THE LIFE-ALTERING CRASH.
BROKEN COLLARBONE
DAMAGED SPINAL COLUMN
DISLOCATED SHOULDER
BROKEN RIBS
BROKEN VERTEBRAE
PUNCTURED ABDOMEN
BROKEN PELVIS
BROKEN LEG
A METAL POLE FROM THE BUS PIERCED FRIDA'S SIDE AND CAME OUT HER FRONT.
CRUSHED FOOT

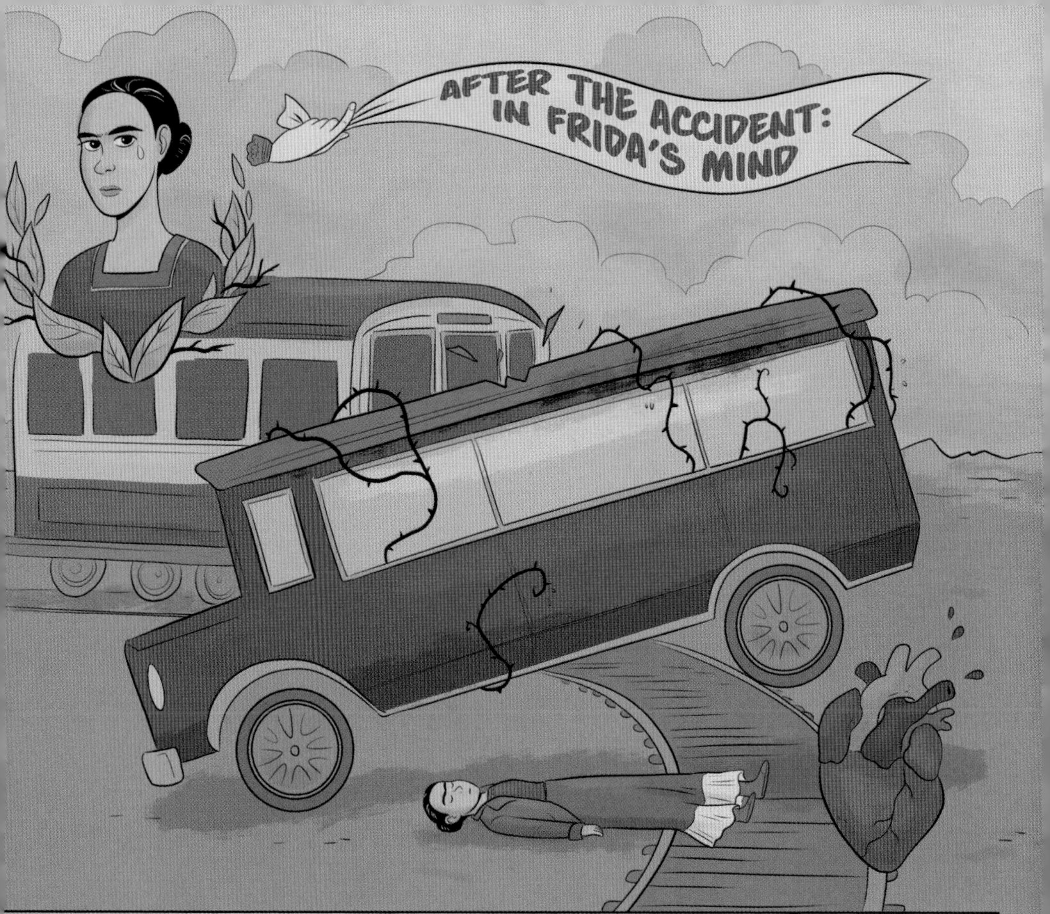
AFTER THE ACCIDENT: IN FRIDA'S MIND

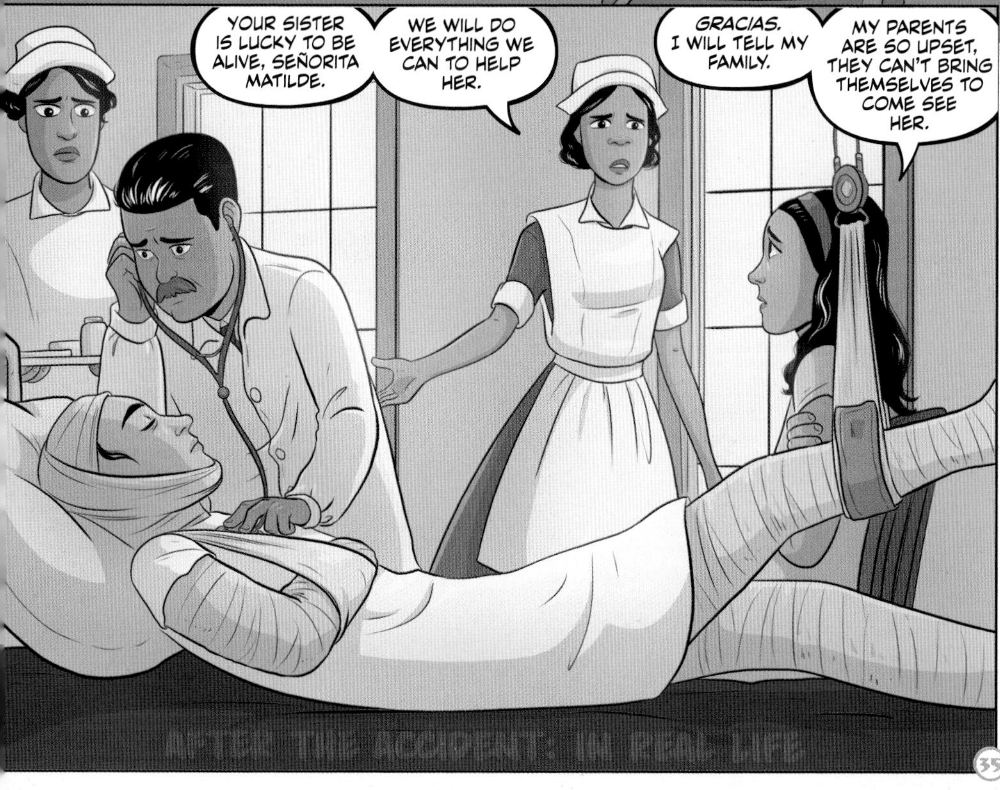
YOUR SISTER IS LUCKY TO BE ALIVE, SEÑORITA MATILDE.
WE WILL DO EVERYTHING WE CAN TO HELP HER.
GRACIAS. I WILL TELL MY FAMILY.
MY PARENTS ARE SO UPSET, THEY CAN'T BRING THEMSELVES TO COME SEE HER.
AFTER THE ACCIDENT: IN REAL LIFE

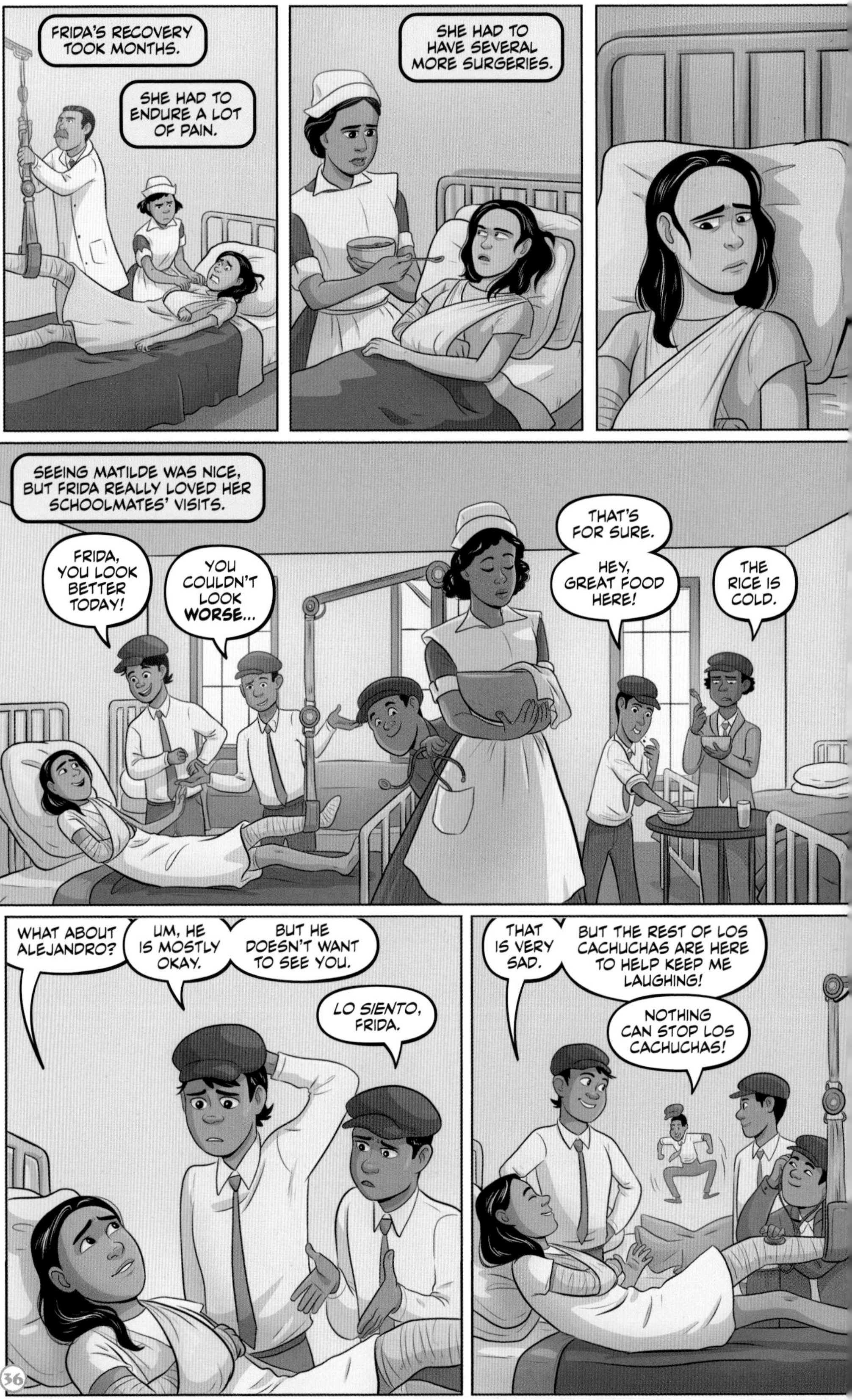
FRIDA'S RECOVERY TOOK MONTHS.
SHE HAD TO ENDURE A LOT OF PAIN.
SHE HAD TO HAVE SEVERAL MORE SURGERIES.
SEEING MATILDE WAS NICE, BUT FRIDA REALLY LOVED HER SCHOOLMATES' VISITS.
FRIDA, YOU LOOK BETTER TODAY!
YOU COULDN'T LOOK **WORSE**...
THAT'S FOR SURE.
HEY, GREAT FOOD HERE!
THE RICE IS COLD.
WHAT ABOUT ALEJANDRO?
UM, HE IS MOSTLY OKAY.
BUT HE DOESN'T WANT TO SEE YOU.
LO SIENTO, FRIDA.
THAT IS VERY SAD.
BUT THE REST OF LOS CACHUCHAS ARE HERE TO HELP KEEP ME LAUGHING!
NOTHING CAN STOP LOS CACHUCHAS!

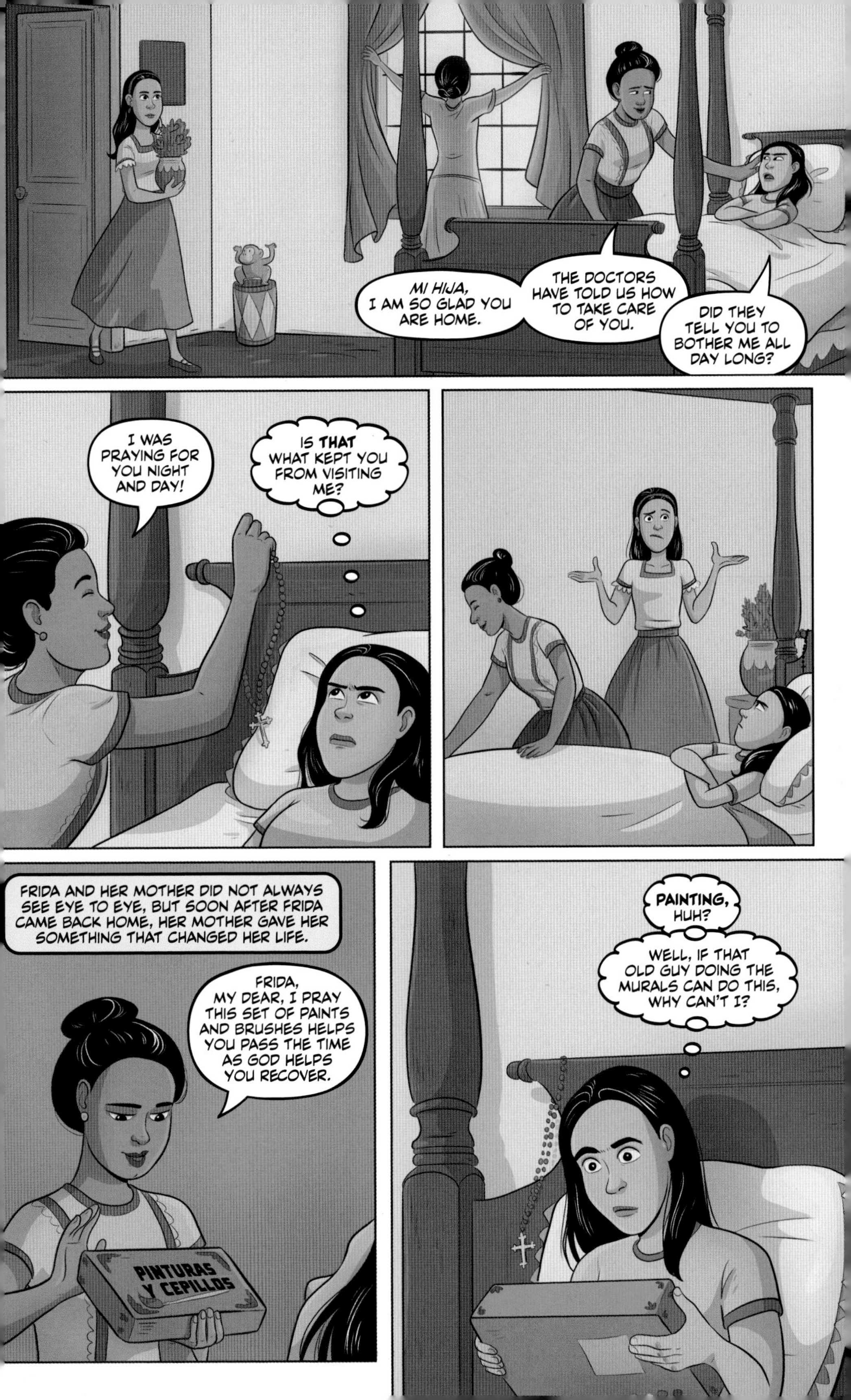

MI HIJA, I AM SO GLAD YOU ARE HOME.
THE DOCTORS HAVE TOLD US HOW TO TAKE CARE OF YOU.
DID THEY TELL YOU TO BOTHER ME ALL DAY LONG?
I WAS PRAYING FOR YOU NIGHT AND DAY!
IS **THAT** WHAT KEPT YOU FROM VISITING ME?
FRIDA AND HER MOTHER DID NOT ALWAYS SEE EYE TO EYE, BUT SOON AFTER FRIDA CAME BACK HOME, HER MOTHER GAVE HER SOMETHING THAT CHANGED HER LIFE.
FRIDA, MY DEAR, I PRAY THIS SET OF PAINTS AND BRUSHES HELPS YOU PASS THE TIME AS GOD HELPS YOU RECOVER.
PINTURAS Y CEPILLOS
PAINTING, HUH?
WELL, IF THAT OLD GUY DOING THE MURALS CAN DO THIS, WHY CAN'T I?

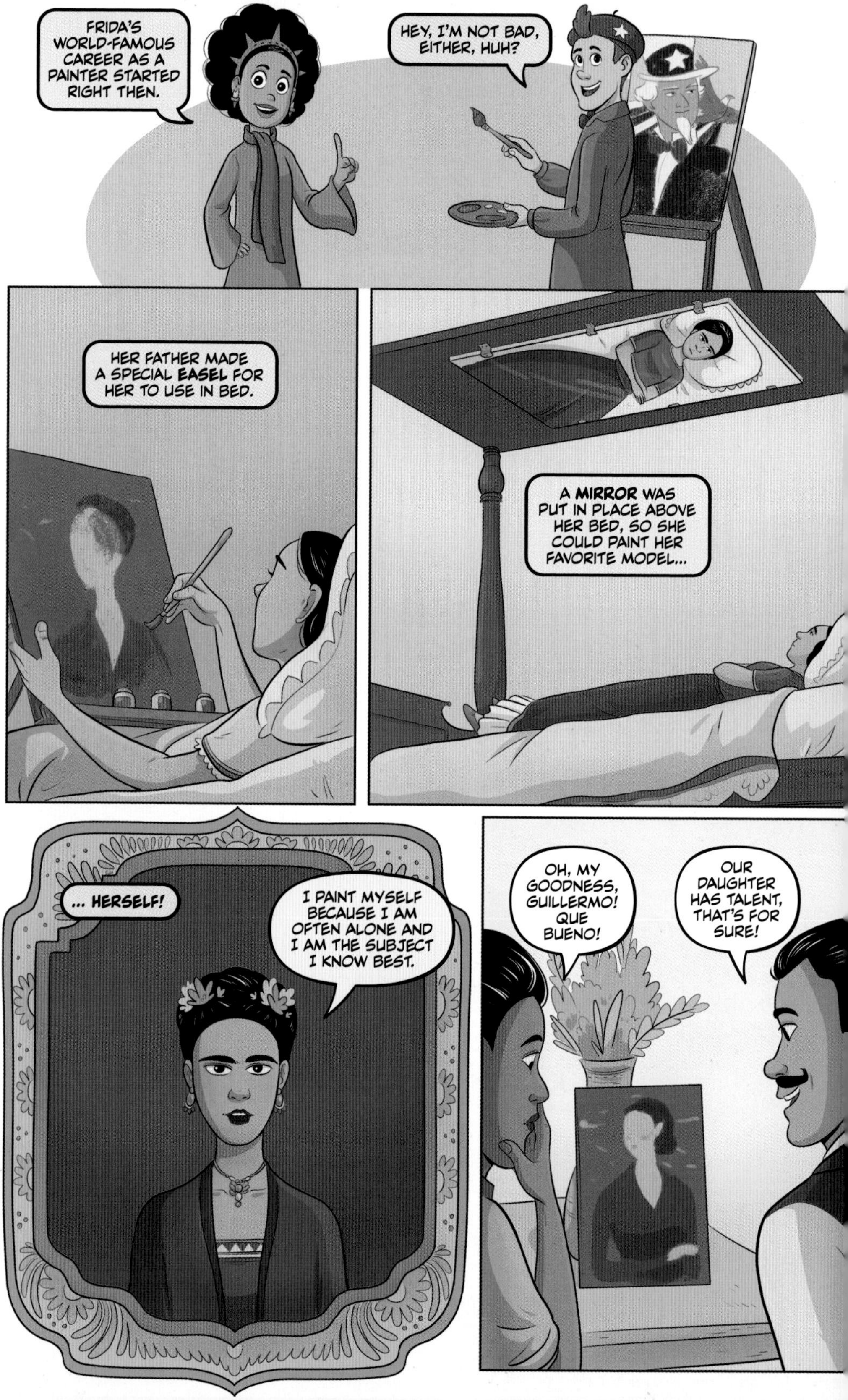
FRIDA'S WORLD-FAMOUS CAREER AS A PAINTER STARTED RIGHT THEN.
HEY, I'M NOT BAD, EITHER, HUH?
HER FATHER MADE A SPECIAL **EASEL** FOR HER TO USE IN BED.
A **MIRROR** WAS PUT IN PLACE ABOVE HER BED, SO SHE COULD PAINT HER FAVORITE MODEL...
... **HERSELF!**
I PAINT MYSELF BECAUSE I AM OFTEN ALONE AND I AM THE SUBJECT I KNOW BEST.
OH, MY GOODNESS, GUILLERMO! QUE BUENO!
OUR DAUGHTER HAS TALENT, THAT'S FOR SURE!

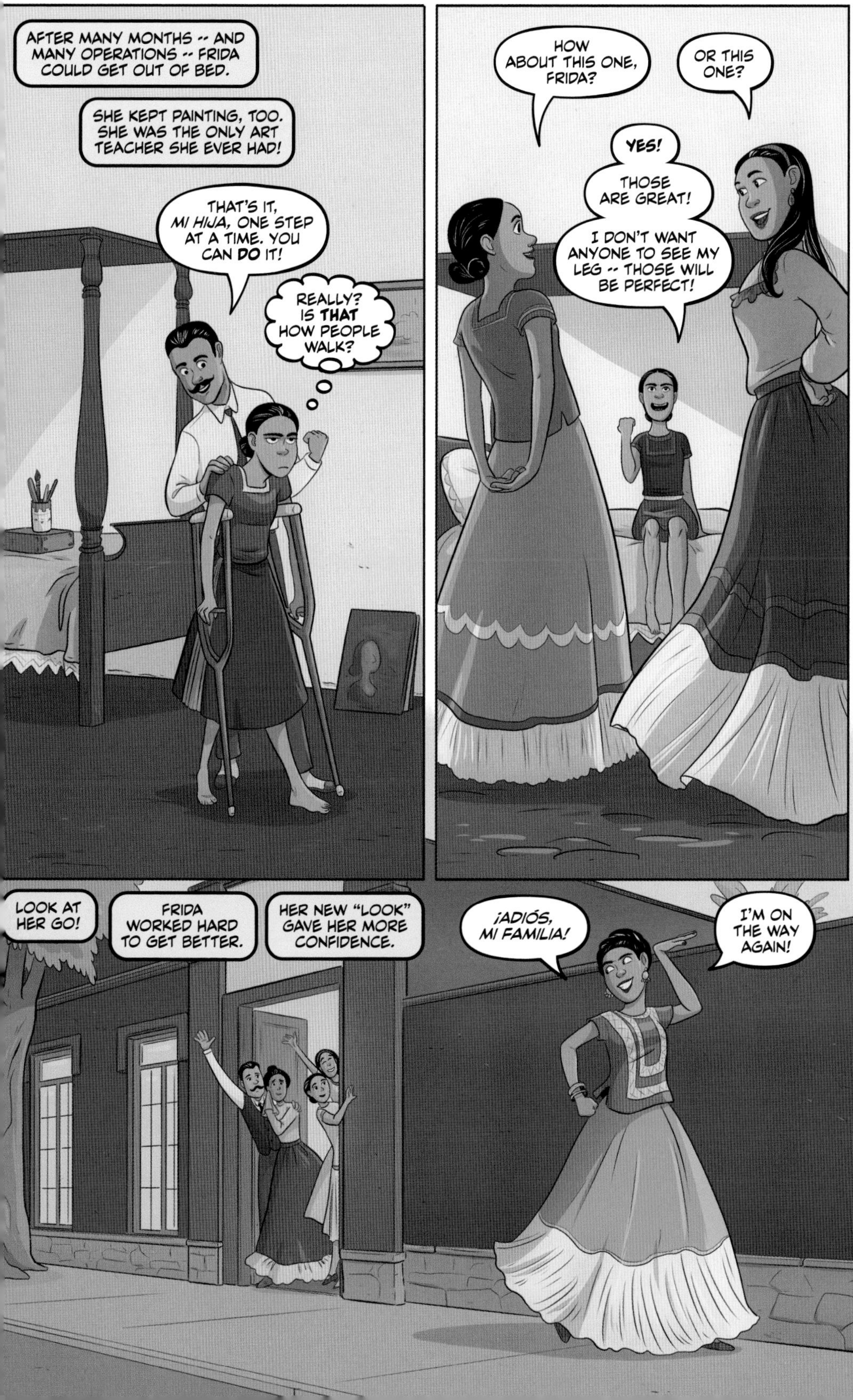
AFTER MANY MONTHS -- AND MANY OPERATIONS -- FRIDA COULD GET OUT OF BED.
SHE KEPT PAINTING, TOO. SHE WAS THE ONLY ART TEACHER SHE EVER HAD!
THAT'S IT, *MI HIJA*, ONE STEP AT A TIME. YOU CAN **DO** IT!
REALLY? IS **THAT** HOW PEOPLE WALK?
HOW ABOUT THIS ONE, FRIDA?
OR THIS ONE?
YES!
THOSE ARE GREAT!
I DON'T WANT ANYONE TO SEE MY LEG -- THOSE WILL BE PERFECT!
LOOK AT HER GO!
FRIDA WORKED HARD TO GET BETTER.
HER NEW "LOOK" GAVE HER MORE CONFIDENCE.
¡ADIÓS, MI FAMILIA!
I'M ON THE WAY AGAIN!

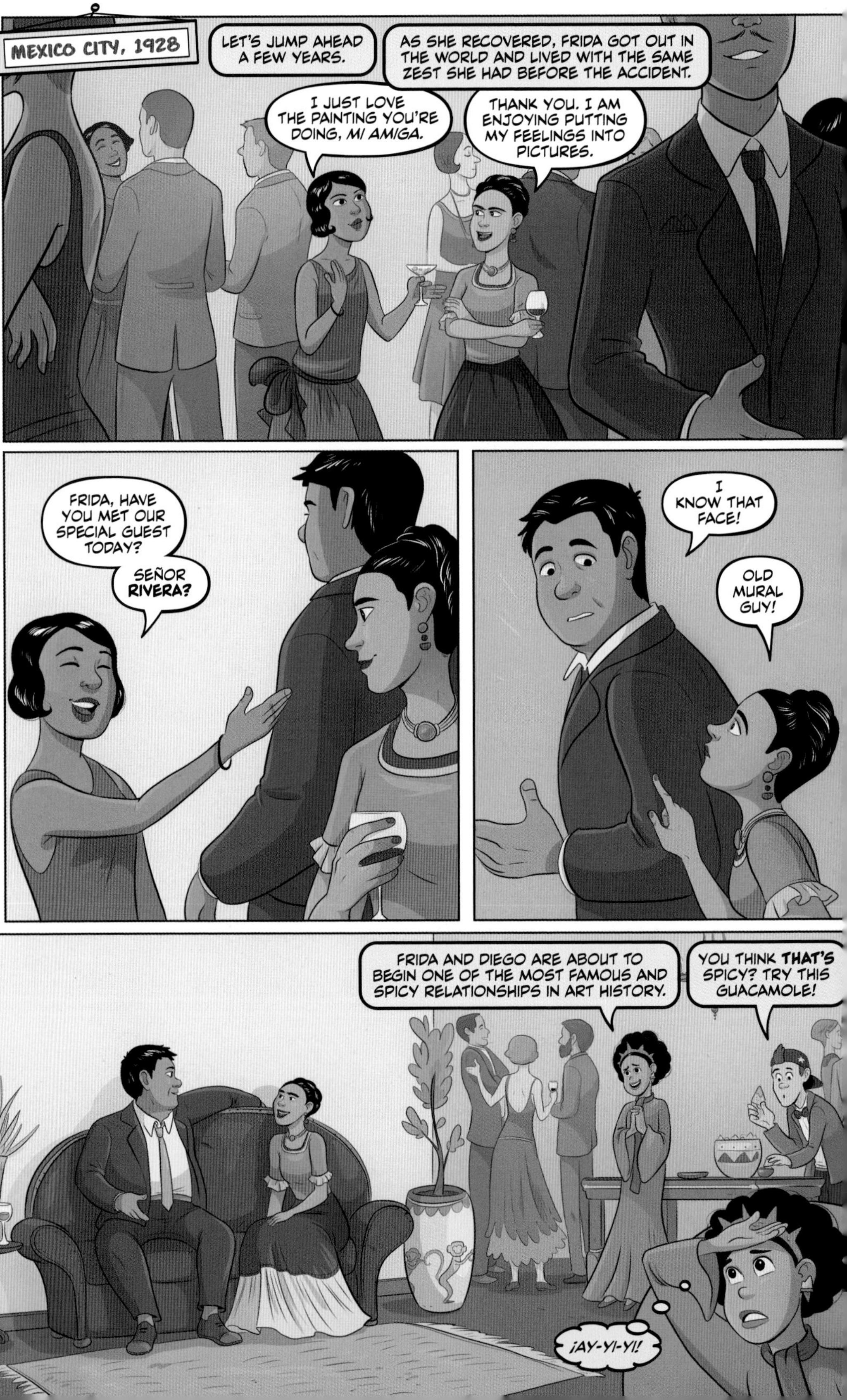
MEXICO CITY, 1928
LET'S JUMP AHEAD A FEW YEARS.
AS SHE RECOVERED, FRIDA GOT OUT IN THE WORLD AND LIVED WITH THE SAME ZEST SHE HAD BEFORE THE ACCIDENT.
I JUST LOVE THE PAINTING YOU'RE DOING, *MI AMIGA*.
THANK YOU. I AM ENJOYING PUTTING MY FEELINGS INTO PICTURES.
FRIDA, HAVE YOU MET OUR SPECIAL GUEST TODAY?
SEÑOR **RIVERA?**
I KNOW THAT FACE!
OLD MURAL GUY!
FRIDA AND DIEGO ARE ABOUT TO BEGIN ONE OF THE MOST FAMOUS AND SPICY RELATIONSHIPS IN ART HISTORY.
YOU THINK **THAT'S** SPICY? TRY THIS GUACAMOLE!
¡AY-YI-YI!

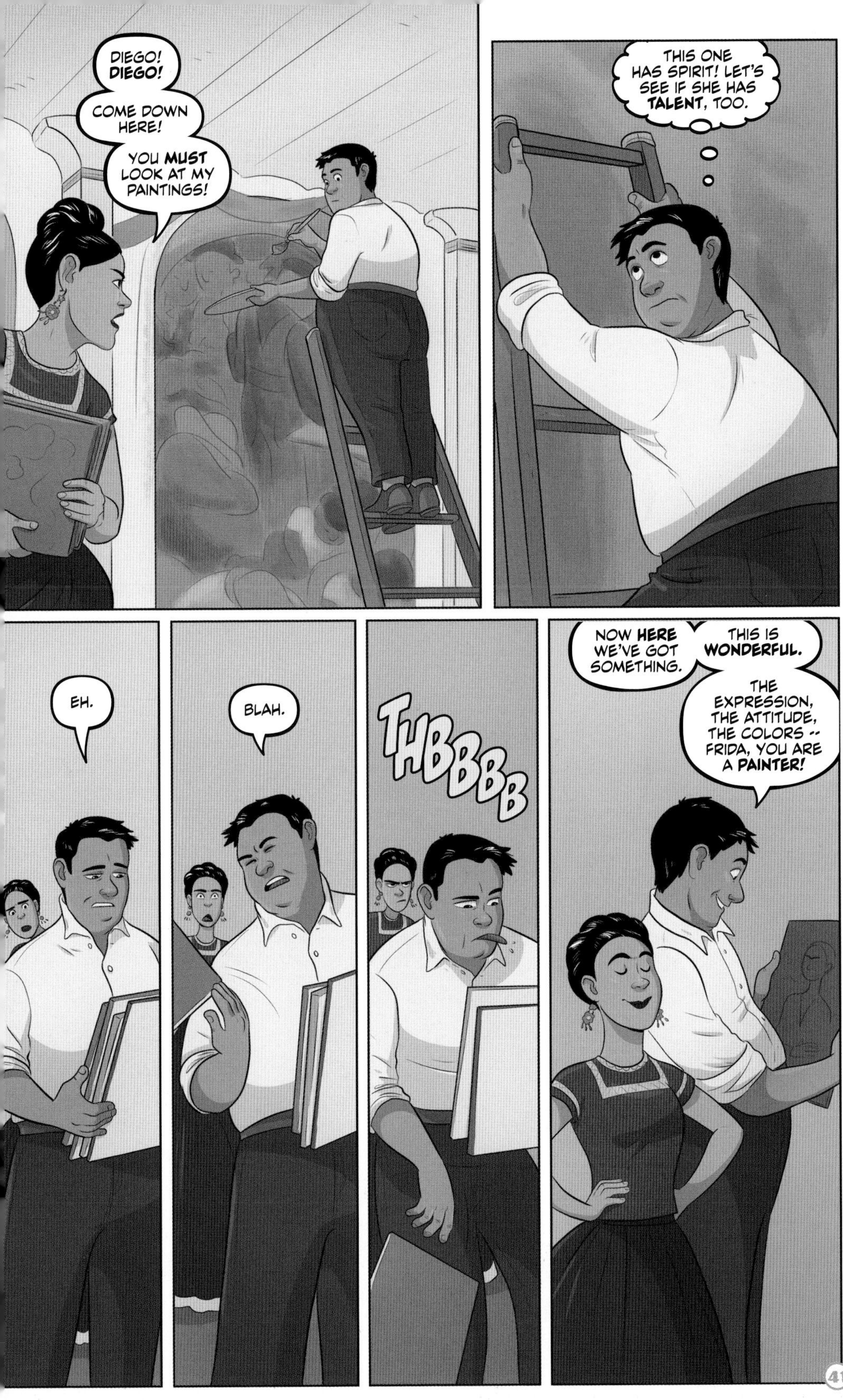
DIEGO! DIEGO!
COME DOWN HERE!
YOU MUST LOOK AT MY PAINTINGS!
THIS ONE HAS SPIRIT! LET'S SEE IF SHE HAS TALENT, TOO.
EH.
BLAH.
THBBBB
NOW HERE WE'VE GOT SOMETHING.
THIS IS WONDERFUL.
THE EXPRESSION, THE ATTITUDE, THE COLORS -- FRIDA, YOU ARE A PAINTER!

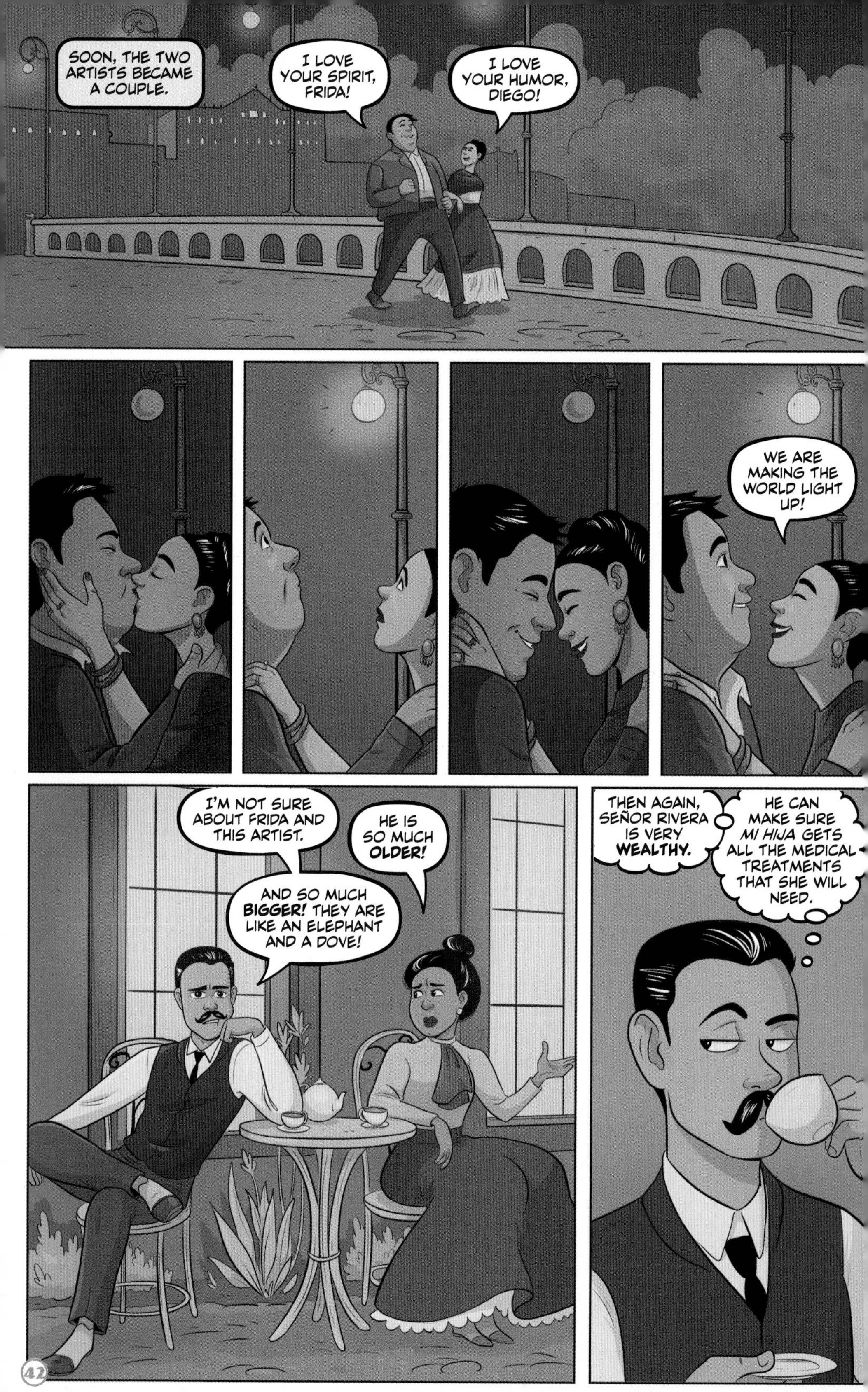
SOON, THE TWO ARTISTS BECAME A COUPLE.
I LOVE YOUR SPIRIT, FRIDA!
I LOVE YOUR HUMOR, DIEGO!
WE ARE MAKING THE WORLD LIGHT UP!
I'M NOT SURE ABOUT FRIDA AND THIS ARTIST.
HE IS SO MUCH **OLDER!**
AND SO MUCH **BIGGER!** THEY ARE LIKE AN ELEPHANT AND A DOVE!
THEN AGAIN, SEÑOR RIVERA IS VERY **WEALTHY.**
HE CAN MAKE SURE *MI HIJA* GETS ALL THE MEDICAL TREATMENTS THAT SHE WILL NEED.

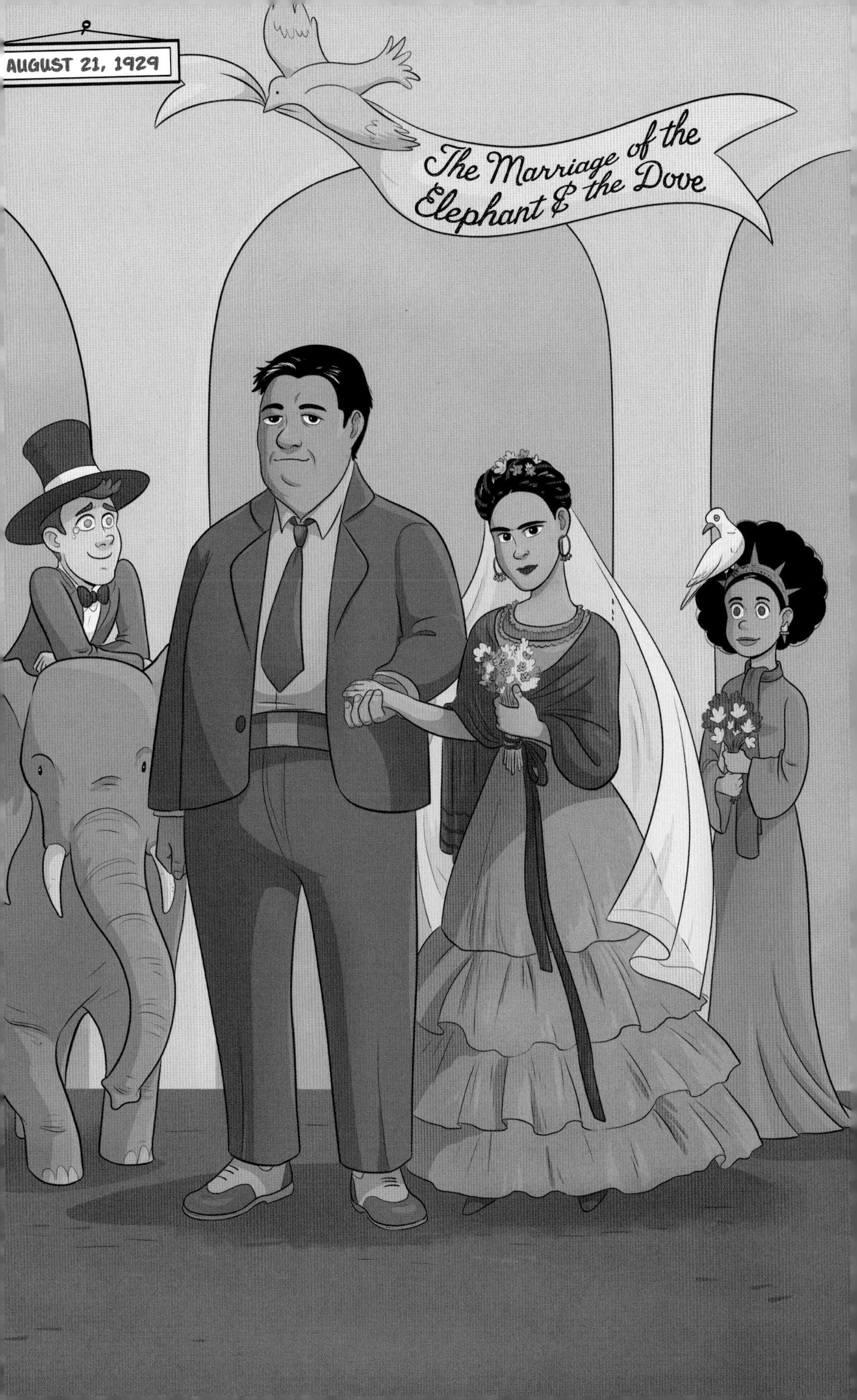
AUGUST 21, 1929
The Marriage of the Elephant & the Dove

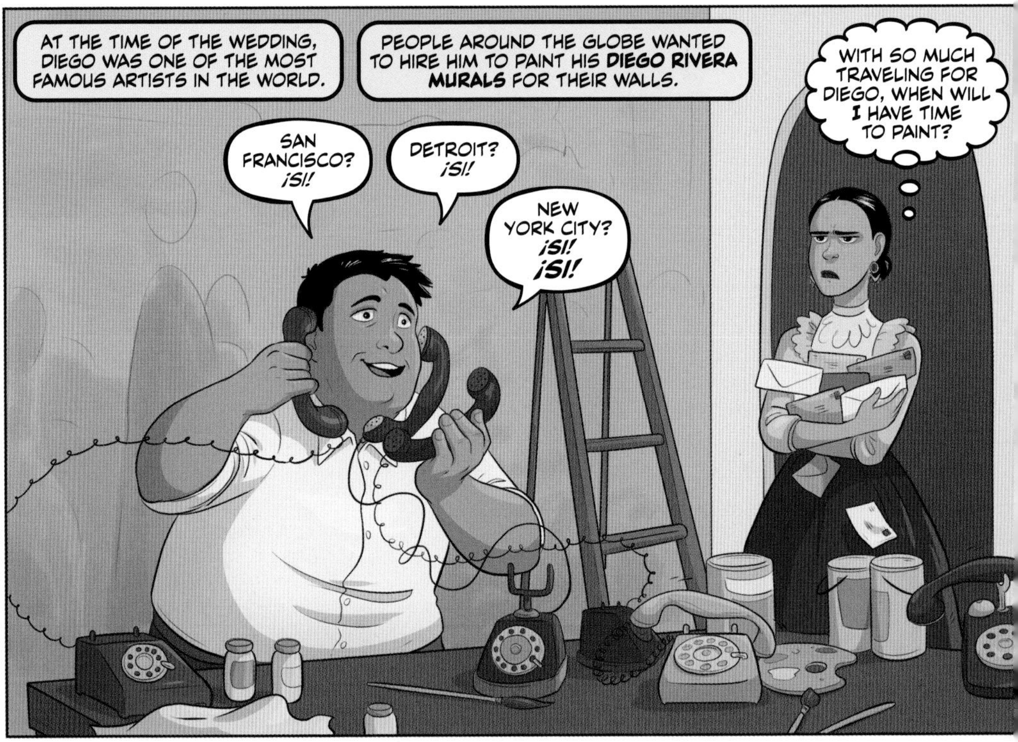
AT THE TIME OF THE WEDDING, DIEGO WAS ONE OF THE MOST FAMOUS ARTISTS IN THE WORLD.
PEOPLE AROUND THE GLOBE WANTED TO HIRE HIM TO PAINT HIS **DIEGO RIVERA MURALS** FOR THEIR WALLS.
SAN FRANCISCO? *¡SI!*
DETROIT? *¡SI!*
NEW YORK CITY? ***¡SI! ¡SI!***
WITH SO MUCH TRAVELING FOR DIEGO, WHEN WILL **I** HAVE TIME TO PAINT?

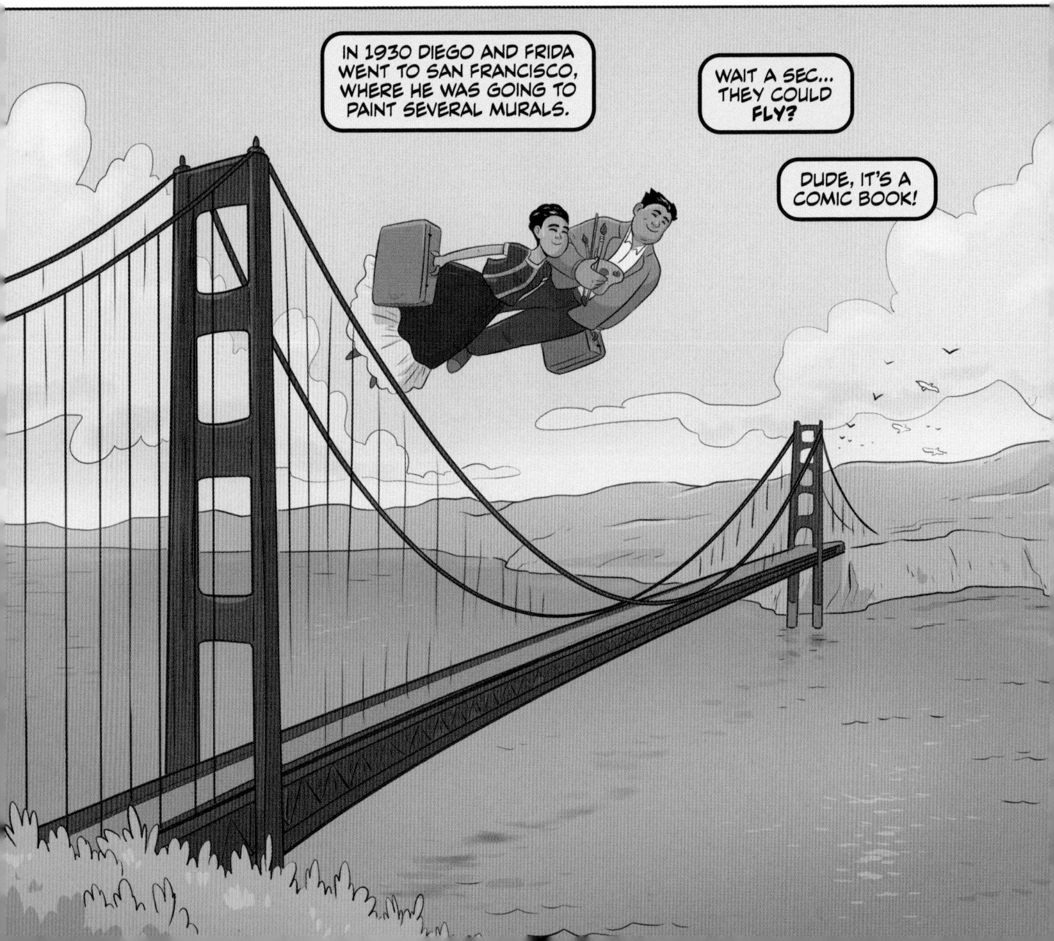
IN 1930 DIEGO AND FRIDA WENT TO SAN FRANCISCO, WHERE HE WAS GOING TO PAINT SEVERAL MURALS.
WAIT A SEC... THEY COULD **FLY?**
DUDE, IT'S A COMIC BOOK!

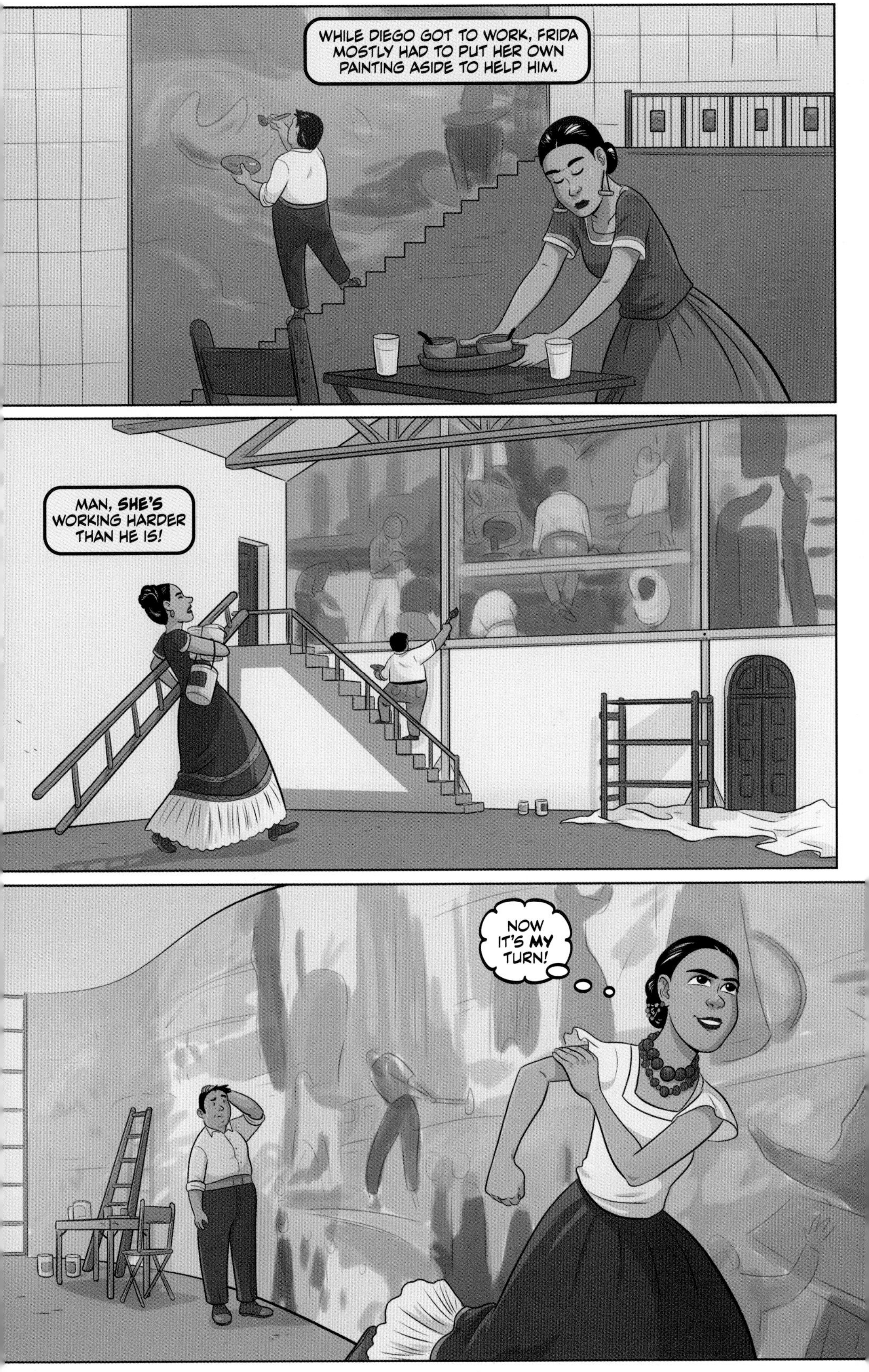
WHILE DIEGO GOT TO WORK, FRIDA MOSTLY HAD TO PUT HER OWN PAINTING ASIDE TO HELP HIM.
MAN, SHE'S WORKING HARDER THAN HE IS!
NOW IT'S MY TURN!

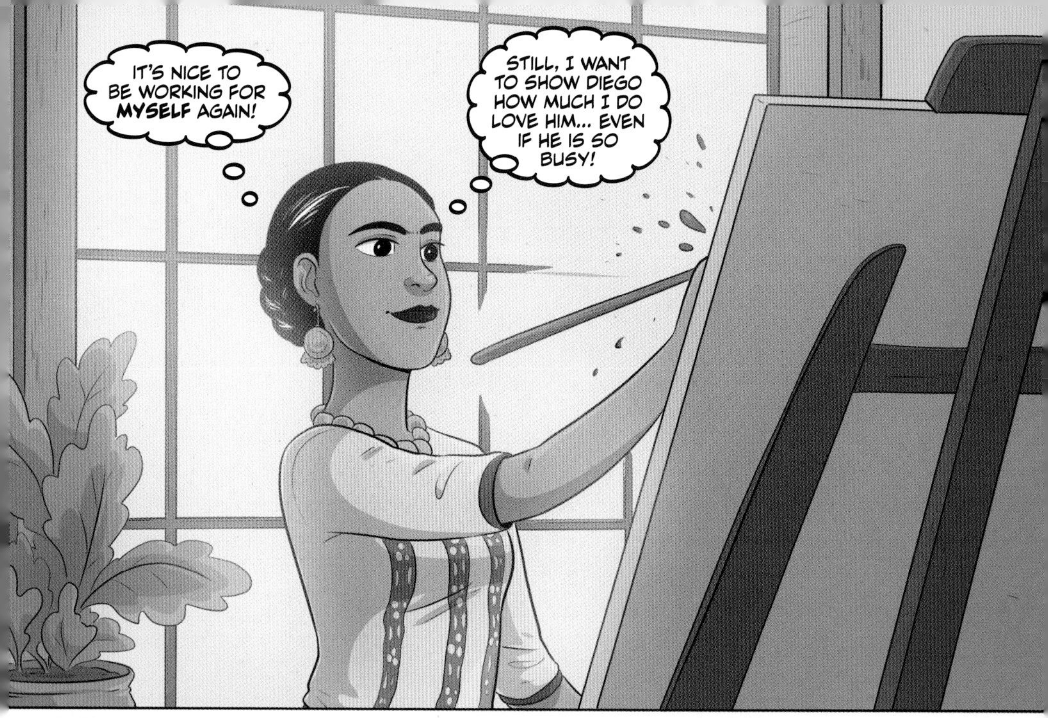
IT'S NICE TO BE WORKING FOR **MYSELF** AGAIN!
STILL, I WANT TO SHOW DIEGO HOW MUCH I DO LOVE HIM... EVEN IF HE IS SO BUSY!

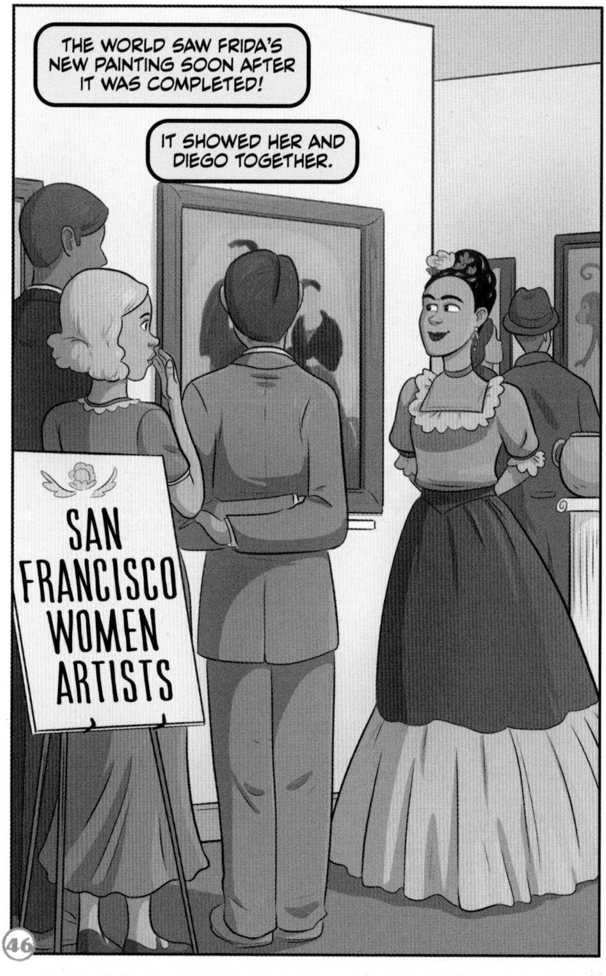
THE WORLD SAW FRIDA'S NEW PAINTING SOON AFTER IT WAS COMPLETED!
IT SHOWED HER AND DIEGO TOGETHER.
SAN FRANCISCO WOMEN ARTISTS

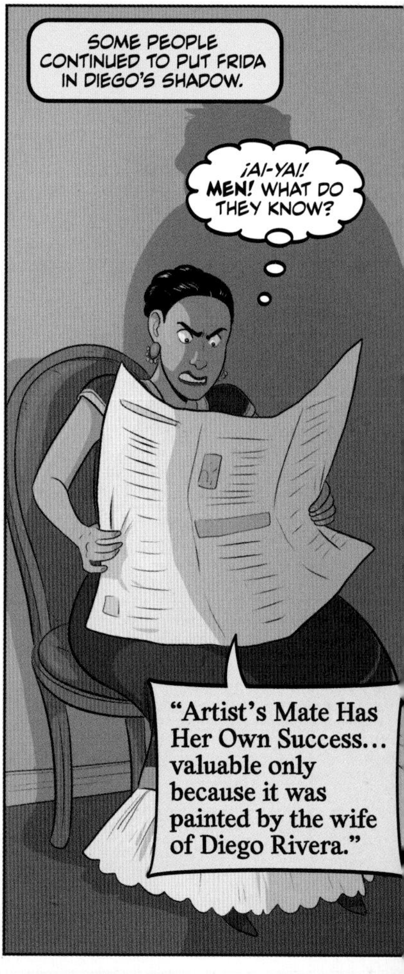
SOME PEOPLE CONTINUED TO PUT FRIDA IN DIEGO'S SHADOW.
¡AI-YAI! **MEN!** WHAT DO THEY KNOW?
"Artist's Mate Has Her Own Success… valuable only because it was painted by the wife of Diego Rivera."

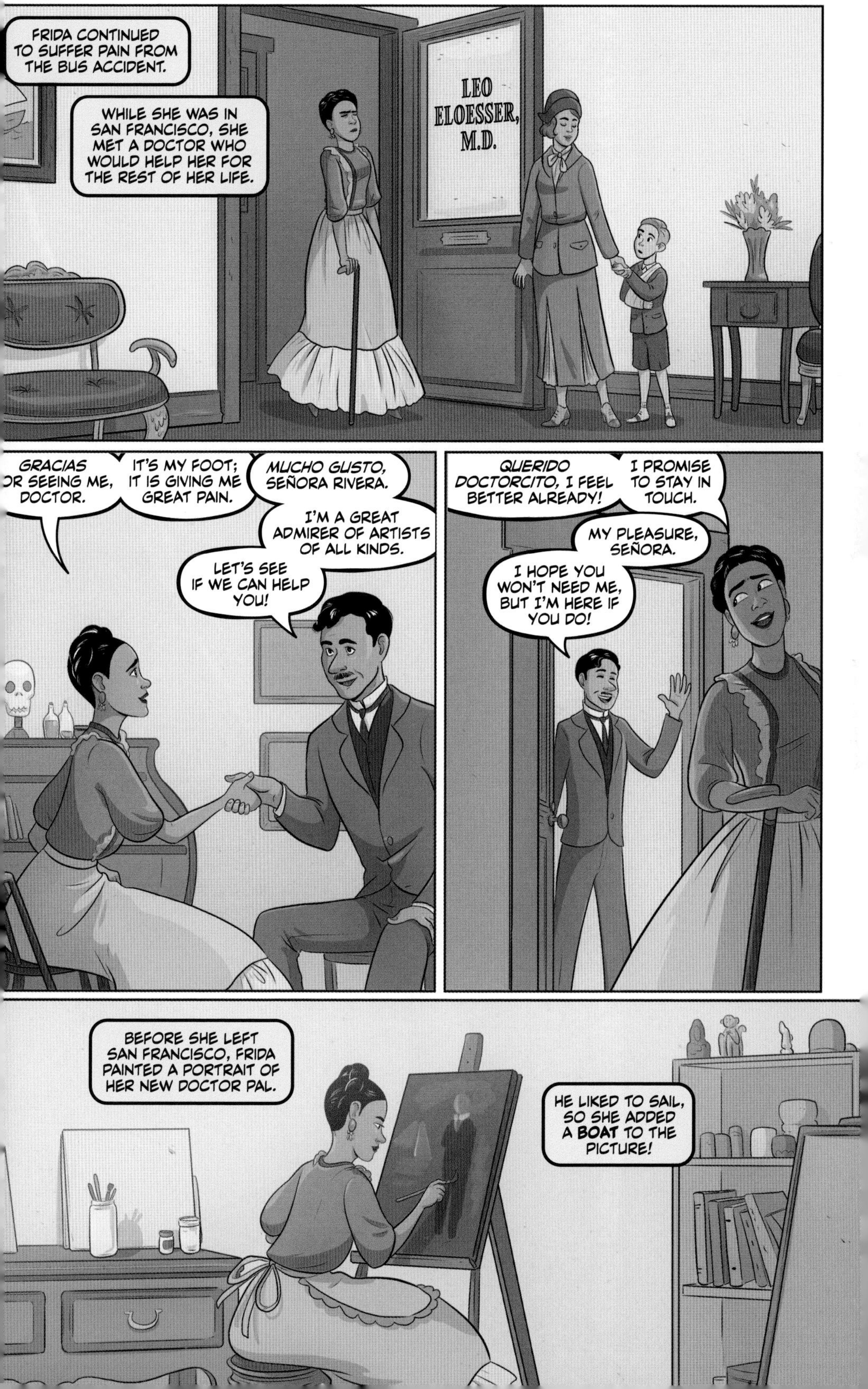
FRIDA CONTINUED TO SUFFER PAIN FROM THE BUS ACCIDENT.
WHILE SHE WAS IN SAN FRANCISCO, SHE MET A DOCTOR WHO WOULD HELP HER FOR THE REST OF HER LIFE.
LEO ELOESSER, M.D.
GRACIAS OR SEEING ME, DOCTOR.
IT'S MY FOOT; IT IS GIVING ME GREAT PAIN.
MUCHO GUSTO, SEÑORA RIVERA.
I'M A GREAT ADMIRER OF ARTISTS OF ALL KINDS.
LET'S SEE IF WE CAN HELP YOU!
QUERIDO DOCTORCITO, I FEEL BETTER ALREADY!
I PROMISE TO STAY IN TOUCH.
MY PLEASURE, SEÑORA.
I HOPE YOU WON'T NEED ME, BUT I'M HERE IF YOU DO!
BEFORE SHE LEFT SAN FRANCISCO, FRIDA PAINTED A PORTRAIT OF HER NEW DOCTOR PAL.
HE LIKED TO SAIL, SO SHE ADDED A **BOAT** TO THE PICTURE!

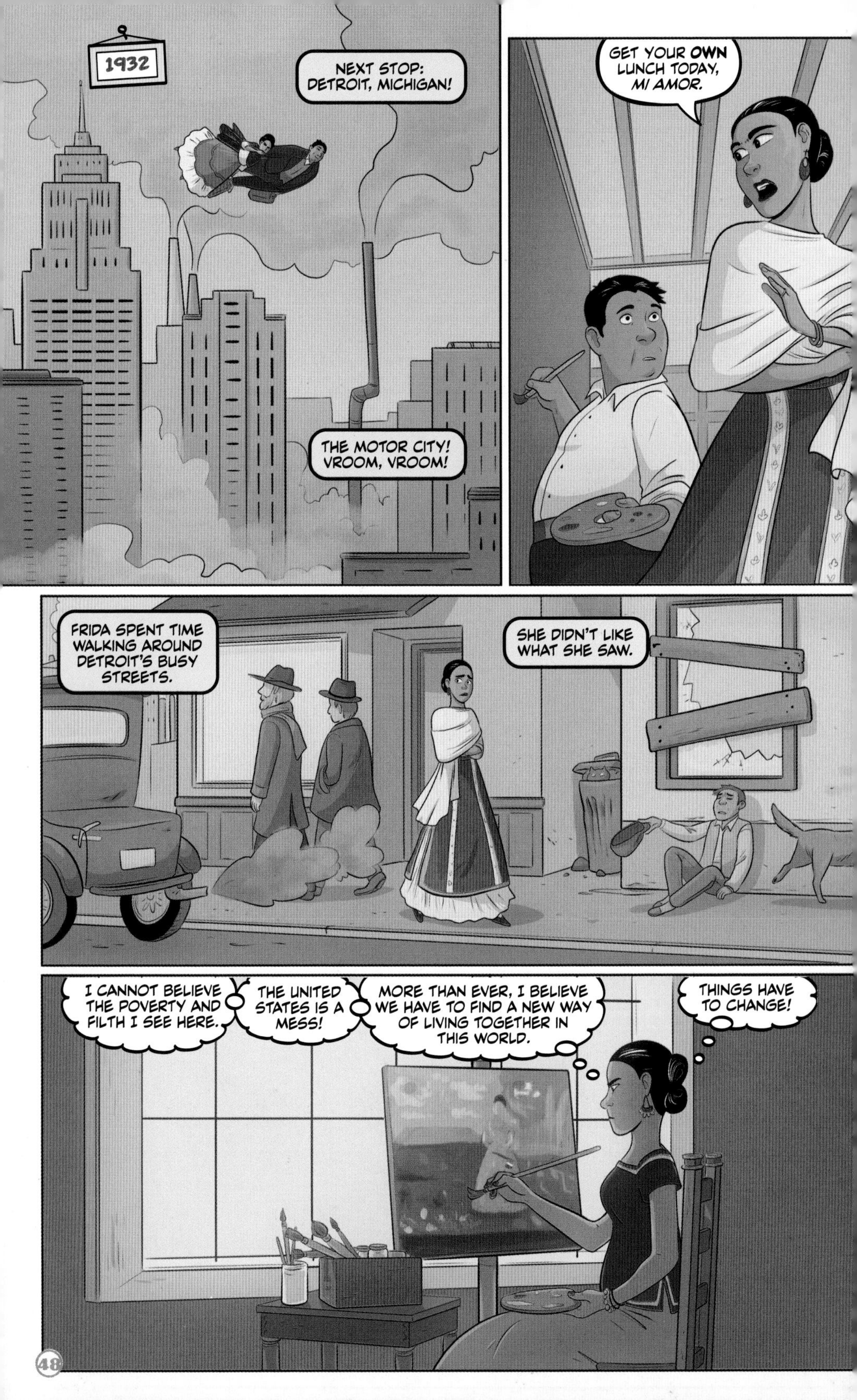
1932
NEXT STOP: DETROIT, MICHIGAN!
THE MOTOR CITY! VROOM, VROOM!
GET YOUR **OWN** LUNCH TODAY, *MI AMOR.*
FRIDA SPENT TIME WALKING AROUND DETROIT'S BUSY STREETS.
SHE DIDN'T LIKE WHAT SHE SAW.
I CANNOT BELIEVE THE POVERTY AND FILTH I SEE HERE.
THE UNITED STATES IS A MESS!
MORE THAN EVER, I BELIEVE WE HAVE TO FIND A NEW WAY OF LIVING TOGETHER IN THIS WORLD.
THINGS HAVE TO CHANGE!

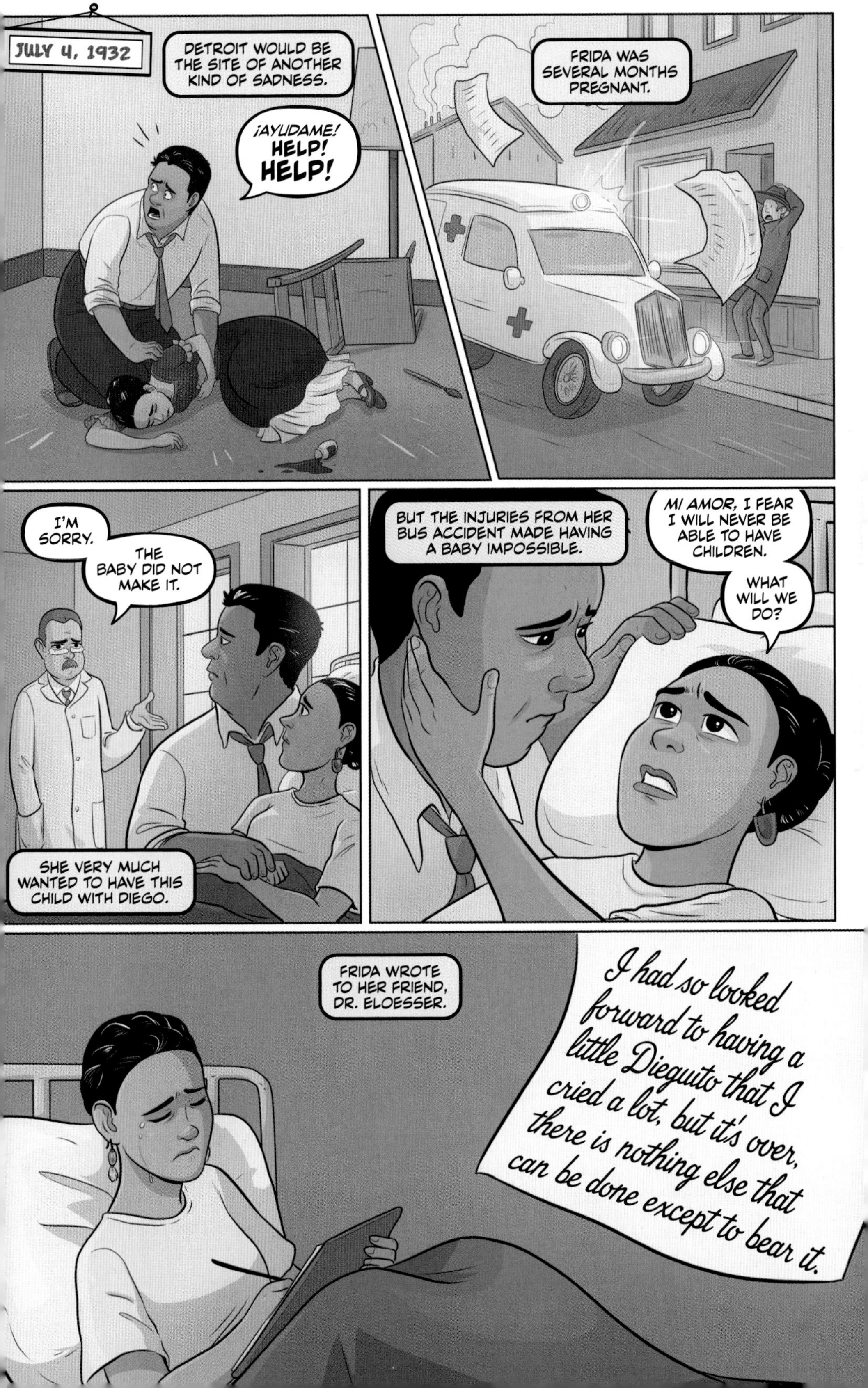
JULY 4, 1932
DETROIT WOULD BE THE SITE OF ANOTHER KIND OF SADNESS.
¡AYUDAME! HELP! HELP!
FRIDA WAS SEVERAL MONTHS PREGNANT.
I'M SORRY.
THE BABY DID NOT MAKE IT.
SHE VERY MUCH WANTED TO HAVE THIS CHILD WITH DIEGO.
BUT THE INJURIES FROM HER BUS ACCIDENT MADE HAVING A BABY IMPOSSIBLE.
MI AMOR, I FEAR I WILL NEVER BE ABLE TO HAVE CHILDREN.
WHAT WILL WE DO?
FRIDA WROTE TO HER FRIEND, DR. ELOESSER.
I had so looked forward to having a little Dieguito that I cried a lot, but it's over, there is nothing else that can be done except to bear it.

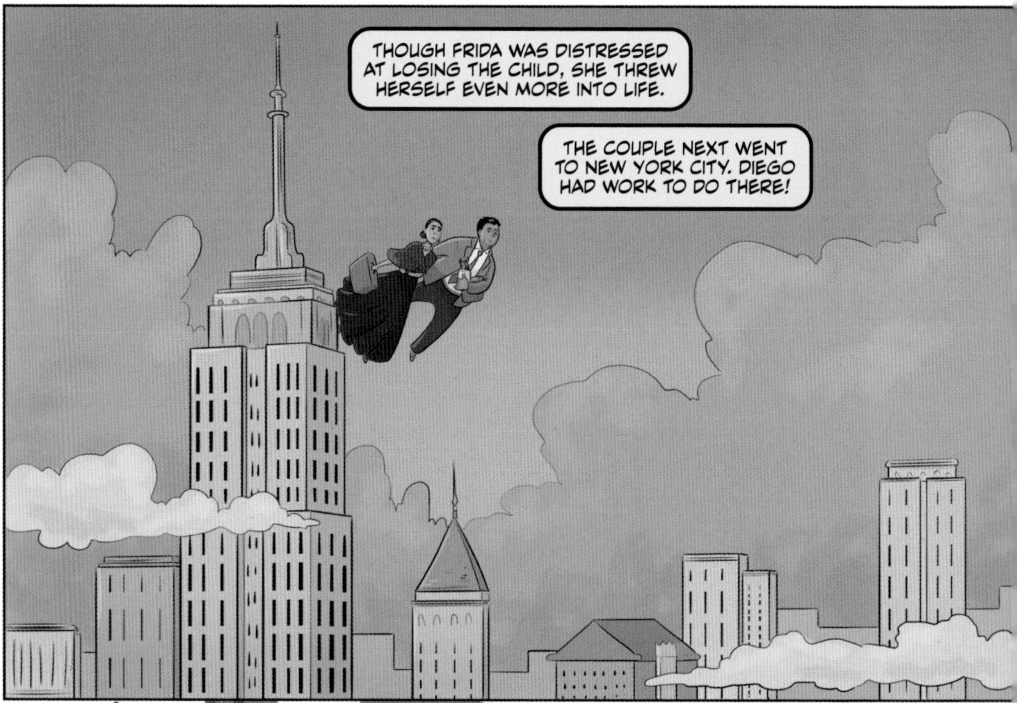
THOUGH FRIDA WAS DISTRESSED AT LOSING THE CHILD, SHE THREW HERSELF EVEN MORE INTO LIFE.
THE COUPLE NEXT WENT TO NEW YORK CITY. DIEGO HAD WORK TO DO THERE!

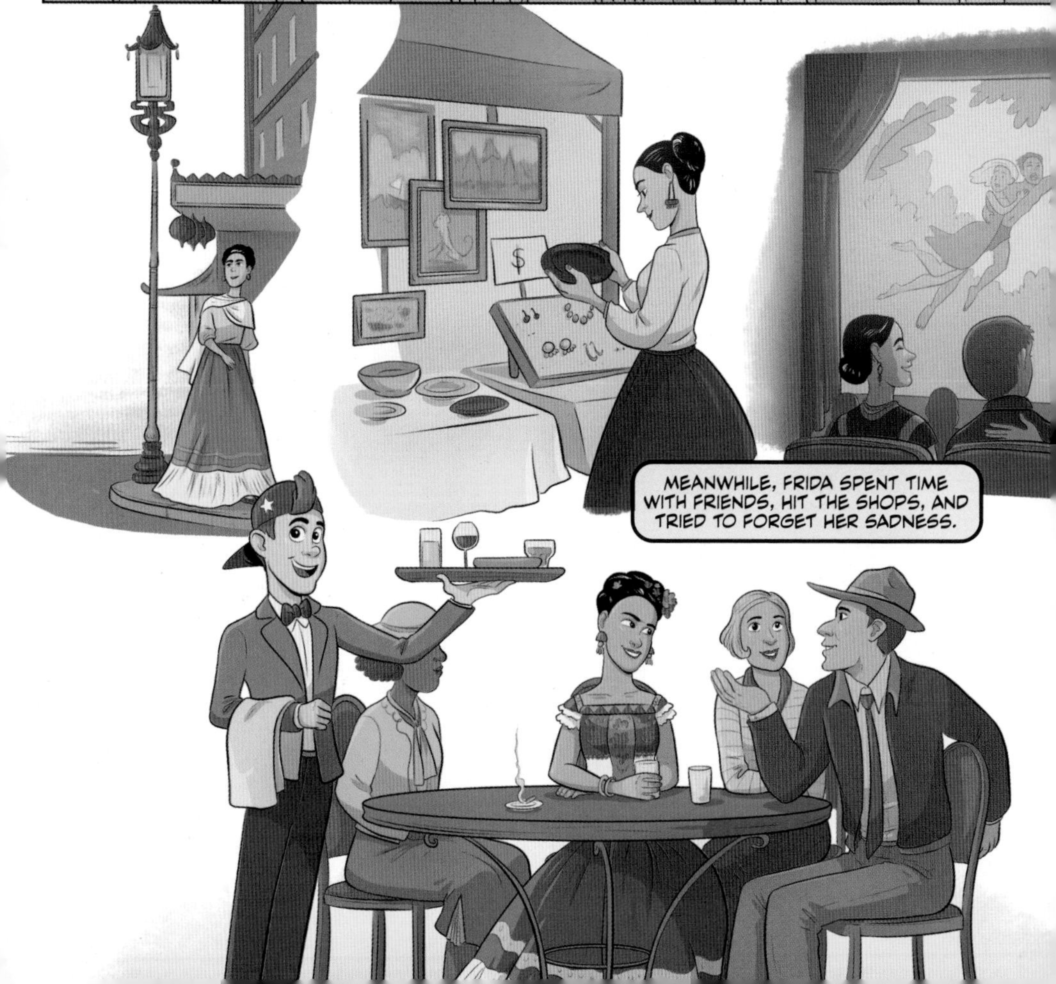
$
MEANWHILE, FRIDA SPENT TIME WITH FRIENDS, HIT THE SHOPS, AND TRIED TO FORGET HER SADNESS.

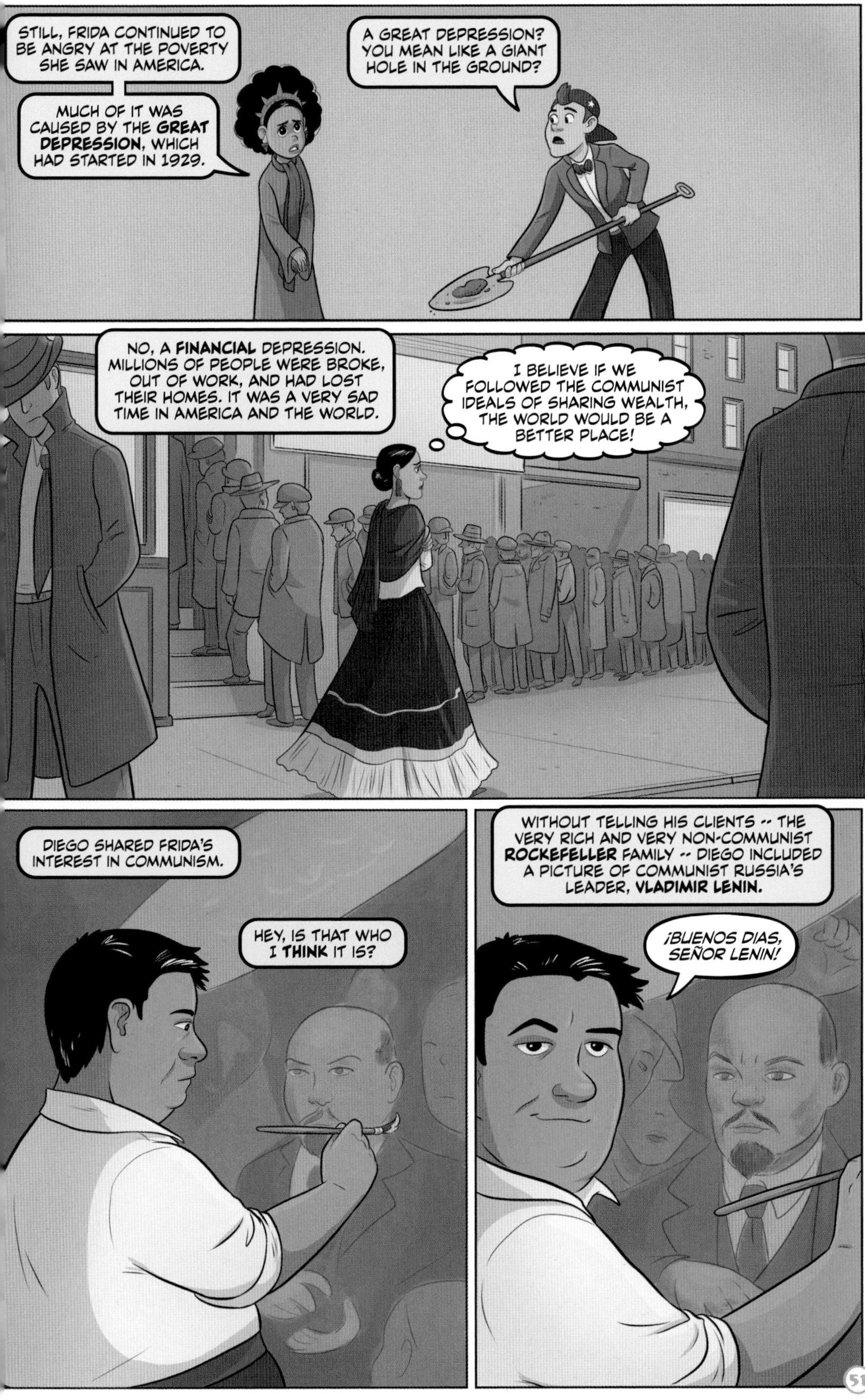

STILL, FRIDA CONTINUED TO BE ANGRY AT THE POVERTY SHE SAW IN AMERICA.
MUCH OF IT WAS CAUSED BY THE **GREAT DEPRESSION**, WHICH HAD STARTED IN 1929.
A GREAT DEPRESSION? YOU MEAN LIKE A GIANT HOLE IN THE GROUND?
NO, A **FINANCIAL** DEPRESSION. MILLIONS OF PEOPLE WERE BROKE, OUT OF WORK, AND HAD LOST THEIR HOMES. IT WAS A VERY SAD TIME IN AMERICA AND THE WORLD.
I BELIEVE IF WE FOLLOWED THE COMMUNIST IDEALS OF SHARING WEALTH, THE WORLD WOULD BE A BETTER PLACE!
DIEGO SHARED FRIDA'S INTEREST IN COMMUNISM.
HEY, IS THAT WHO I **THINK** IT IS?
WITHOUT TELLING HIS CLIENTS -- THE VERY RICH AND VERY NON-COMMUNIST **ROCKEFELLER** FAMILY -- DIEGO INCLUDED A PICTURE OF COMMUNIST RUSSIA'S LEADER, **VLADIMIR LENIN.**
¡BUENOS DIAS, SEÑOR LENIN!

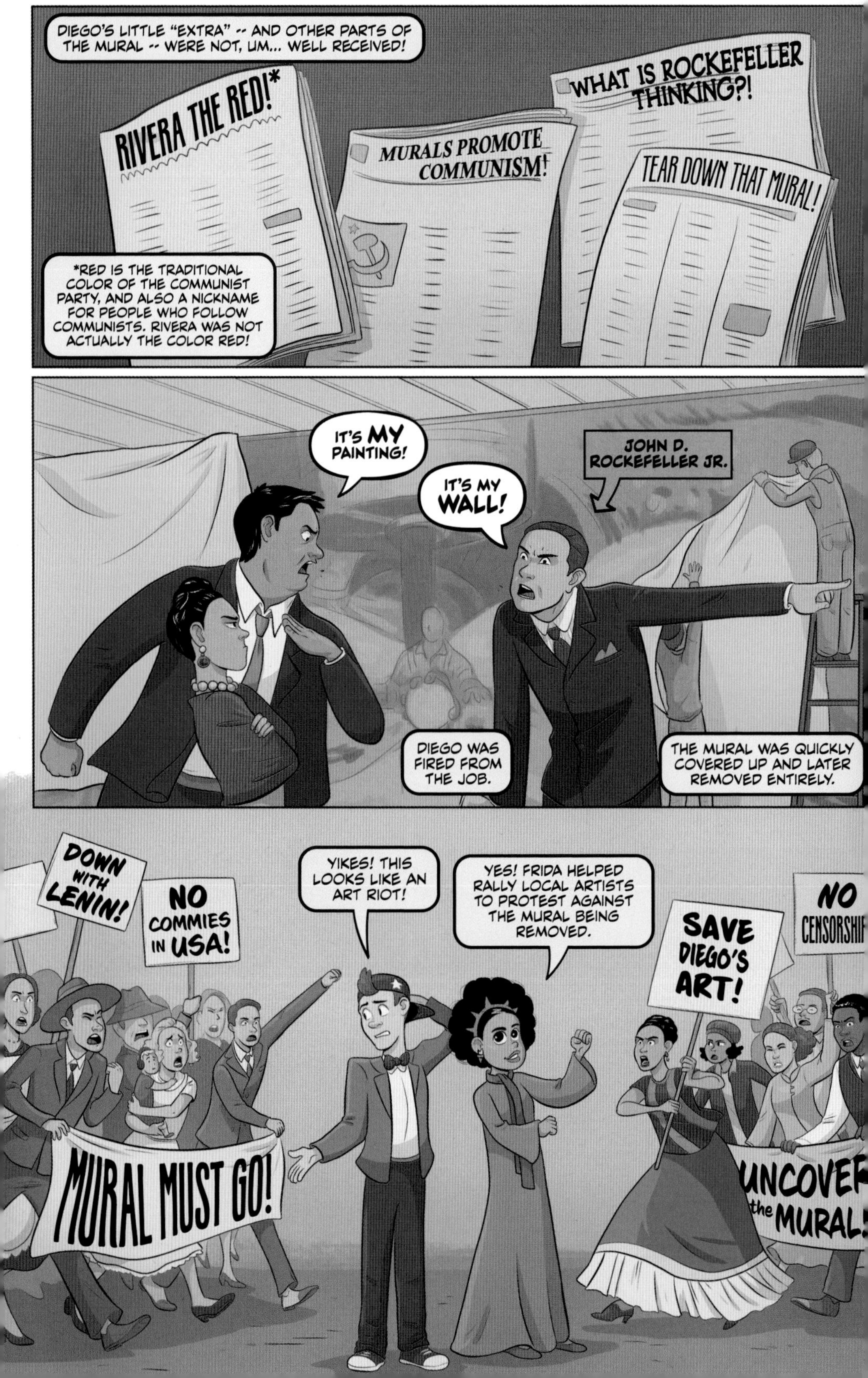
DIEGO'S LITTLE "EXTRA" -- AND OTHER PARTS OF THE MURAL -- WERE NOT, UM... WELL RECEIVED!
RIVERA THE RED!*
MURALS PROMOTE COMMUNISM!
WHAT IS ROCKEFELLER THINKING?!
TEAR DOWN THAT MURAL!
*RED IS THE TRADITIONAL COLOR OF THE COMMUNIST PARTY, AND ALSO A NICKNAME FOR PEOPLE WHO FOLLOW COMMUNISTS. RIVERA WAS NOT ACTUALLY THE COLOR RED!
IT'S MY PAINTING!
IT'S MY WALL!
JOHN D. ROCKEFELLER JR.
DIEGO WAS FIRED FROM THE JOB.
THE MURAL WAS QUICKLY COVERED UP AND LATER REMOVED ENTIRELY.
DOWN WITH LENIN!
NO COMMIES IN USA!
YIKES! THIS LOOKS LIKE AN ART RIOT!
YES! FRIDA HELPED RALLY LOCAL ARTISTS TO PROTEST AGAINST THE MURAL BEING REMOVED.
SAVE DIEGO'S ART!
NO CENSORSHIP
MURAL MUST GO!
UNCOVER the MURAL!

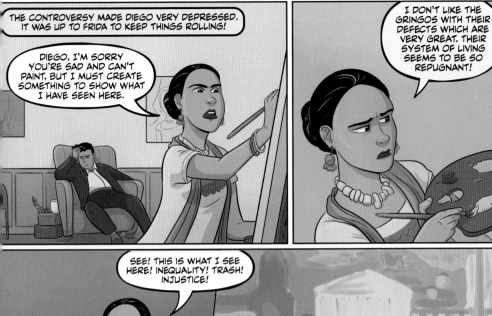

THE CONTROVERSY MADE DIEGO VERY DEPRESSED. IT WAS UP TO FRIDA TO KEEP THINGS ROLLING!

DIEGO, I'M SORRY YOU'RE SAD AND CAN'T PAINT, BUT I MUST CREATE SOMETHING TO SHOW WHAT I HAVE SEEN HERE.

I DON'T LIKE THE GRINGOS WITH THEIR DEFECTS WHICH ARE VERY GREAT. THEIR SYSTEM OF LIVING SEEMS TO BE SO REPUGNANT!

SEE! THIS IS WHAT I SEE HERE! INEQUALITY! TRASH! INJUSTICE!

I WILL CALL THIS *MY DRESS HANGS THERE,* BECAUSE I DON'T WANT **MYSELF** TO BE THERE.

DIEGO? MI AMOR, CAN WE GO HOME?

SORRY YOU DIDN'T LIKE AMERICA VERY MUCH, FRIDA. I HOPE YOU COME BACK ANOTHER TIME SO WE CAN TRY AGAIN!

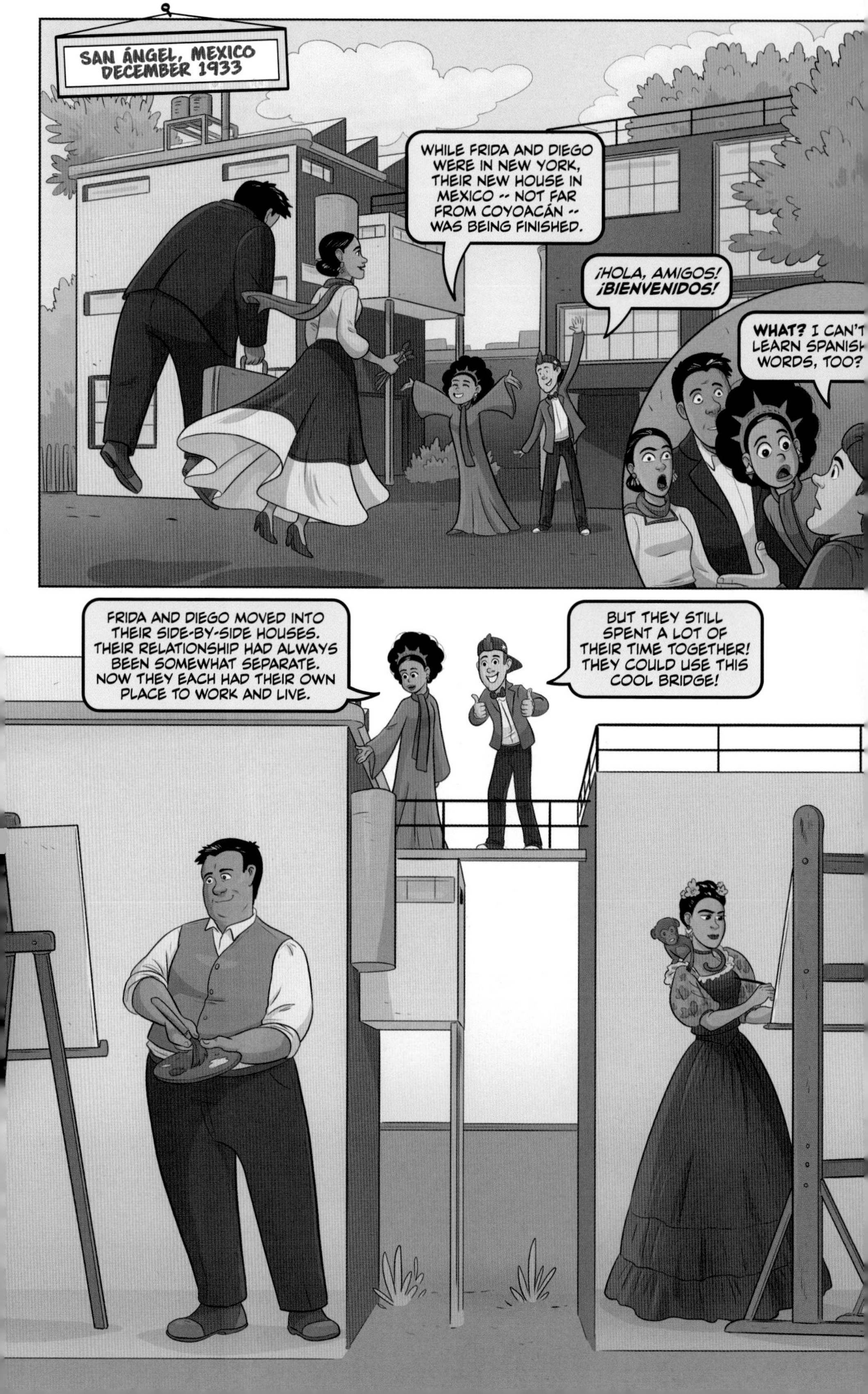
SAN ÁNGEL, MEXICO
DECEMBER 1933
WHILE FRIDA AND DIEGO WERE IN NEW YORK, THEIR NEW HOUSE IN MEXICO -- NOT FAR FROM COYOACÁN -- WAS BEING FINISHED.
¡HOLA, AMIGOS! ¡BIENVENIDOS!
WHAT? I CAN'T LEARN SPANISH WORDS, TOO?
FRIDA AND DIEGO MOVED INTO THEIR SIDE-BY-SIDE HOUSES. THEIR RELATIONSHIP HAD ALWAYS BEEN SOMEWHAT SEPARATE. NOW THEY EACH HAD THEIR OWN PLACE TO WORK AND LIVE.
BUT THEY STILL SPENT A LOT OF THEIR TIME TOGETHER! THEY COULD USE THIS COOL BRIDGE!

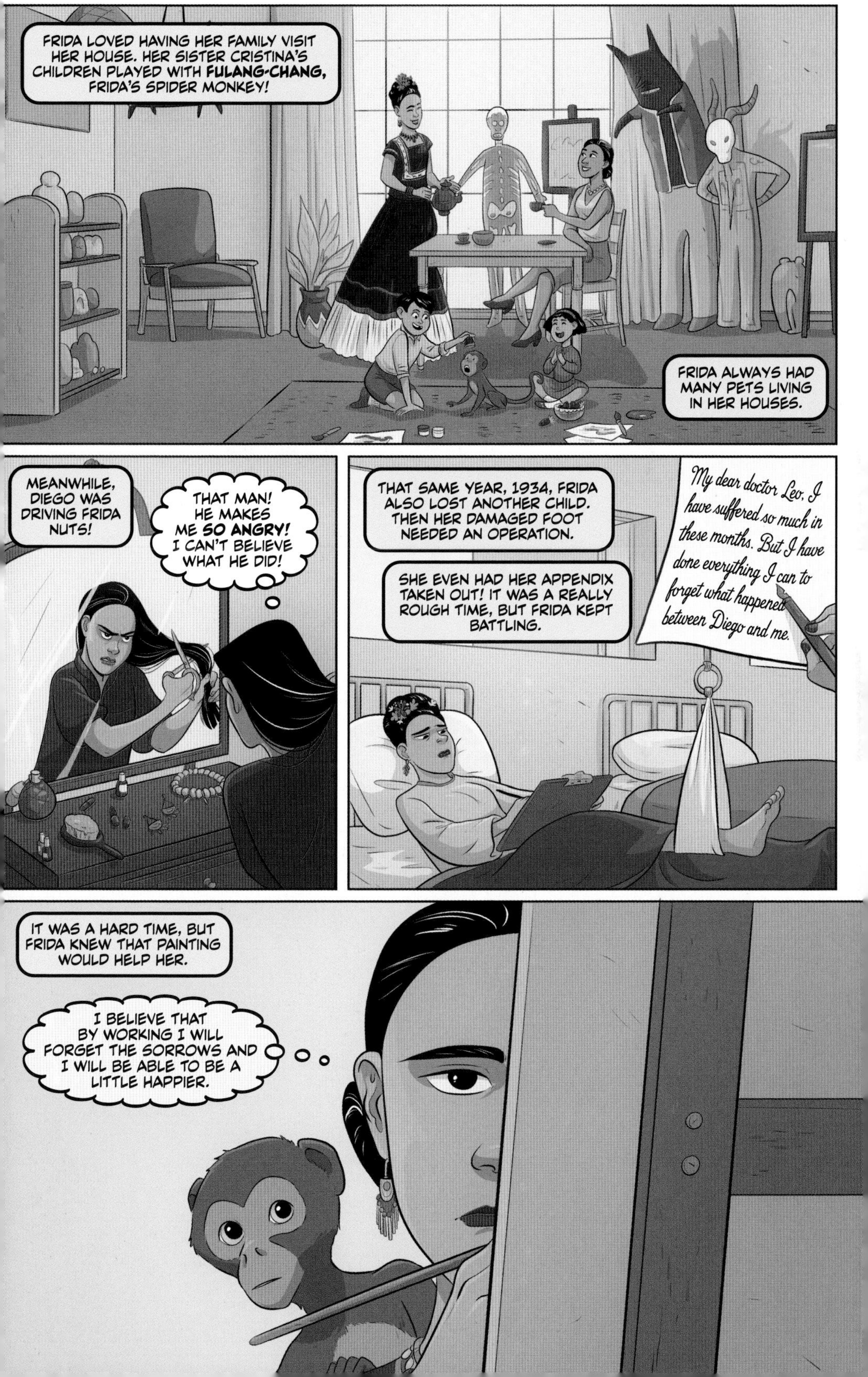
FRIDA LOVED HAVING HER FAMILY VISIT HER HOUSE. HER SISTER CRISTINA'S CHILDREN PLAYED WITH **FULANG-CHANG,** FRIDA'S SPIDER MONKEY!
FRIDA ALWAYS HAD MANY PETS LIVING IN HER HOUSES.
MEANWHILE, DIEGO WAS DRIVING FRIDA NUTS!
THAT MAN! HE MAKES ME **SO ANGRY!** I CAN'T BELIEVE WHAT HE DID!
THAT SAME YEAR, 1934, FRIDA ALSO LOST ANOTHER CHILD. THEN HER DAMAGED FOOT NEEDED AN OPERATION.
SHE EVEN HAD HER APPENDIX TAKEN OUT! IT WAS A REALLY ROUGH TIME, BUT FRIDA KEPT BATTLING.
My dear doctor Leo, I have suffered so much in these months. But I have done everything I can to forget what happened between Diego and me.
IT WAS A HARD TIME, BUT FRIDA KNEW THAT PAINTING WOULD HELP HER.
I BELIEVE THAT BY WORKING I WILL FORGET THE SORROWS AND I WILL BE ABLE TO BE A LITTLE HAPPIER.

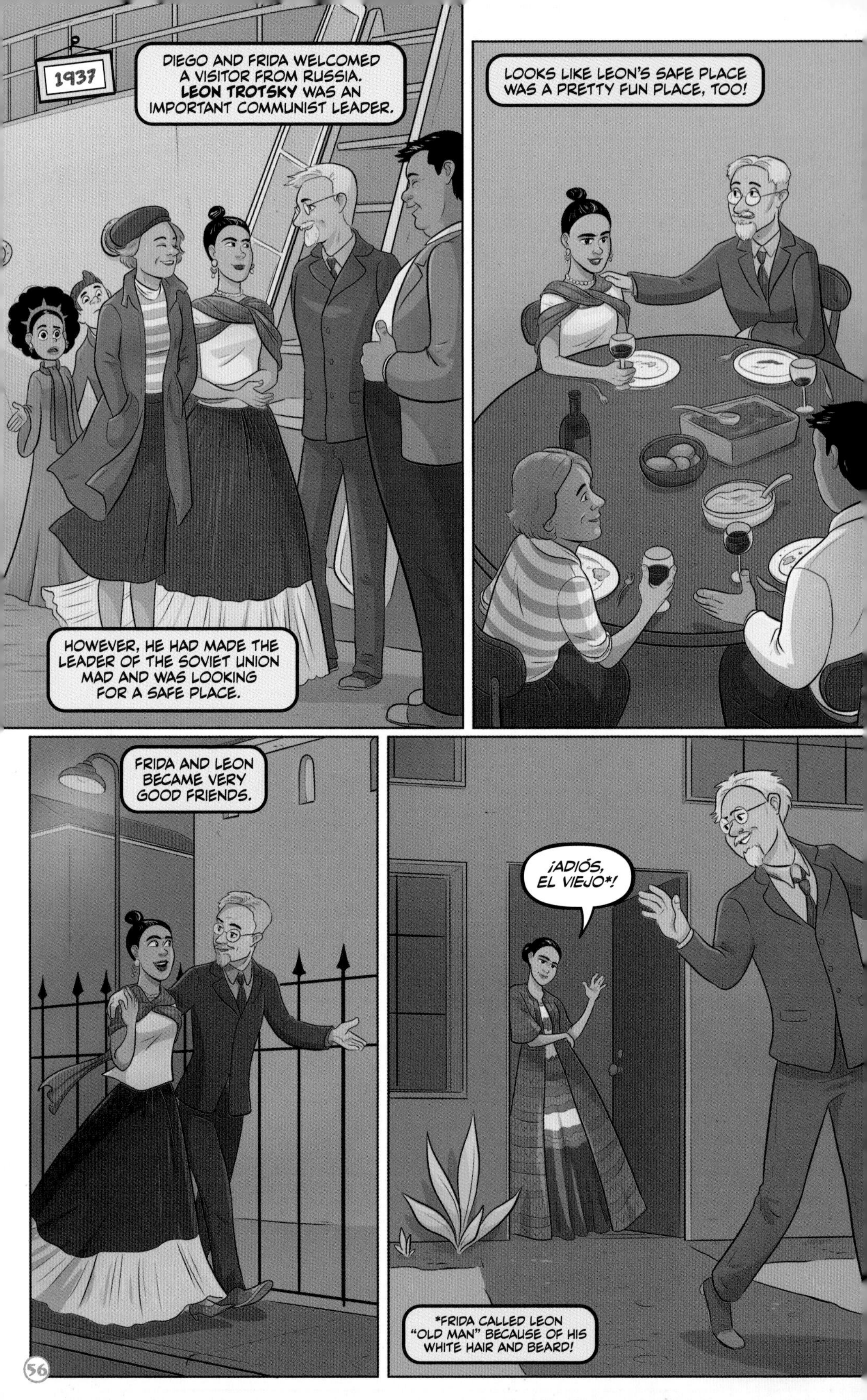
1937
DIEGO AND FRIDA WELCOMED A VISITOR FROM RUSSIA. **LEON TROTSKY** WAS AN IMPORTANT COMMUNIST LEADER.
HOWEVER, HE HAD MADE THE LEADER OF THE SOVIET UNION MAD AND WAS LOOKING FOR A SAFE PLACE.
LOOKS LIKE LEON'S SAFE PLACE WAS A PRETTY FUN PLACE, TOO!
FRIDA AND LEON BECAME VERY GOOD FRIENDS.
¡ADIÓS, EL VIEJO*!
*FRIDA CALLED LEON "OLD MAN" BECAUSE OF HIS WHITE HAIR AND BEARD!

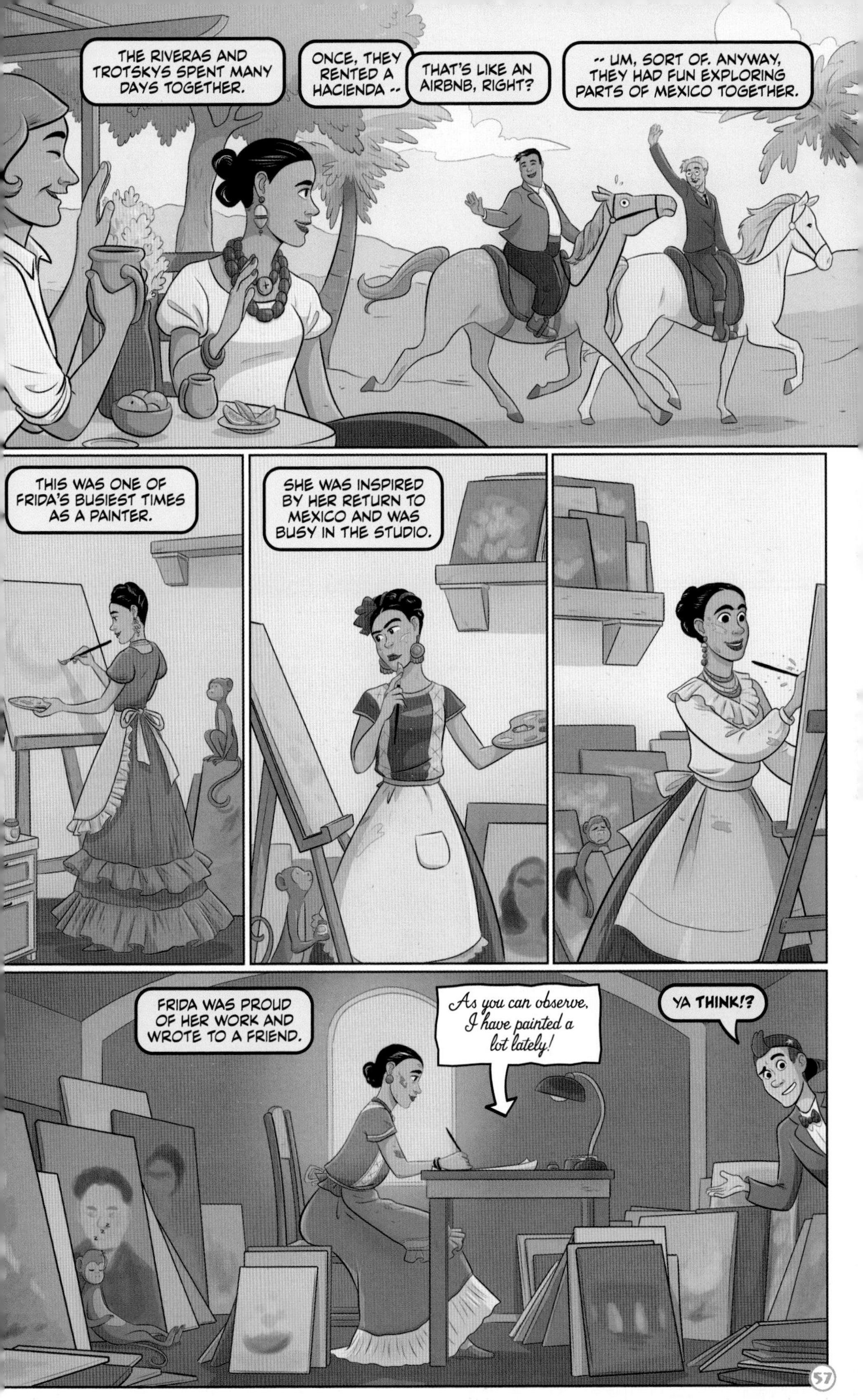
THE RIVERAS AND TROTSKYS SPENT MANY DAYS TOGETHER.
ONCE, THEY RENTED A HACIENDA --
THAT'S LIKE AN AIRBNB, RIGHT?
-- UM, SORT OF. ANYWAY, THEY HAD FUN EXPLORING PARTS OF MEXICO TOGETHER.
THIS WAS ONE OF FRIDA'S BUSIEST TIMES AS A PAINTER.
SHE WAS INSPIRED BY HER RETURN TO MEXICO AND WAS BUSY IN THE STUDIO.
FRIDA WAS PROUD OF HER WORK AND WROTE TO A FRIEND.
As you can observe, I have painted a lot lately!
YA THINK!?

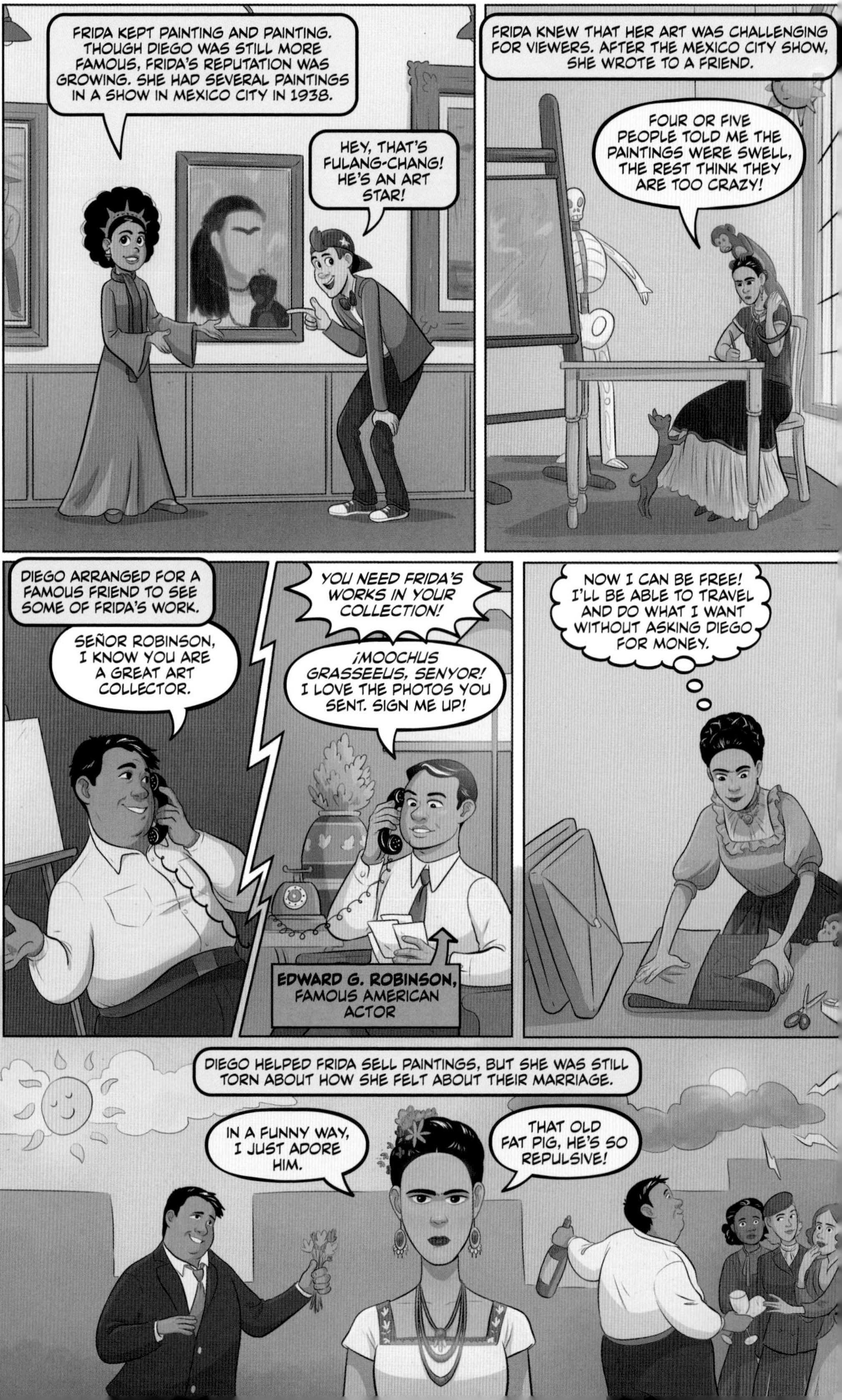
FRIDA KEPT PAINTING AND PAINTING. THOUGH DIEGO WAS STILL MORE FAMOUS, FRIDA'S REPUTATION WAS GROWING. SHE HAD SEVERAL PAINTINGS IN A SHOW IN MEXICO CITY IN 1938.
HEY, THAT'S FULANG-CHANG! HE'S AN ART STAR!
FRIDA KNEW THAT HER ART WAS CHALLENGING FOR VIEWERS. AFTER THE MEXICO CITY SHOW, SHE WROTE TO A FRIEND.
FOUR OR FIVE PEOPLE TOLD ME THE PAINTINGS WERE SWELL, THE REST THINK THEY ARE TOO CRAZY!
DIEGO ARRANGED FOR A FAMOUS FRIEND TO SEE SOME OF FRIDA'S WORK.
SEÑOR ROBINSON, I KNOW YOU ARE A GREAT ART COLLECTOR.
YOU NEED FRIDA'S WORKS IN YOUR COLLECTION!
¡MOOCHUS GRASSEEUS, SENYOR! I LOVE THE PHOTOS YOU SENT. SIGN ME UP!
EDWARD G. ROBINSON, FAMOUS AMERICAN ACTOR
NOW I CAN BE FREE! I'LL BE ABLE TO TRAVEL AND DO WHAT I WANT WITHOUT ASKING DIEGO FOR MONEY.
DIEGO HELPED FRIDA SELL PAINTINGS, BUT SHE WAS STILL TORN ABOUT HOW SHE FELT ABOUT THEIR MARRIAGE.
IN A FUNNY WAY, I JUST ADORE HIM.
THAT OLD FAT PIG, HE'S SO REPULSIVE!

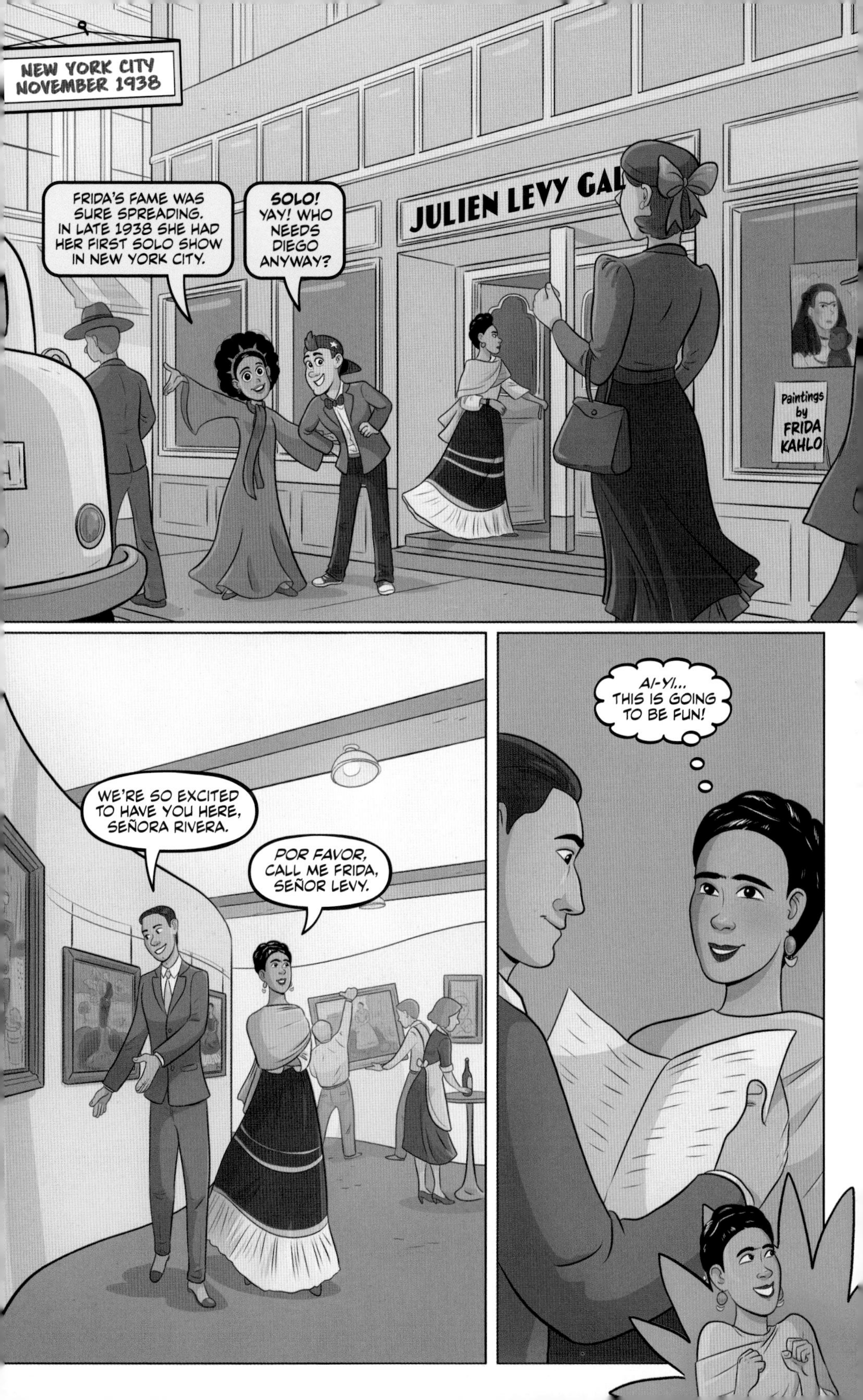
NEW YORK CITY
NOVEMBER 1938
FRIDA'S FAME WAS SURE SPREADING. IN LATE 1938 SHE HAD HER FIRST SOLO SHOW IN NEW YORK CITY.
SOLO! YAY! WHO NEEDS DIEGO ANYWAY?
JULIEN LEVY GAL
Paintings by FRIDA KAHLO
WE'RE SO EXCITED TO HAVE YOU HERE, SEÑORA RIVERA.
POR FAVOR, CALL ME FRIDA, SEÑOR LEVY.
AI-YI... THIS IS GOING TO BE FUN!

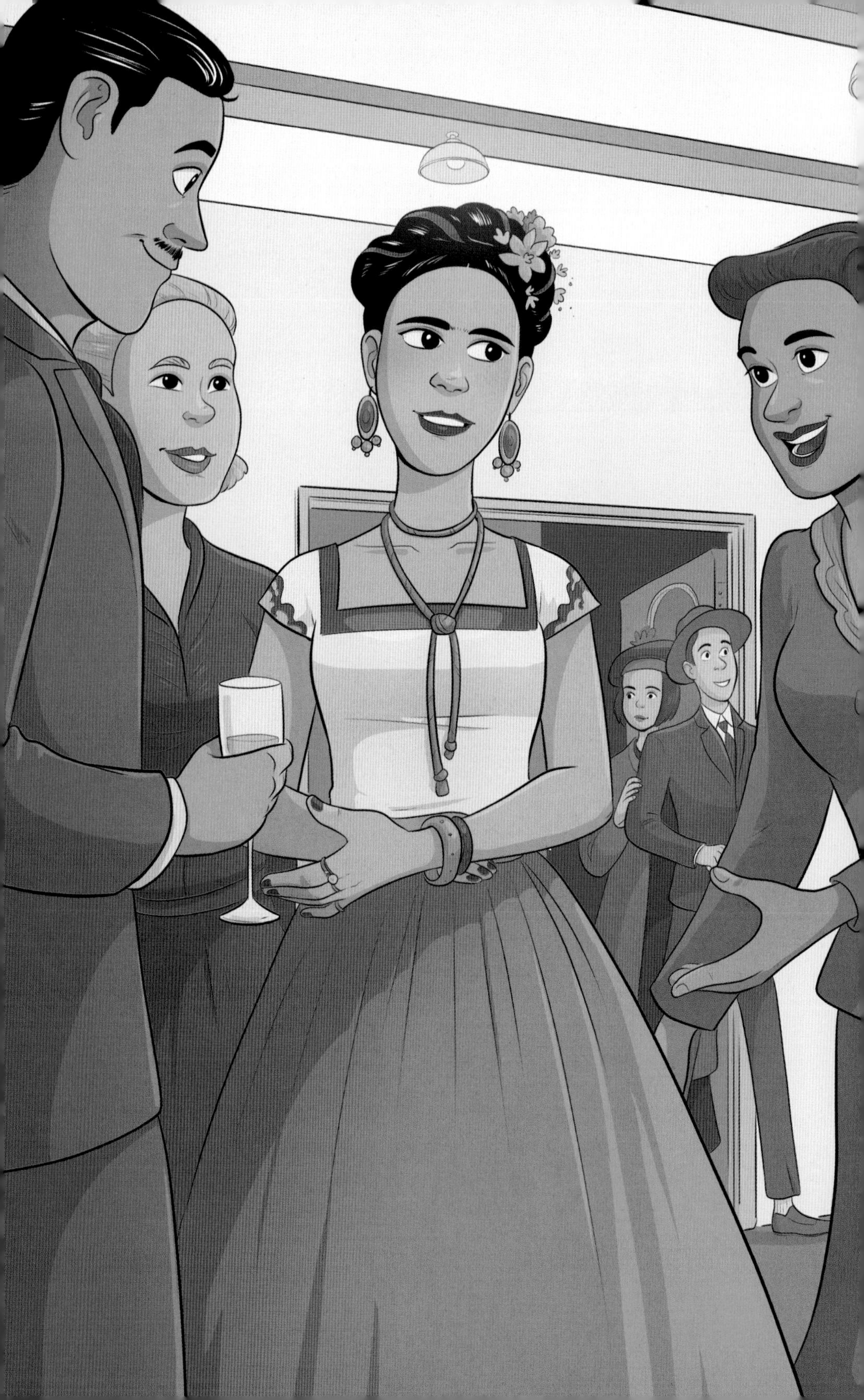

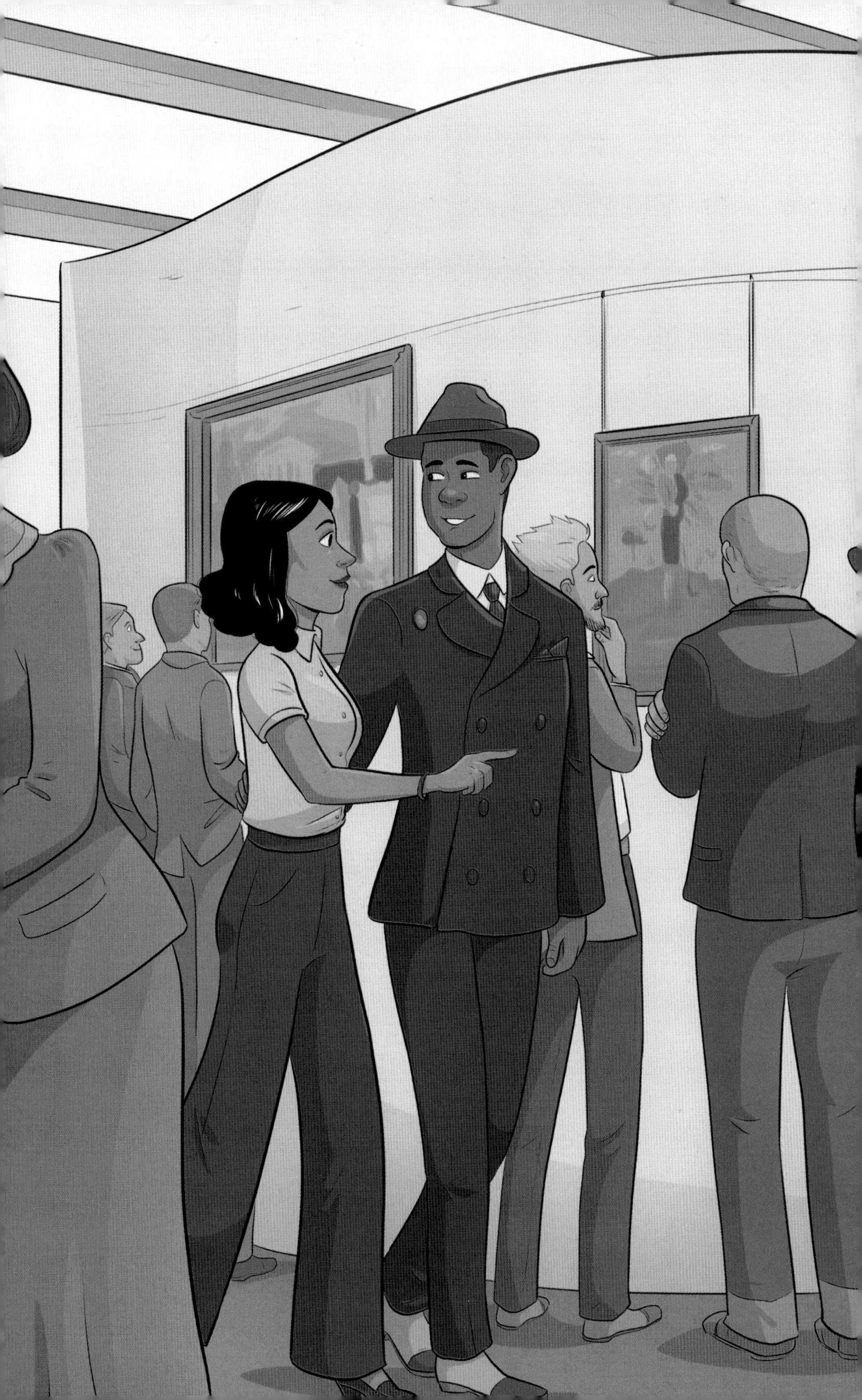

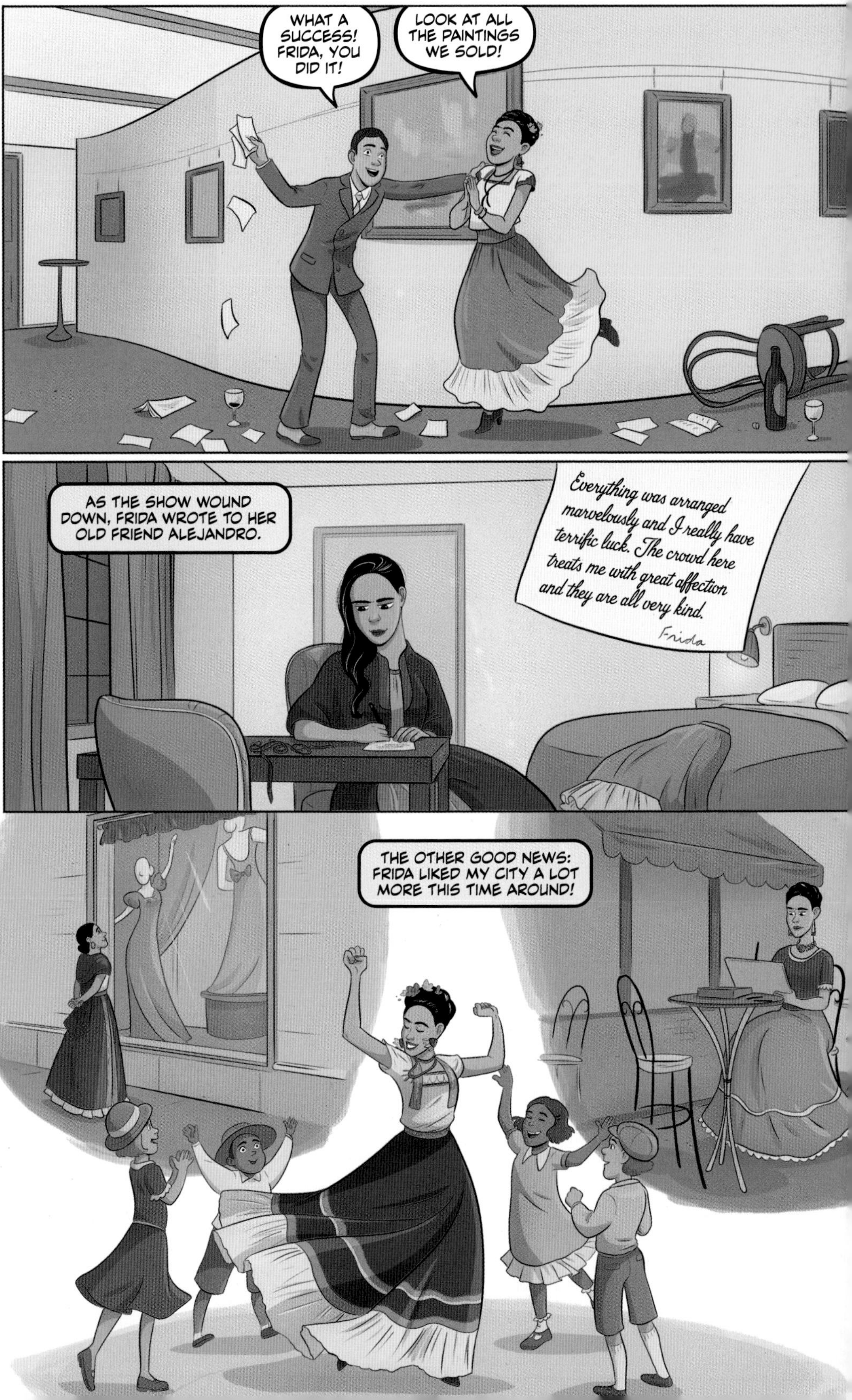
WHAT A SUCCESS! FRIDA, YOU DID IT!
LOOK AT ALL THE PAINTINGS WE SOLD!
AS THE SHOW WOUND DOWN, FRIDA WROTE TO HER OLD FRIEND ALEJANDRO.
Everything was arranged marvelously and I really have terrific luck. The crowd here treats me with great affection and they are all very kind.
Frida
THE OTHER GOOD NEWS: FRIDA LIKED MY CITY A LOT MORE THIS TIME AROUND!

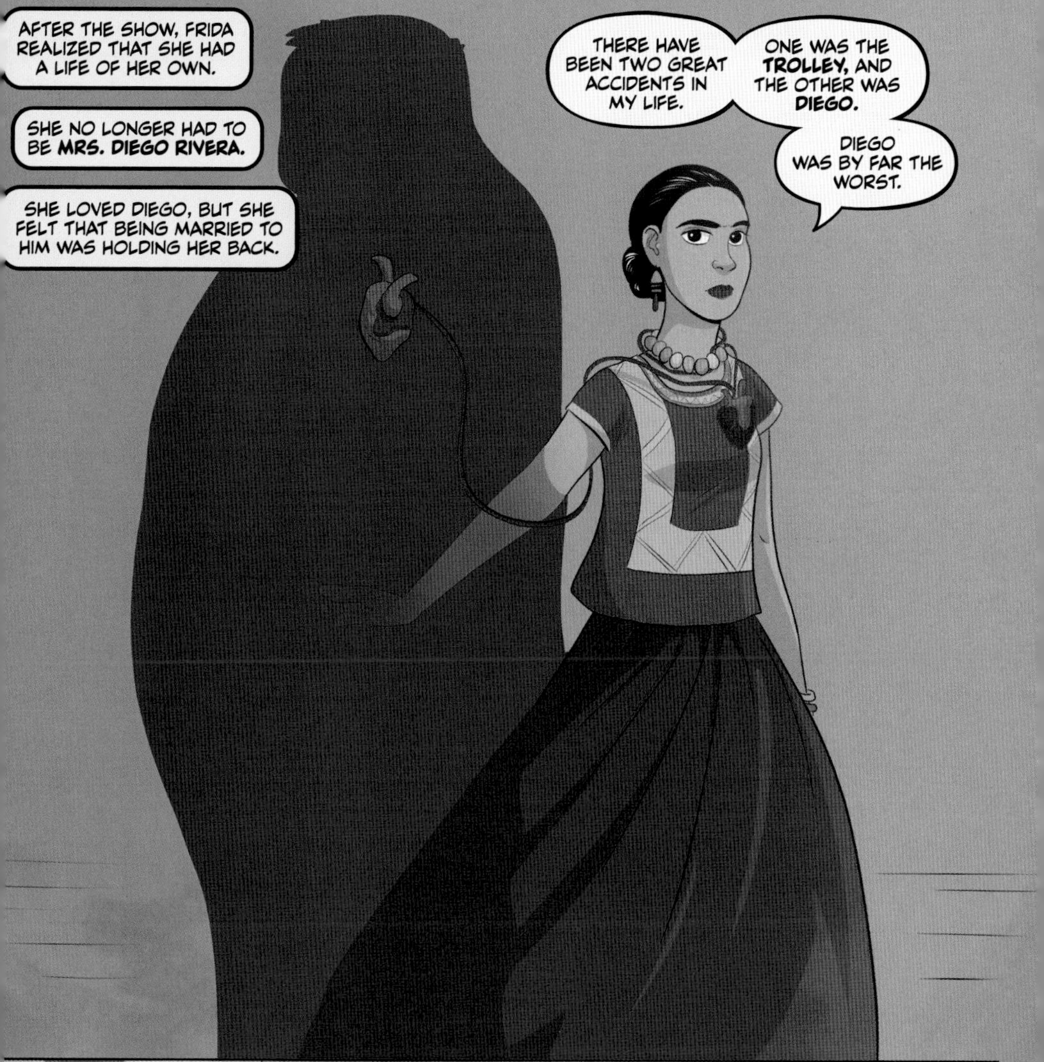
AFTER THE SHOW, FRIDA REALIZED THAT SHE HAD A LIFE OF HER OWN.
SHE NO LONGER HAD TO BE **MRS. DIEGO RIVERA.**
SHE LOVED DIEGO, BUT SHE FELT THAT BEING MARRIED TO HIM WAS HOLDING HER BACK.
THERE HAVE BEEN TWO GREAT ACCIDENTS IN MY LIFE.
ONE WAS THE **TROLLEY,** AND THE OTHER WAS **DIEGO.**
DIEGO WAS BY FAR THE WORST.

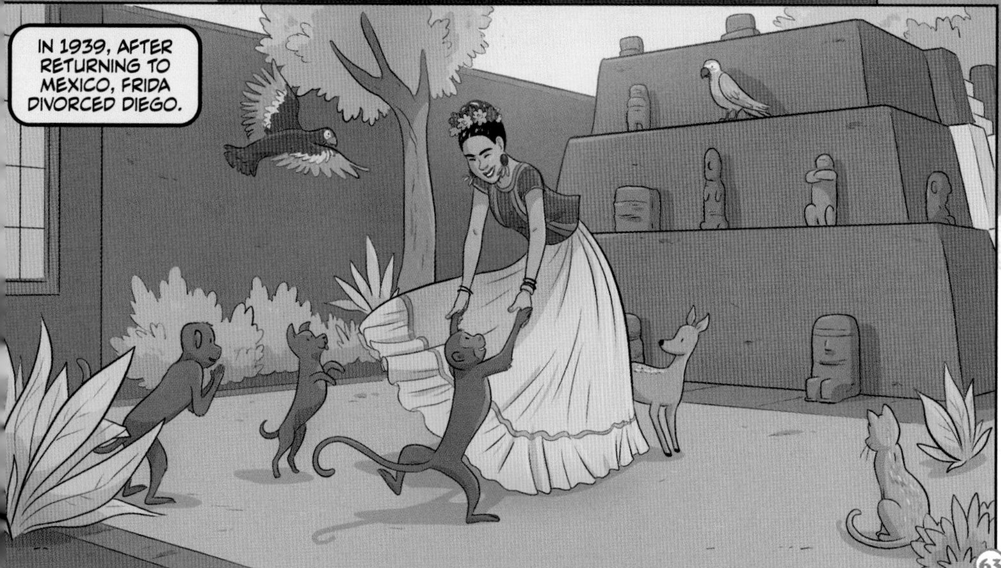
IN 1939, AFTER RETURNING TO MEXICO, FRIDA DIVORCED DIEGO.

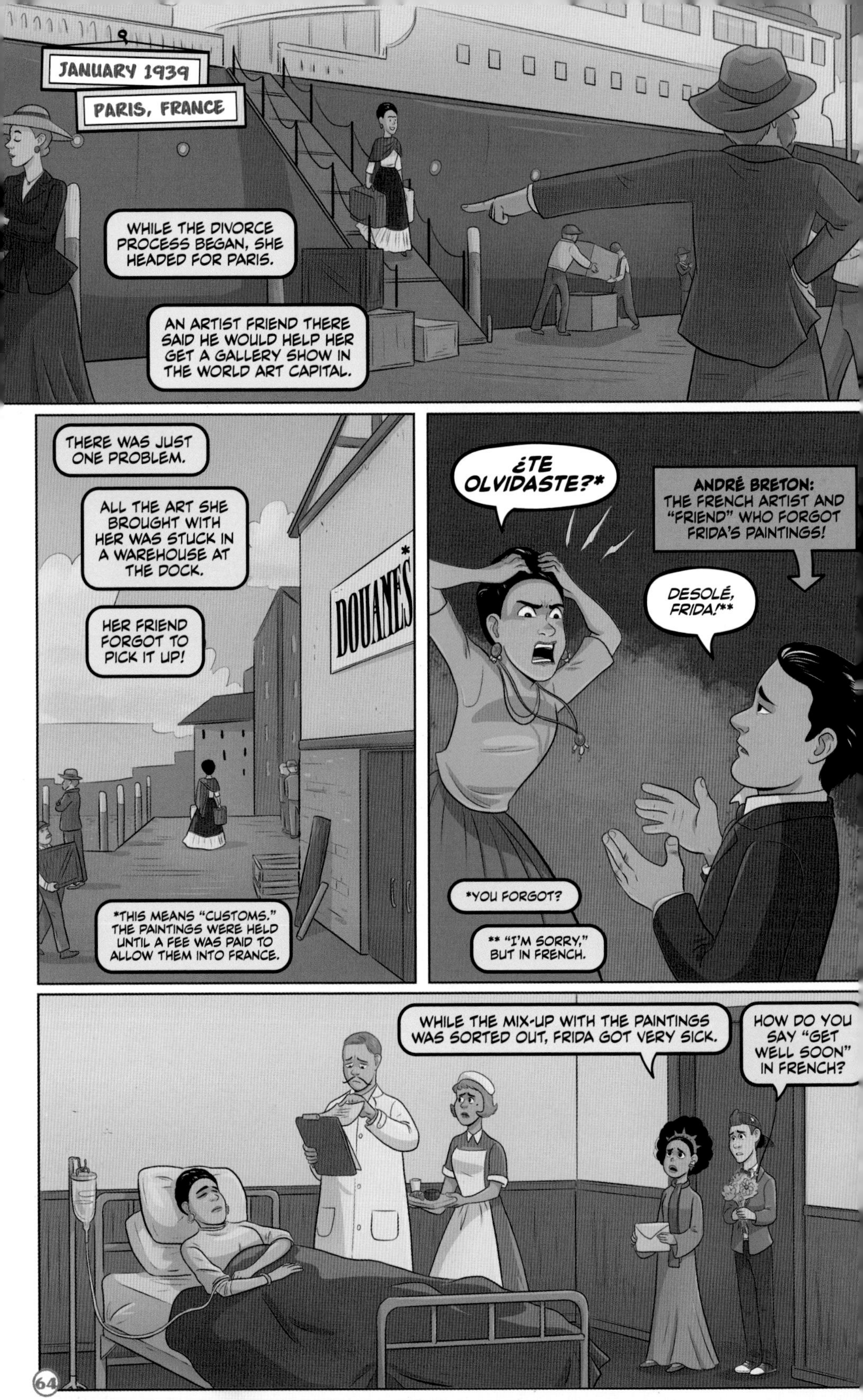

JANUARY 1939
PARIS, FRANCE
WHILE THE DIVORCE PROCESS BEGAN, SHE HEADED FOR PARIS.
AN ARTIST FRIEND THERE SAID HE WOULD HELP HER GET A GALLERY SHOW IN THE WORLD ART CAPITAL.
THERE WAS JUST ONE PROBLEM.
ALL THE ART SHE BROUGHT WITH HER WAS STUCK IN A WAREHOUSE AT THE DOCK.
HER FRIEND FORGOT TO PICK IT UP!
DOUANES*
*THIS MEANS "CUSTOMS." THE PAINTINGS WERE HELD UNTIL A FEE WAS PAID TO ALLOW THEM INTO FRANCE.
¿TE OLVIDASTE?*
ANDRÉ BRETON: THE FRENCH ARTIST AND "FRIEND" WHO FORGOT FRIDA'S PAINTINGS!
DESOLÉ, FRIDA!**
*YOU FORGOT?
** "I'M SORRY," BUT IN FRENCH.
WHILE THE MIX-UP WITH THE PAINTINGS WAS SORTED OUT, FRIDA GOT VERY SICK.
HOW DO YOU SAY "GET WELL SOON" IN FRENCH?

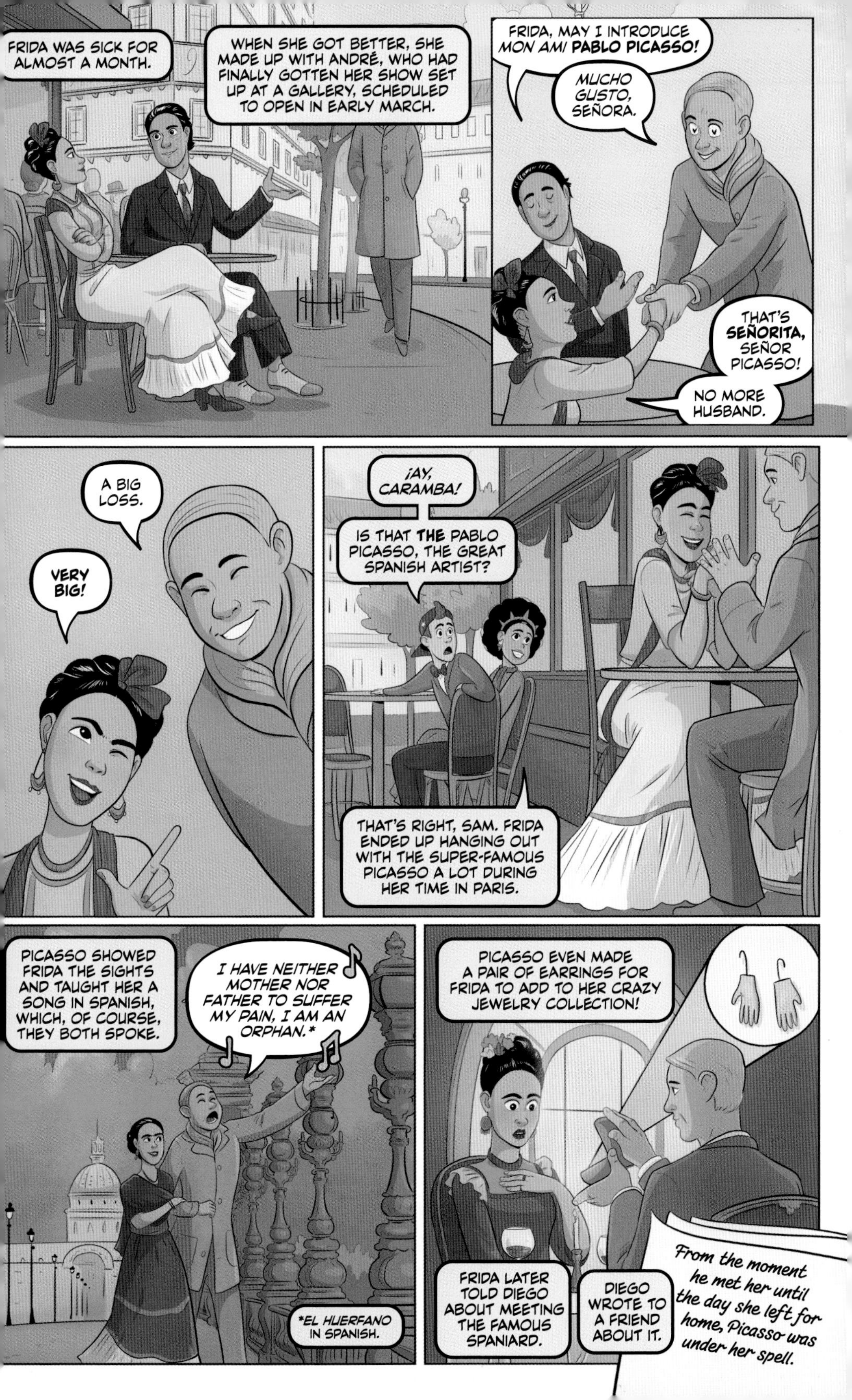
FRIDA WAS SICK FOR ALMOST A MONTH.
WHEN SHE GOT BETTER, SHE MADE UP WITH ANDRÉ, WHO HAD FINALLY GOTTEN HER SHOW SET UP AT A GALLERY, SCHEDULED TO OPEN IN EARLY MARCH.
FRIDA, MAY I INTRODUCE *MON AMI* **PABLO PICASSO!**
MUCHO GUSTO, SEÑORA.
THAT'S **SEÑORITA,** SEÑOR PICASSO!
NO MORE HUSBAND.
A BIG LOSS.
VERY BIG!
¡AY, CARAMBA!
IS THAT **THE** PABLO PICASSO, THE GREAT SPANISH ARTIST?
THAT'S RIGHT, SAM. FRIDA ENDED UP HANGING OUT WITH THE SUPER-FAMOUS PICASSO A LOT DURING HER TIME IN PARIS.
PICASSO SHOWED FRIDA THE SIGHTS AND TAUGHT HER A SONG IN SPANISH, WHICH, OF COURSE, THEY BOTH SPOKE.
*I HAVE NEITHER MOTHER NOR FATHER TO SUFFER MY PAIN, I AM AN ORPHAN.**
**EL HUERFANO* IN SPANISH.
PICASSO EVEN MADE A PAIR OF EARRINGS FOR FRIDA TO ADD TO HER CRAZY JEWELRY COLLECTION!
FRIDA LATER TOLD DIEGO ABOUT MEETING THE FAMOUS SPANIARD.
DIEGO WROTE TO A FRIEND ABOUT IT.
From the moment he met her until the day she left for home, Picasso was under her spell.

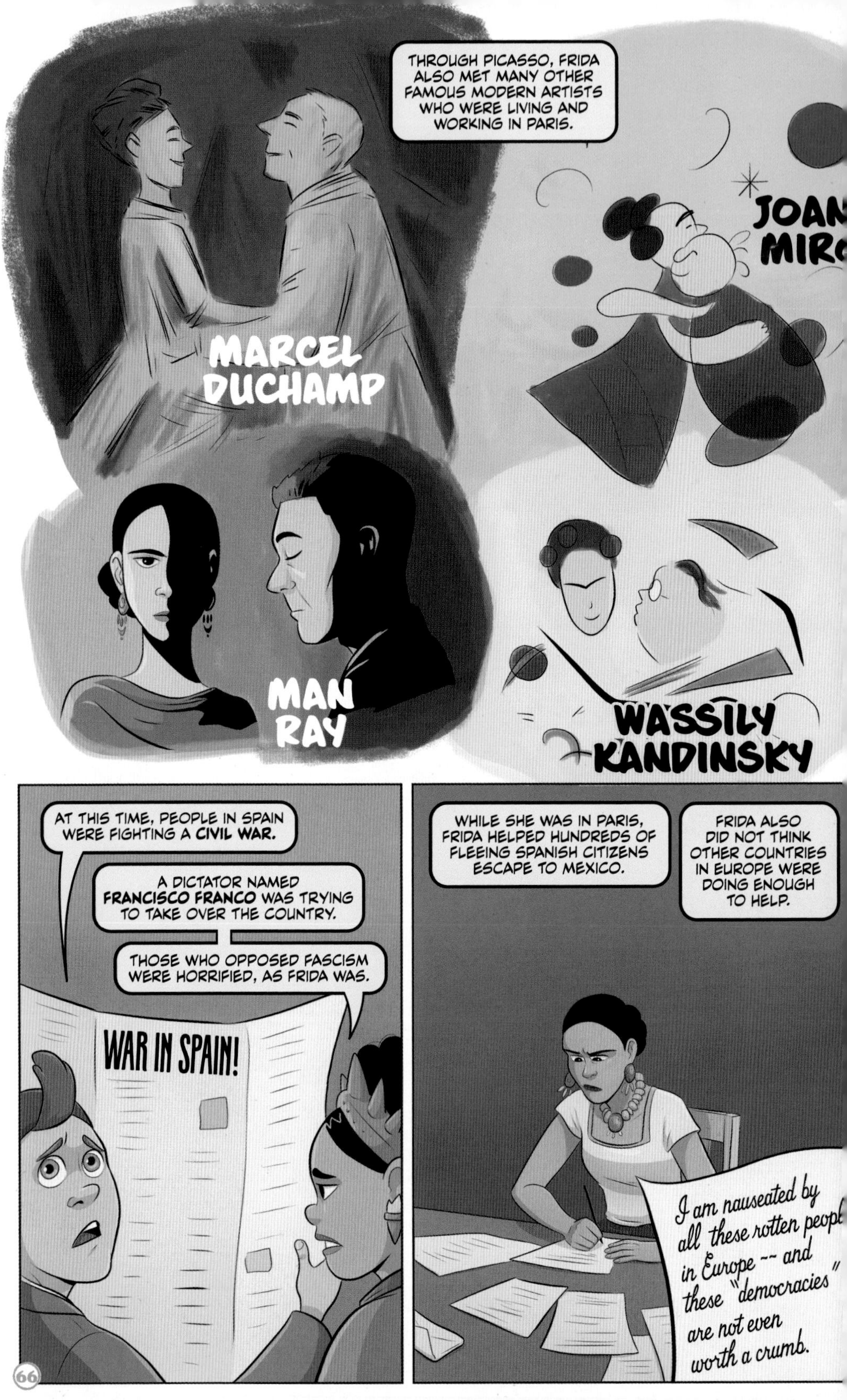
THROUGH PICASSO, FRIDA ALSO MET MANY OTHER FAMOUS MODERN ARTISTS WHO WERE LIVING AND WORKING IN PARIS.
MARCEL DUCHAMP
JOAN MIRÓ
MAN RAY
WASSILY KANDINSKY
AT THIS TIME, PEOPLE IN SPAIN WERE FIGHTING A **CIVIL WAR.**
A DICTATOR NAMED **FRANCISCO FRANCO** WAS TRYING TO TAKE OVER THE COUNTRY.
THOSE WHO OPPOSED FASCISM WERE HORRIFIED, AS FRIDA WAS.
WAR IN SPAIN!
WHILE SHE WAS IN PARIS, FRIDA HELPED HUNDREDS OF FLEEING SPANISH CITIZENS ESCAPE TO MEXICO.
FRIDA ALSO DID NOT THINK OTHER COUNTRIES IN EUROPE WERE DOING ENOUGH TO HELP.
I am nauseated by all these rotten people in Europe -- and these "democracies" are not even worth a crumb.

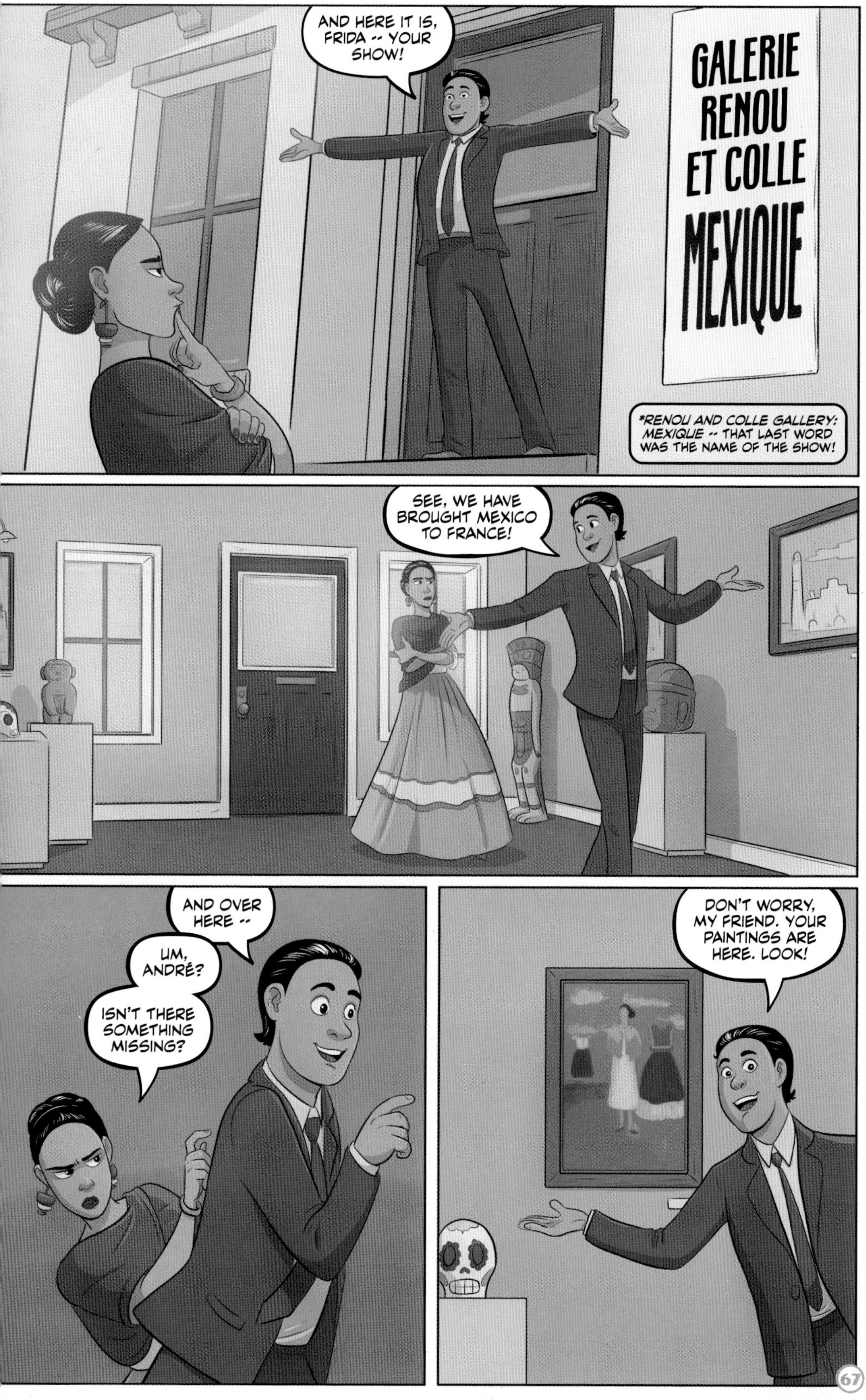
AND HERE IT IS, FRIDA -- YOUR SHOW!
GALERIE RENOU ET COLLE
MEXIQUE
*RENOU AND COLLE GALLERY: MEXIQUE -- THAT LAST WORD WAS THE NAME OF THE SHOW!
SEE, WE HAVE BROUGHT MEXICO TO FRANCE!
AND OVER HERE --
UM, ANDRÉ?
ISN'T THERE SOMETHING MISSING?
DON'T WORRY, MY FRIEND. YOUR PAINTINGS ARE HERE. LOOK!

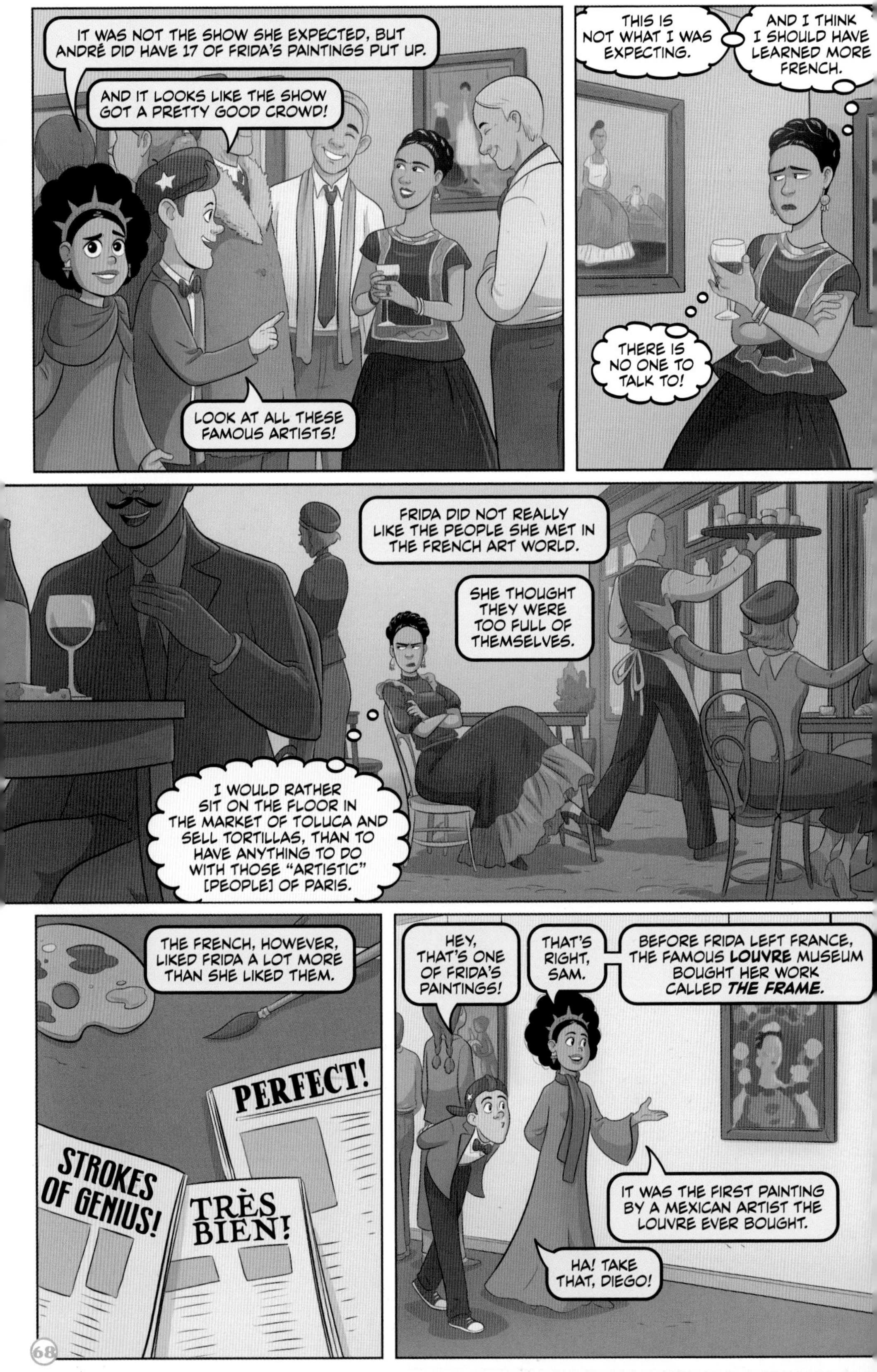
IT WAS NOT THE SHOW SHE EXPECTED, BUT ANDRÉ DID HAVE 17 OF FRIDA'S PAINTINGS PUT UP.
AND IT LOOKS LIKE THE SHOW GOT A PRETTY GOOD CROWD!
LOOK AT ALL THESE FAMOUS ARTISTS!
THIS IS NOT WHAT I WAS EXPECTING.
AND I THINK I SHOULD HAVE LEARNED MORE FRENCH.
THERE IS NO ONE TO TALK TO!
FRIDA DID NOT REALLY LIKE THE PEOPLE SHE MET IN THE FRENCH ART WORLD.
SHE THOUGHT THEY WERE TOO FULL OF THEMSELVES.
I WOULD RATHER SIT ON THE FLOOR IN THE MARKET OF TOLUCA AND SELL TORTILLAS, THAN TO HAVE ANYTHING TO DO WITH THOSE "ARTISTIC" [PEOPLE] OF PARIS.
THE FRENCH, HOWEVER, LIKED FRIDA A LOT MORE THAN SHE LIKED THEM.
PERFECT!
STROKES OF GENIUS!
TRÈS BIEN!
HEY, THAT'S ONE OF FRIDA'S PAINTINGS!
THAT'S RIGHT, SAM.
BEFORE FRIDA LEFT FRANCE, THE FAMOUS **LOUVRE** MUSEUM BOUGHT HER WORK CALLED ***THE FRAME.***
IT WAS THE FIRST PAINTING BY A MEXICAN ARTIST THE LOUVRE EVER BOUGHT.
HA! TAKE THAT, DIEGO!

NOT LONG AFTER HER SHOW WAS OVER, FRIDA HEADED BACK TO MEXICO AND MOVED BACK INTO HER FAMILY HOME.

SHE HOPED FOR BETTER TIMES, BUT THAT'S NOT WHAT SHE GOT.

HER DIVORCE FROM DIEGO WAS FINALIZED.

SHE HAD WANTED IT, BUT IT STILL MADE HER VERY SAD.

THEN A MAN SHE HAD BEEN DATING BROKE UP WITH HER.

AND THEN IN AUGUST 1940, LEON TROTSKY WAS KILLED IN MEXICO CITY.

BECAUSE SHE KNEW HIM, FRIDA WAS INTERROGATED BY THE POLICE!

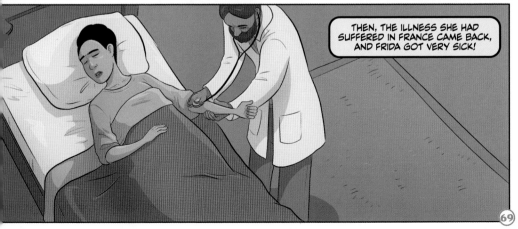

THEN, THE ILLNESS SHE HAD SUFFERED IN FRANCE CAME BACK, AND FRIDA GOT VERY SICK!

69

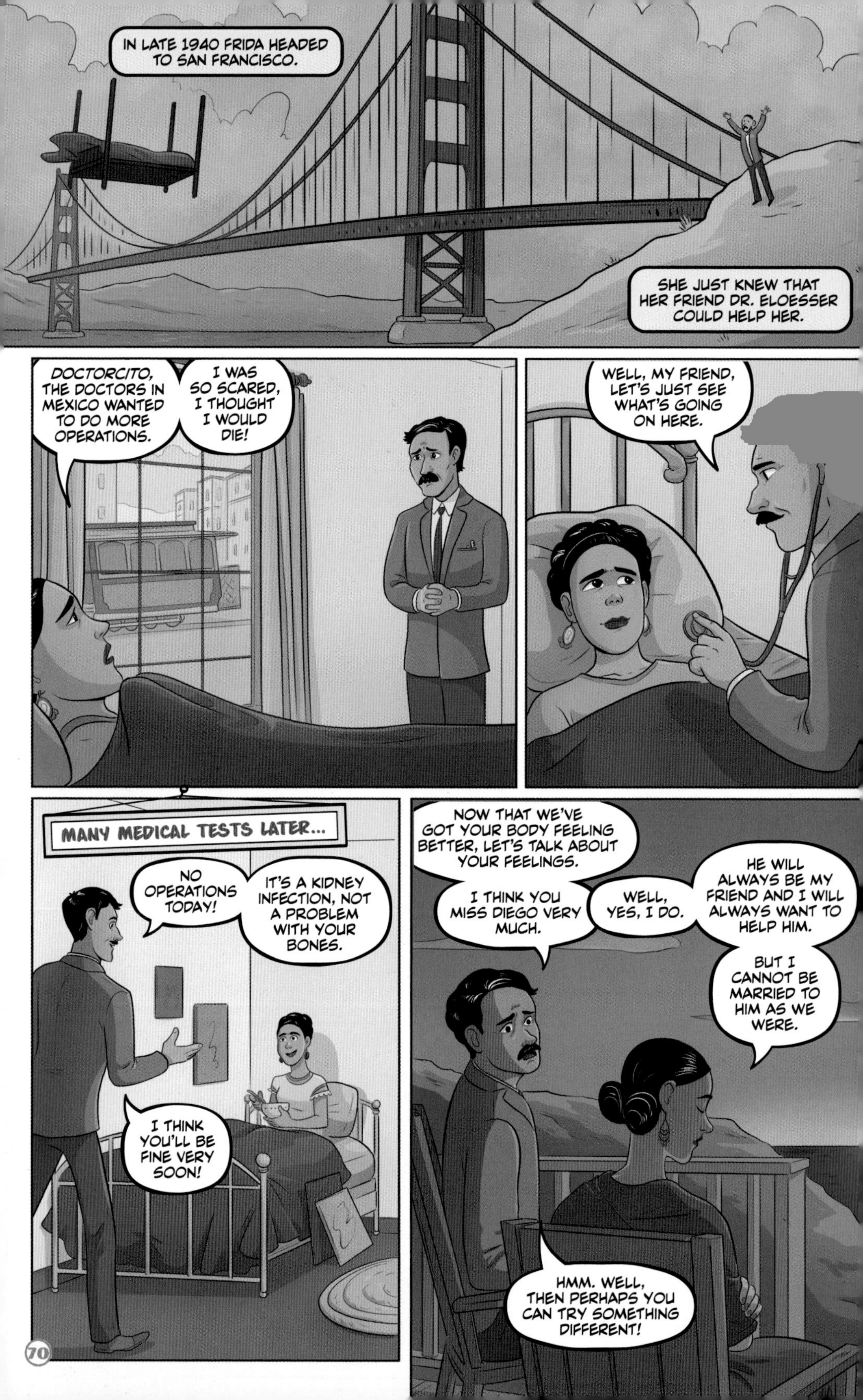
IN LATE 1940 FRIDA HEADED TO SAN FRANCISCO.
SHE JUST KNEW THAT HER FRIEND DR. ELOESSER COULD HELP HER.
DOCTORCITO, THE DOCTORS IN MEXICO WANTED TO DO MORE OPERATIONS.
I WAS SO SCARED, I THOUGHT I WOULD DIE!
WELL, MY FRIEND, LET'S JUST SEE WHAT'S GOING ON HERE.
MANY MEDICAL TESTS LATER...
NO OPERATIONS TODAY!
IT'S A KIDNEY INFECTION, NOT A PROBLEM WITH YOUR BONES.
I THINK YOU'LL BE FINE VERY SOON!
NOW THAT WE'VE GOT YOUR BODY FEELING BETTER, LET'S TALK ABOUT YOUR FEELINGS.
I THINK YOU MISS DIEGO VERY MUCH.
WELL, YES, I DO.
HE WILL ALWAYS BE MY FRIEND AND I WILL ALWAYS WANT TO HELP HIM.
BUT I CANNOT BE MARRIED TO HIM AS WE WERE.
HMM. WELL, THEN PERHAPS YOU CAN TRY SOMETHING DIFFERENT!

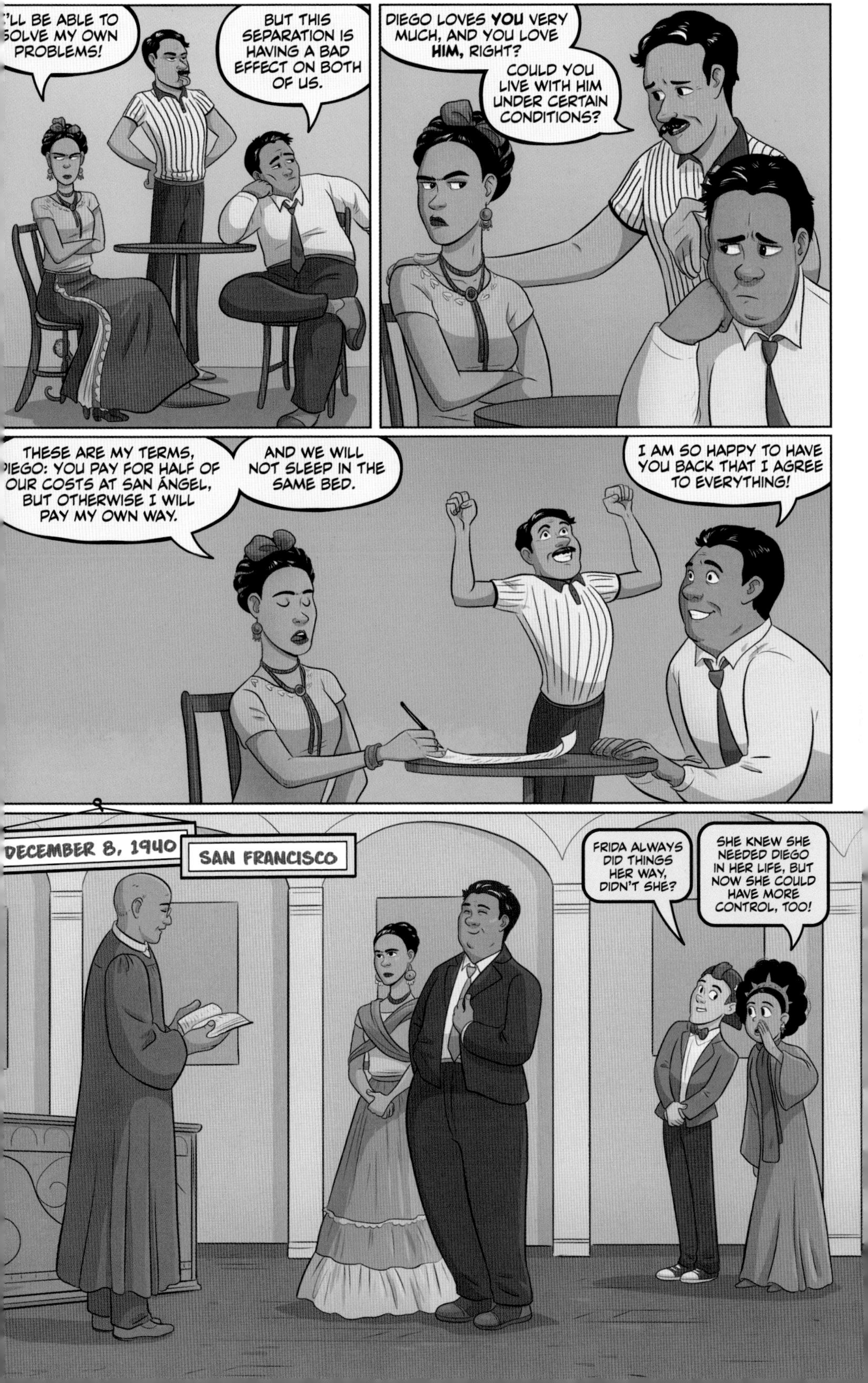
I'LL BE ABLE TO SOLVE MY OWN PROBLEMS!
BUT THIS SEPARATION IS HAVING A BAD EFFECT ON BOTH OF US.
DIEGO LOVES **YOU** VERY MUCH, AND YOU LOVE **HIM,** RIGHT?
COULD YOU LIVE WITH HIM UNDER CERTAIN CONDITIONS?
THESE ARE MY TERMS, DIEGO: YOU PAY FOR HALF OF OUR COSTS AT SAN ÁNGEL, BUT OTHERWISE I WILL PAY MY OWN WAY.
AND WE WILL NOT SLEEP IN THE SAME BED.
I AM SO HAPPY TO HAVE YOU BACK THAT I AGREE TO EVERYTHING!
DECEMBER 8, 1940
SAN FRANCISCO
FRIDA ALWAYS DID THINGS HER WAY, DIDN'T SHE?
SHE KNEW SHE NEEDED DIEGO IN HER LIFE, BUT NOW SHE COULD HAVE MORE CONTROL, TOO!

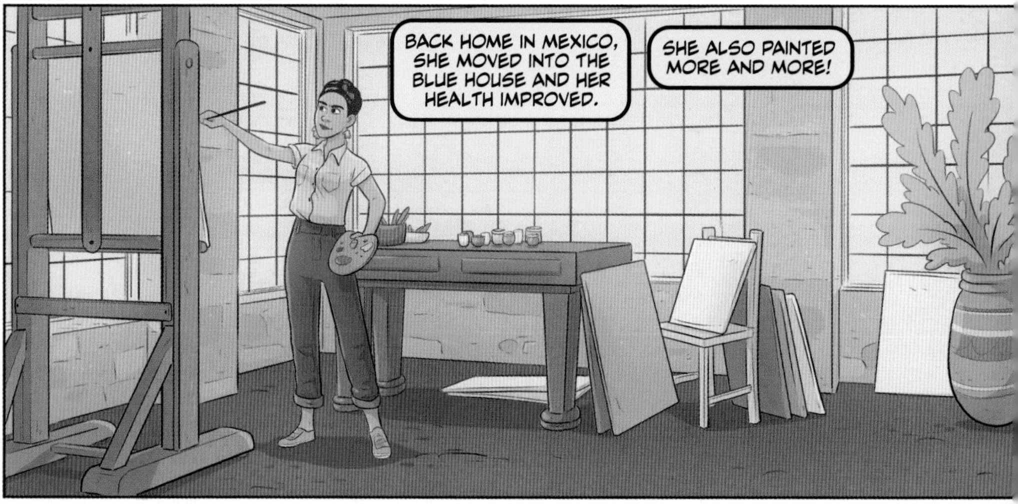
BACK HOME IN MEXICO, SHE MOVED INTO THE BLUE HOUSE AND HER HEALTH IMPROVED.
SHE ALSO PAINTED MORE AND MORE!

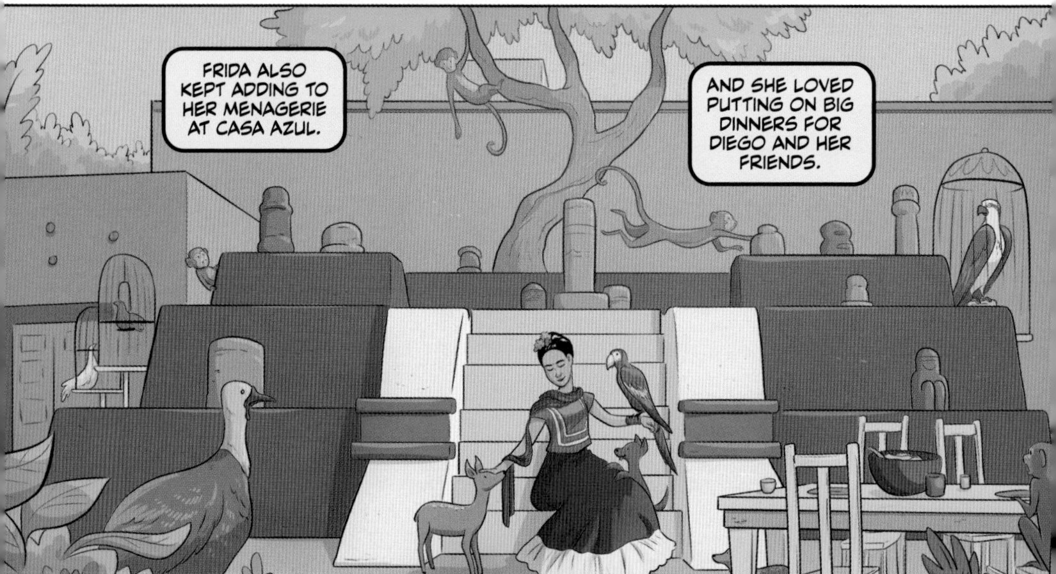
FRIDA ALSO KEPT ADDING TO HER MENAGERIE AT CASA AZUL.
AND SHE LOVED PUTTING ON BIG DINNERS FOR DIEGO AND HER FRIENDS.

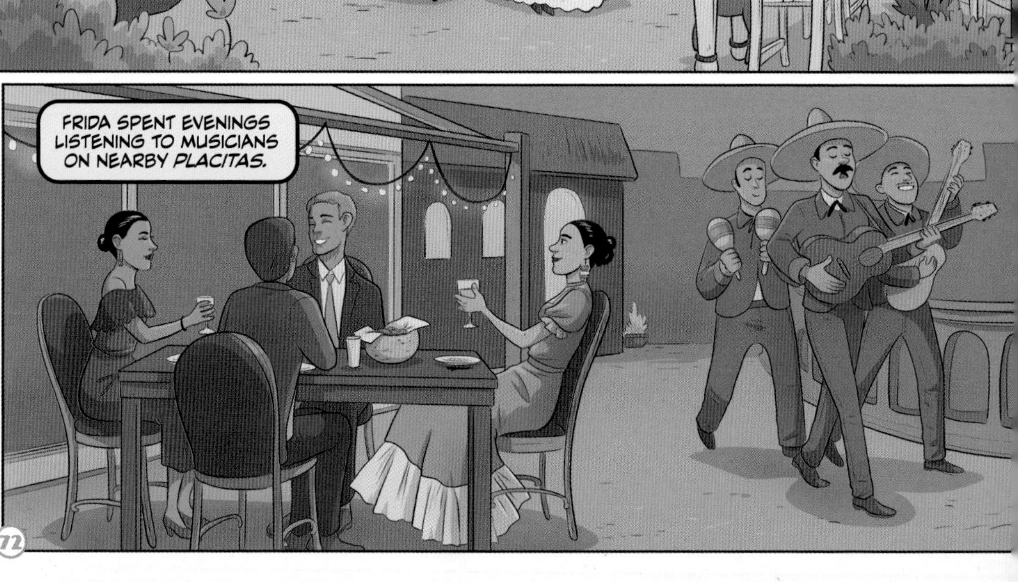
FRIDA SPENT EVENINGS LISTENING TO MUSICIANS ON NEARBY *PLACITAS*.

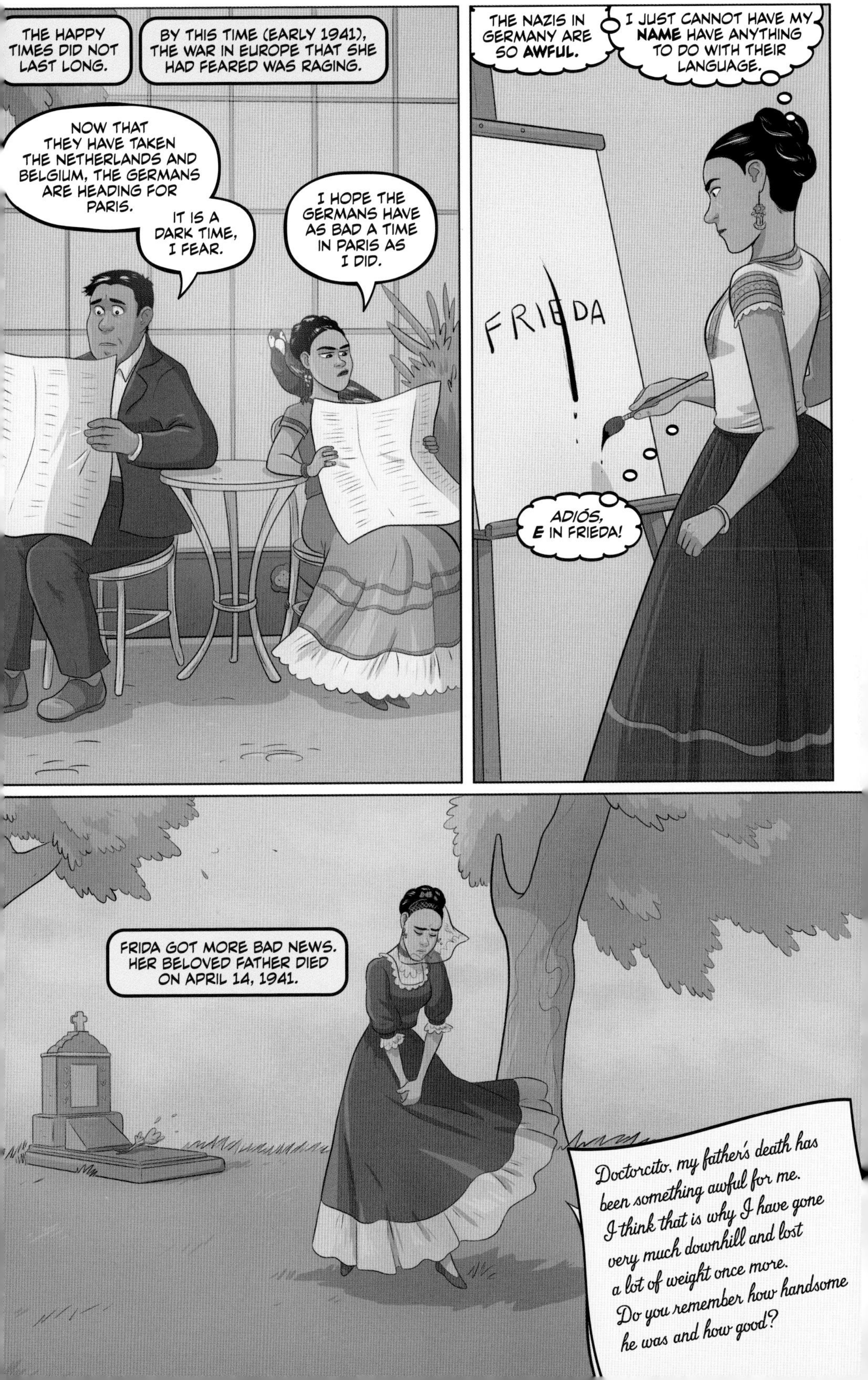
THE HAPPY TIMES DID NOT LAST LONG.
BY THIS TIME (EARLY 1941), THE WAR IN EUROPE THAT SHE HAD FEARED WAS RAGING.
NOW THAT THEY HAVE TAKEN THE NETHERLANDS AND BELGIUM, THE GERMANS ARE HEADING FOR PARIS.
IT IS A DARK TIME, I FEAR.
I HOPE THE GERMANS HAVE AS BAD A TIME IN PARIS AS I DID.
THE NAZIS IN GERMANY ARE SO **AWFUL.**
I JUST CANNOT HAVE MY **NAME** HAVE ANYTHING TO DO WITH THEIR LANGUAGE.
FRIEDA
ADIÓS, **E** IN FRIEDA!
FRIDA GOT MORE BAD NEWS. HER BELOVED FATHER DIED ON APRIL 14, 1941.
Doctorcito, my father's death has been something awful for me. I think that is why I have gone very much downhill and lost a lot of weight once more. Do you remember how handsome he was and how good?

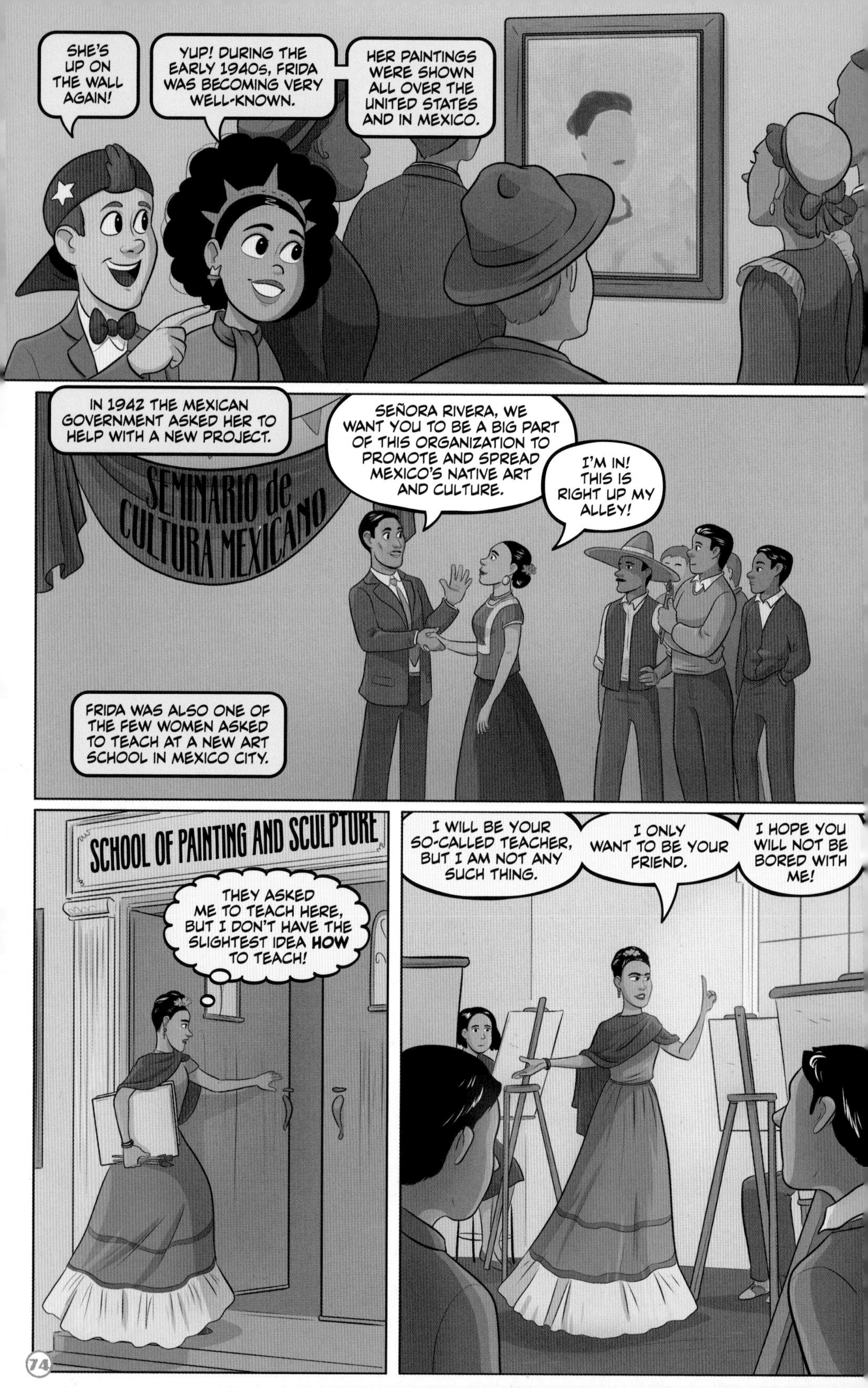
SHE'S UP ON THE WALL AGAIN!
YUP! DURING THE EARLY 1940s, FRIDA WAS BECOMING VERY WELL-KNOWN.
HER PAINTINGS WERE SHOWN ALL OVER THE UNITED STATES AND IN MEXICO.
IN 1942 THE MEXICAN GOVERNMENT ASKED HER TO HELP WITH A NEW PROJECT.
SEMINARIO de CULTURA MEXICANO
SEÑORA RIVERA, WE WANT YOU TO BE A BIG PART OF THIS ORGANIZATION TO PROMOTE AND SPREAD MEXICO'S NATIVE ART AND CULTURE.
I'M IN! THIS IS RIGHT UP MY ALLEY!
FRIDA WAS ALSO ONE OF THE FEW WOMEN ASKED TO TEACH AT A NEW ART SCHOOL IN MEXICO CITY.
SCHOOL OF PAINTING AND SCULPTURE
THEY ASKED ME TO TEACH HERE, BUT I DON'T HAVE THE SLIGHTEST IDEA **HOW** TO TEACH!
I WILL BE YOUR SO-CALLED TEACHER, BUT I AM NOT ANY SUCH THING.
I ONLY WANT TO BE YOUR FRIEND.
I HOPE YOU WILL NOT BE BORED WITH ME!

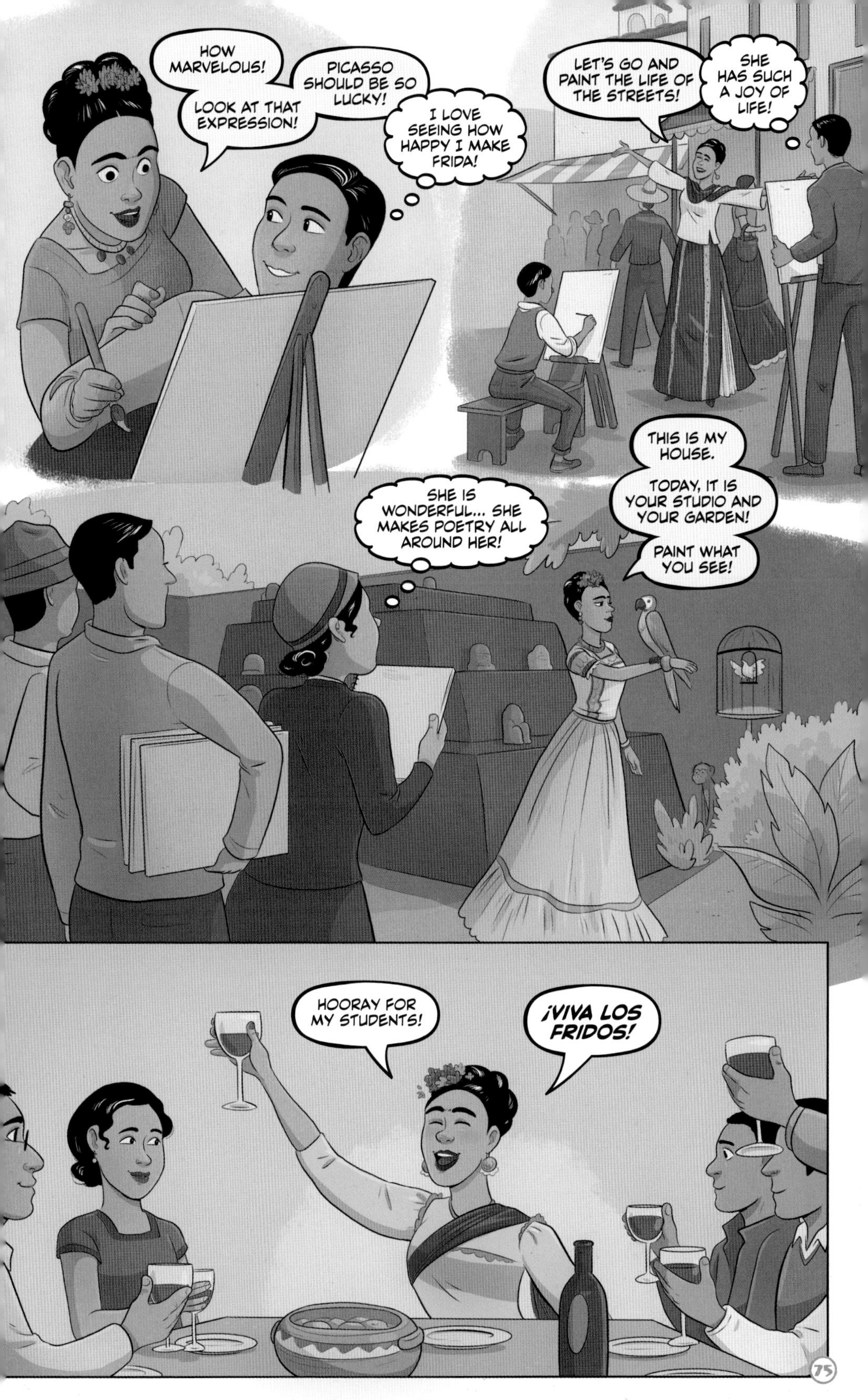
HOW MARVELOUS!
LOOK AT THAT EXPRESSION!
PICASSO SHOULD BE SO LUCKY!
I LOVE SEEING HOW HAPPY I MAKE FRIDA!
LET'S GO AND PAINT THE LIFE OF THE STREETS!
SHE HAS SUCH A JOY OF LIFE!
SHE IS WONDERFUL... SHE MAKES POETRY ALL AROUND HER!
THIS IS MY HOUSE.
TODAY, IT IS YOUR STUDIO AND YOUR GARDEN!
PAINT WHAT YOU SEE!
HOORAY FOR MY STUDENTS!
¡VIVA LOS FRIDOS!

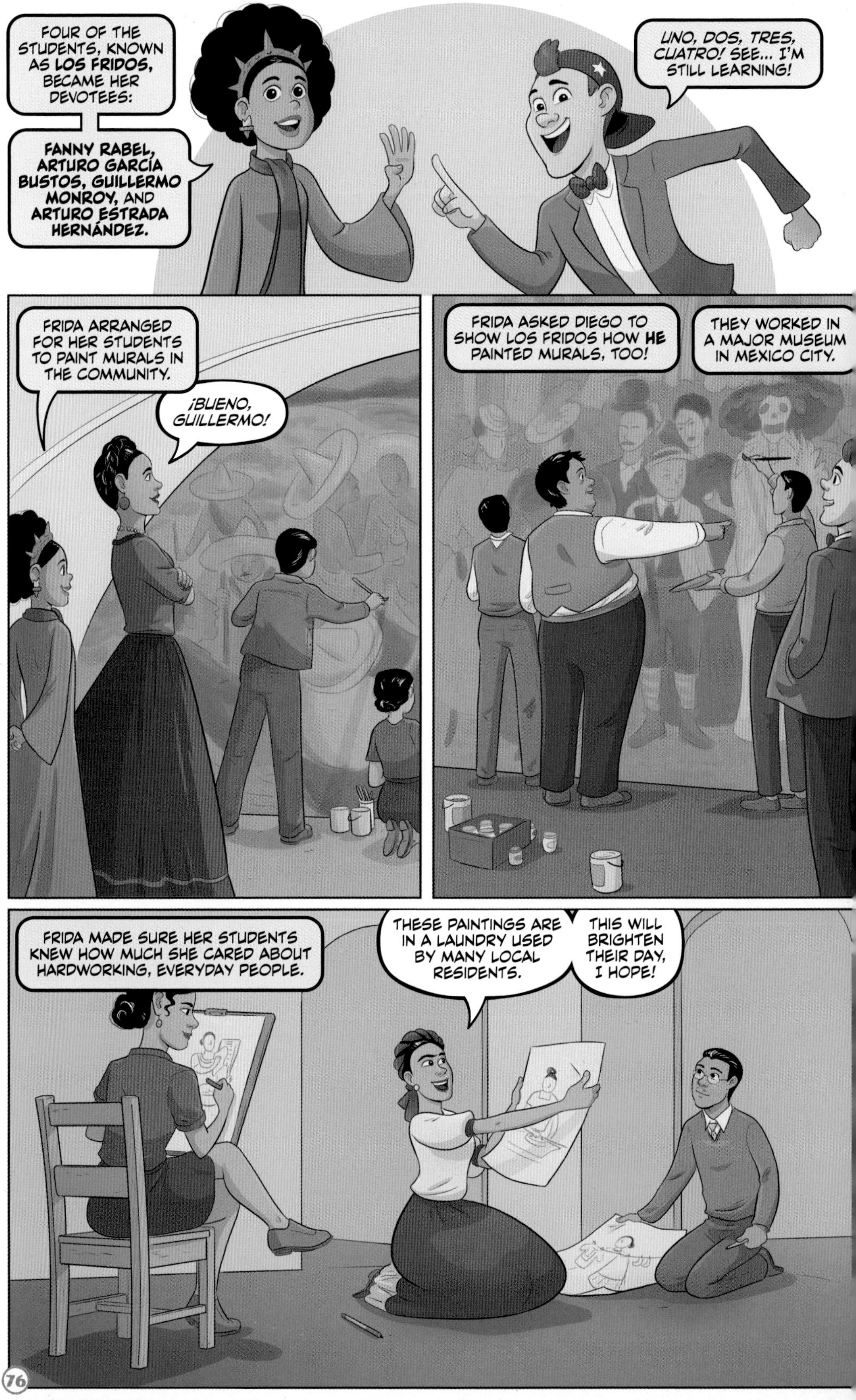
FOUR OF THE STUDENTS, KNOWN AS **LOS FRIDOS**, BECAME HER DEVOTEES:
FANNY RABEL, ARTURO GARCÍA BUSTOS, GUILLERMO MONROY, AND **ARTURO ESTRADA HERNÁNDEZ.**
UNO, DOS, TRES, CUATRO! SEE... I'M STILL LEARNING!
FRIDA ARRANGED FOR HER STUDENTS TO PAINT MURALS IN THE COMMUNITY.
¡BUENO, GUILLERMO!
FRIDA ASKED DIEGO TO SHOW LOS FRIDOS HOW **HE** PAINTED MURALS, TOO!
THEY WORKED IN A MAJOR MUSEUM IN MEXICO CITY.
FRIDA MADE SURE HER STUDENTS KNEW HOW MUCH SHE CARED ABOUT HARDWORKING, EVERYDAY PEOPLE.
THESE PAINTINGS ARE IN A LAUNDRY USED BY MANY LOCAL RESIDENTS.
THIS WILL BRIGHTEN THEIR DAY, I HOPE!

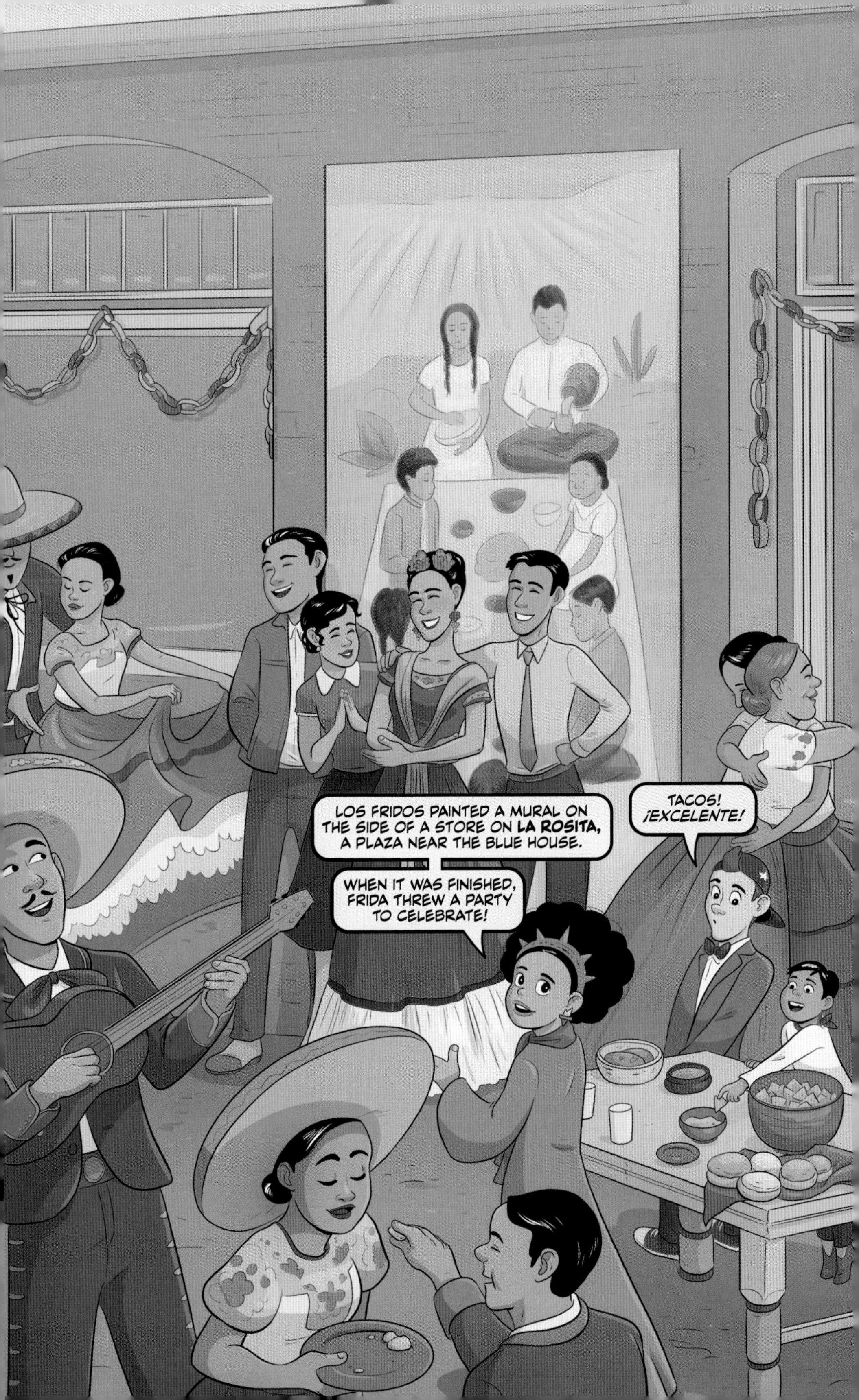
LOS FRIDOS PAINTED A MURAL ON THE SIDE OF A STORE ON **LA ROSITA,** A PLAZA NEAR THE BLUE HOUSE.
WHEN IT WAS FINISHED, FRIDA THREW A PARTY TO CELEBRATE!
TACOS! ¡EXCELENTE!

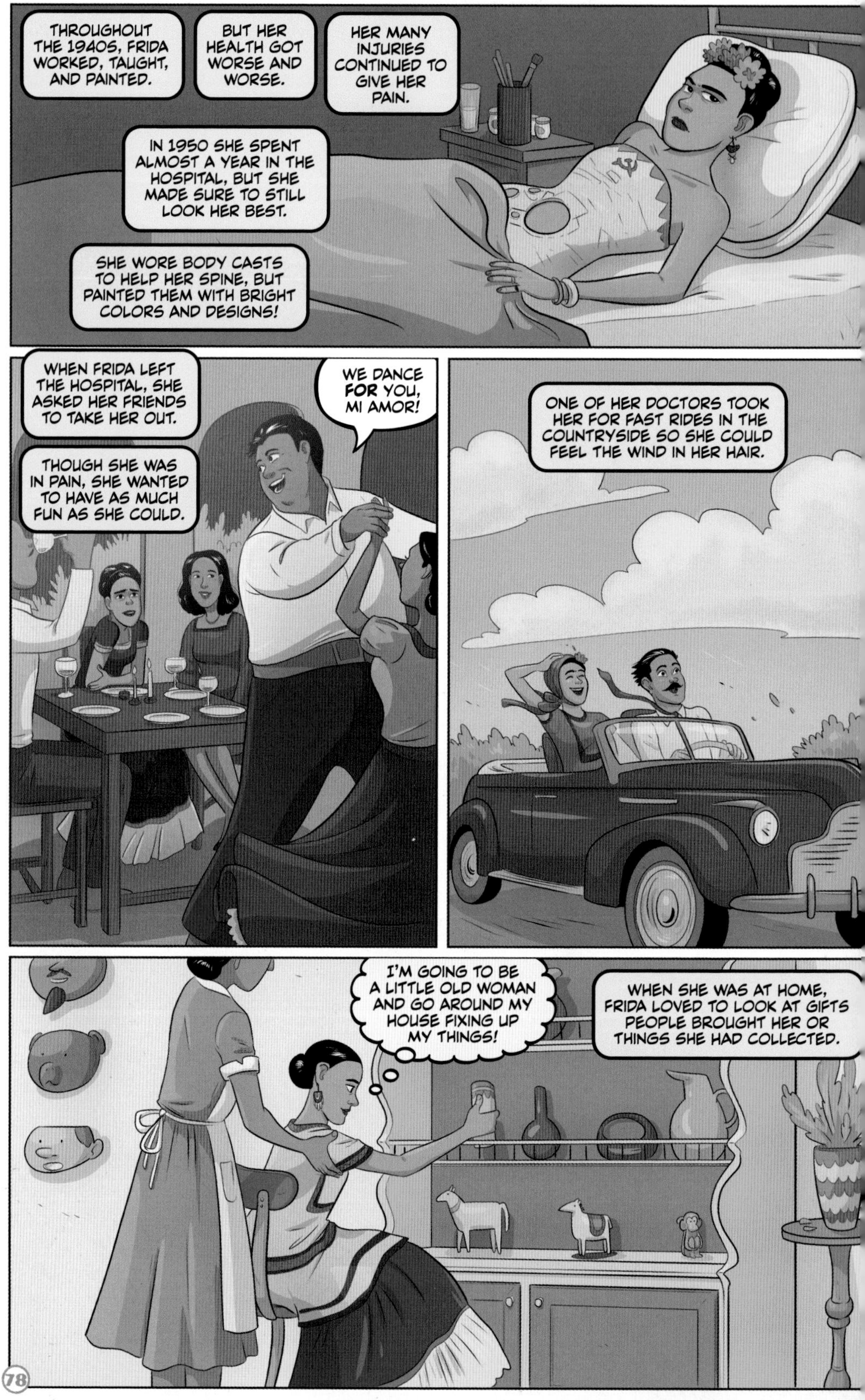
THROUGHOUT THE 1940S, FRIDA WORKED, TAUGHT, AND PAINTED.
BUT HER HEALTH GOT WORSE AND WORSE.
HER MANY INJURIES CONTINUED TO GIVE HER PAIN.
IN 1950 SHE SPENT ALMOST A YEAR IN THE HOSPITAL, BUT SHE MADE SURE TO STILL LOOK HER BEST.
SHE WORE BODY CASTS TO HELP HER SPINE, BUT PAINTED THEM WITH BRIGHT COLORS AND DESIGNS!
WHEN FRIDA LEFT THE HOSPITAL, SHE ASKED HER FRIENDS TO TAKE HER OUT.
THOUGH SHE WAS IN PAIN, SHE WANTED TO HAVE AS MUCH FUN AS SHE COULD.
WE DANCE **FOR** YOU, MI AMOR!
ONE OF HER DOCTORS TOOK HER FOR FAST RIDES IN THE COUNTRYSIDE SO SHE COULD FEEL THE WIND IN HER HAIR.
I'M GOING TO BE A LITTLE OLD WOMAN AND GO AROUND MY HOUSE FIXING UP MY THINGS!
WHEN SHE WAS AT HOME, FRIDA LOVED TO LOOK AT GIFTS PEOPLE BROUGHT HER OR THINGS SHE HAD COLLECTED.

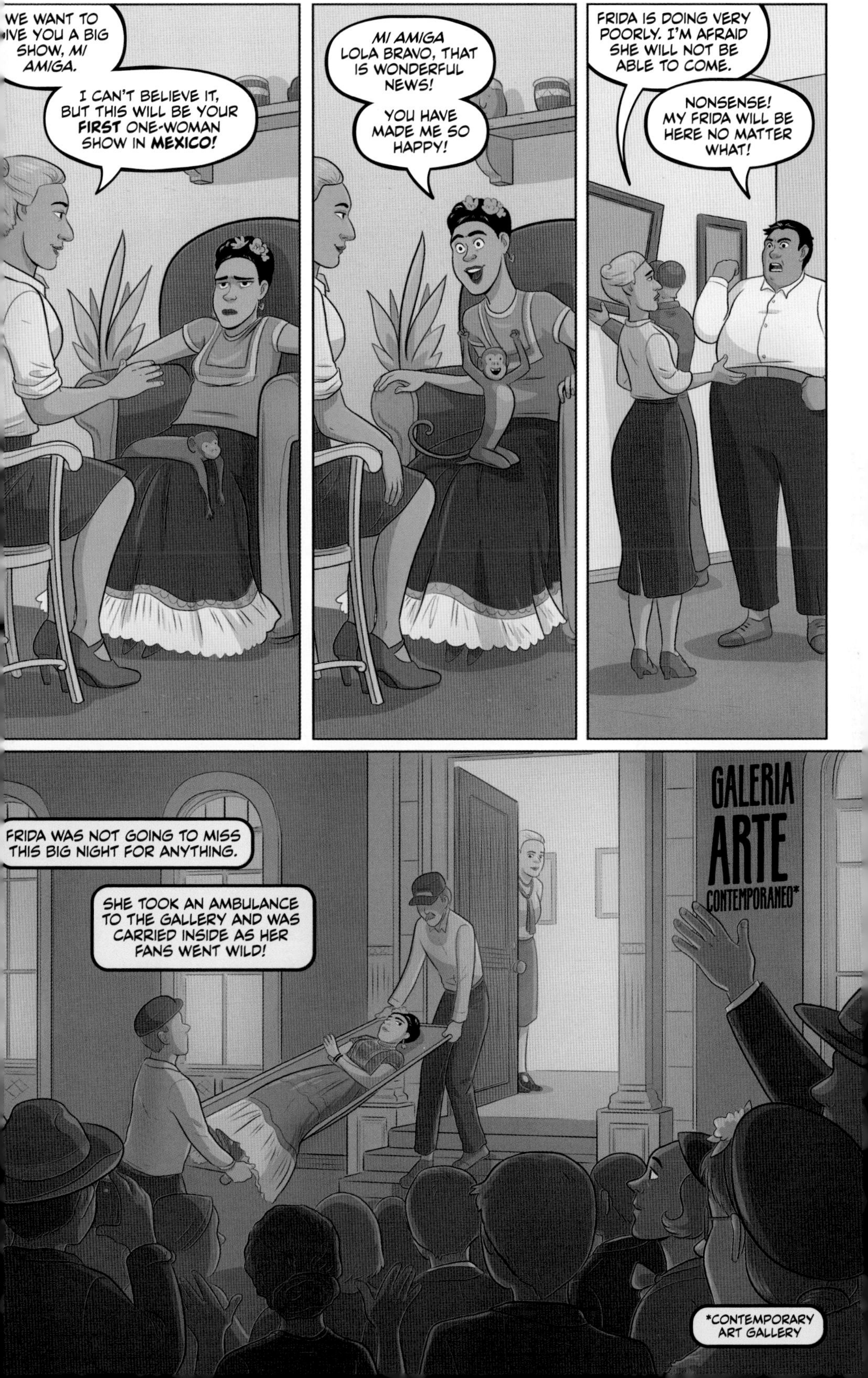
WE WANT TO
IVE YOU A BIG
SHOW, MI
AMIGA.
I CAN'T BELIEVE IT,
BUT THIS WILL BE YOUR
FIRST ONE-WOMAN
SHOW IN MEXICO!
MI AMIGA
LOLA BRAVO, THAT
IS WONDERFUL
NEWS!
YOU HAVE
MADE ME SO
HAPPY!
FRIDA IS DOING VERY
POORLY. I'M AFRAID
SHE WILL NOT BE
ABLE TO COME.
NONSENSE!
MY FRIDA WILL BE
HERE NO MATTER
WHAT!
GALERIA
ARTE
CONTEMPORANEO*
FRIDA WAS NOT GOING TO MISS
THIS BIG NIGHT FOR ANYTHING.
SHE TOOK AN AMBULANCE
TO THE GALLERY AND WAS
CARRIED INSIDE AS HER
FANS WENT WILD!
*CONTEMPORARY
ART GALLERY

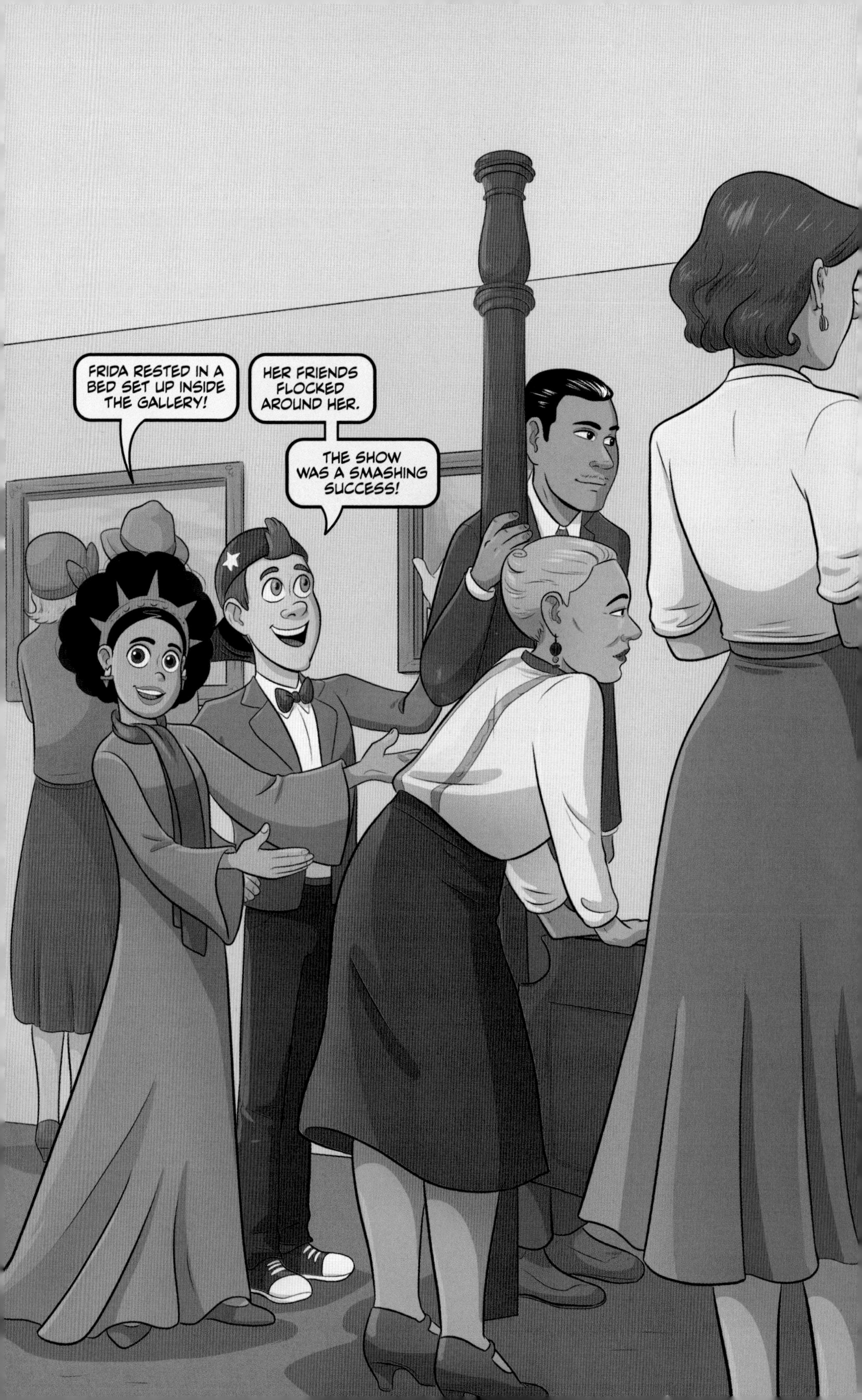
FRIDA RESTED IN A BED SET UP INSIDE THE GALLERY!
HER FRIENDS FLOCKED AROUND HER.
THE SHOW WAS A SMASHING SUCCESS!

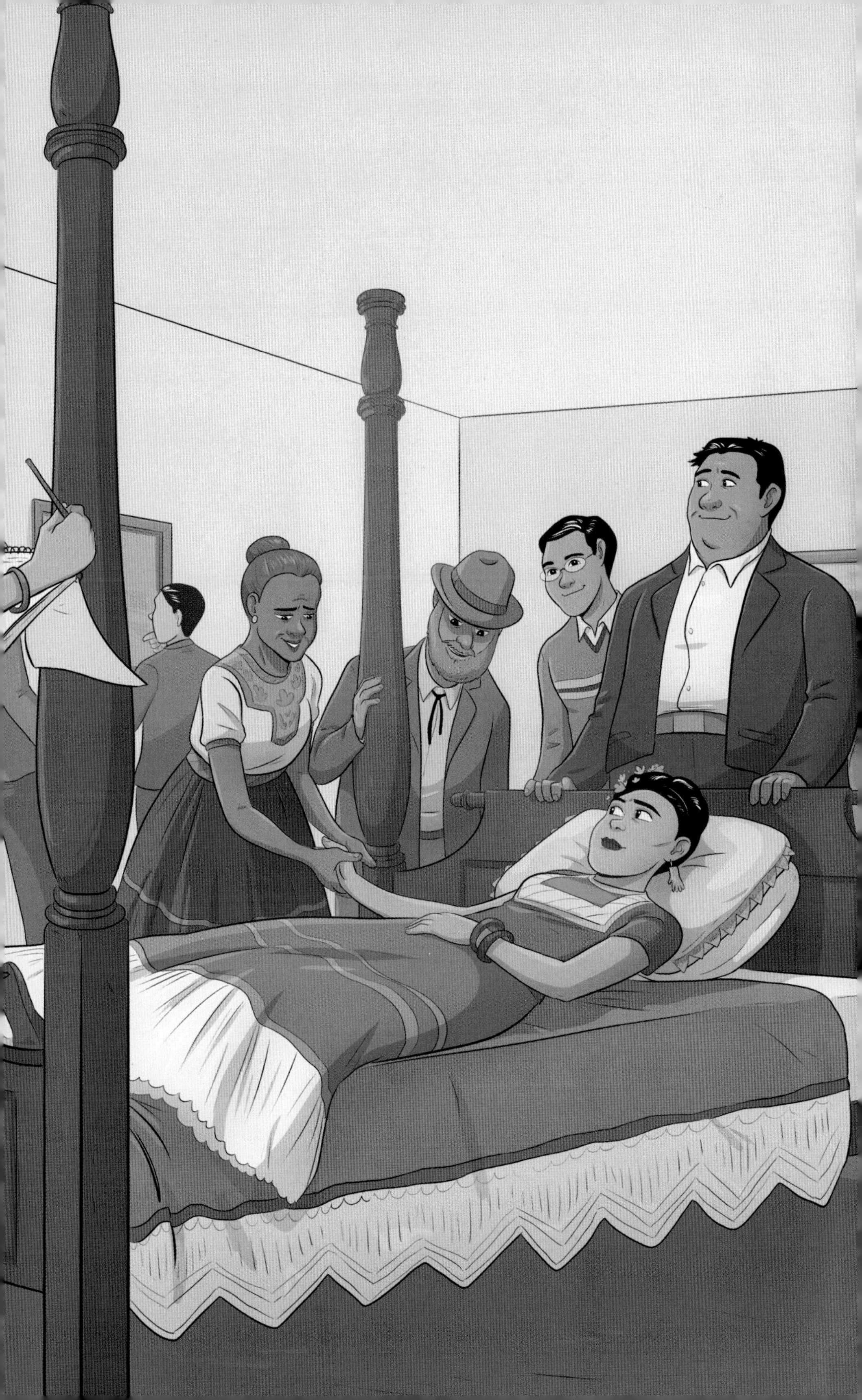

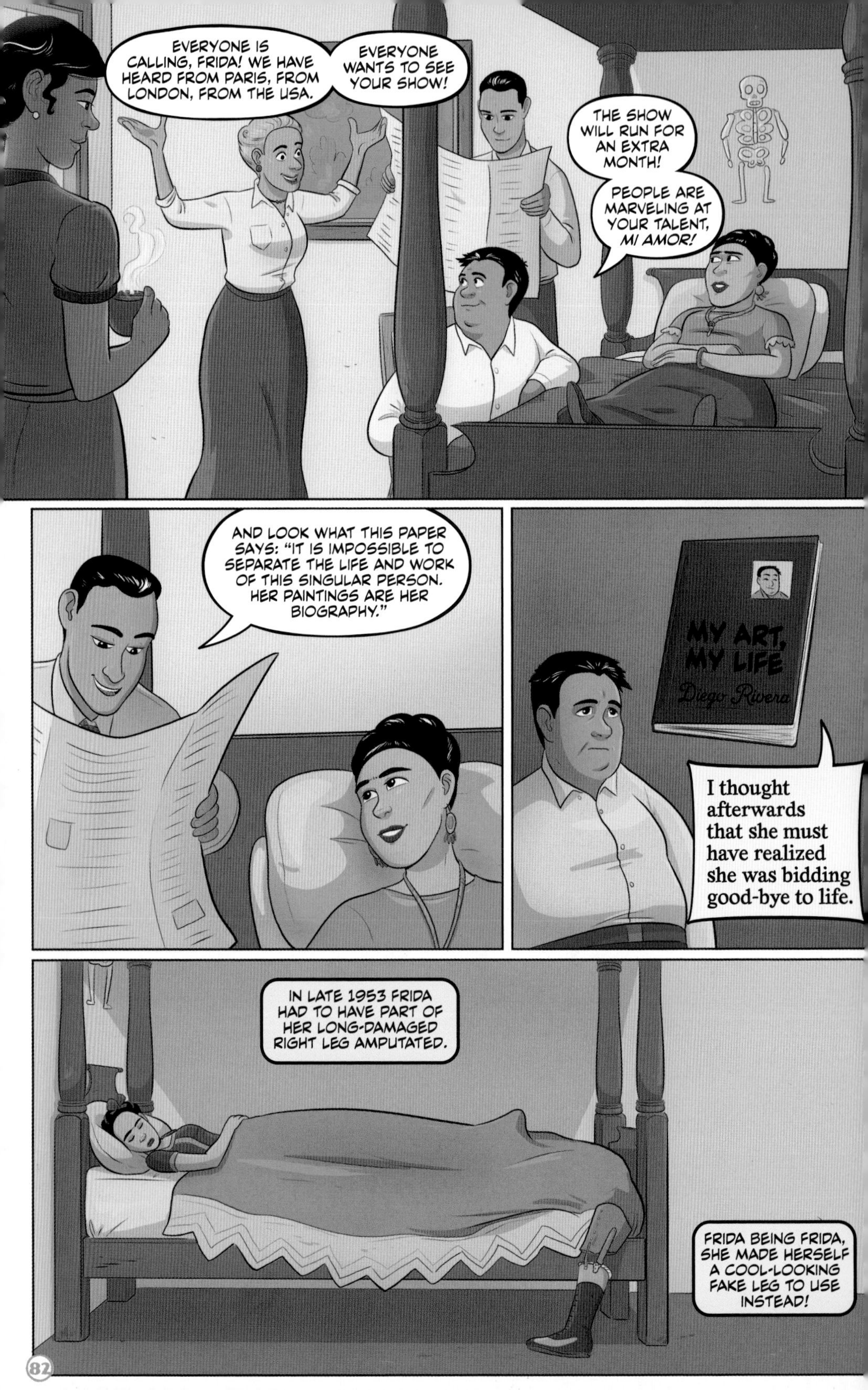
EVERYONE IS CALLING, FRIDA! WE HAVE HEARD FROM PARIS, FROM LONDON, FROM THE USA.
EVERYONE WANTS TO SEE YOUR SHOW!
THE SHOW WILL RUN FOR AN EXTRA MONTH!
PEOPLE ARE MARVELING AT YOUR TALENT, *MI AMOR!*
AND LOOK WHAT THIS PAPER SAYS: "IT IS IMPOSSIBLE TO SEPARATE THE LIFE AND WORK OF THIS SINGULAR PERSON. HER PAINTINGS ARE HER BIOGRAPHY."
MY ART, MY LIFE
Diego Rivera
I thought afterwards that she must have realized she was bidding good-bye to life.
IN LATE 1953 FRIDA HAD TO HAVE PART OF HER LONG-DAMAGED RIGHT LEG AMPUTATED.
FRIDA BEING FRIDA, SHE MADE HERSELF A COOL-LOOKING FAKE LEG TO USE INSTEAD!

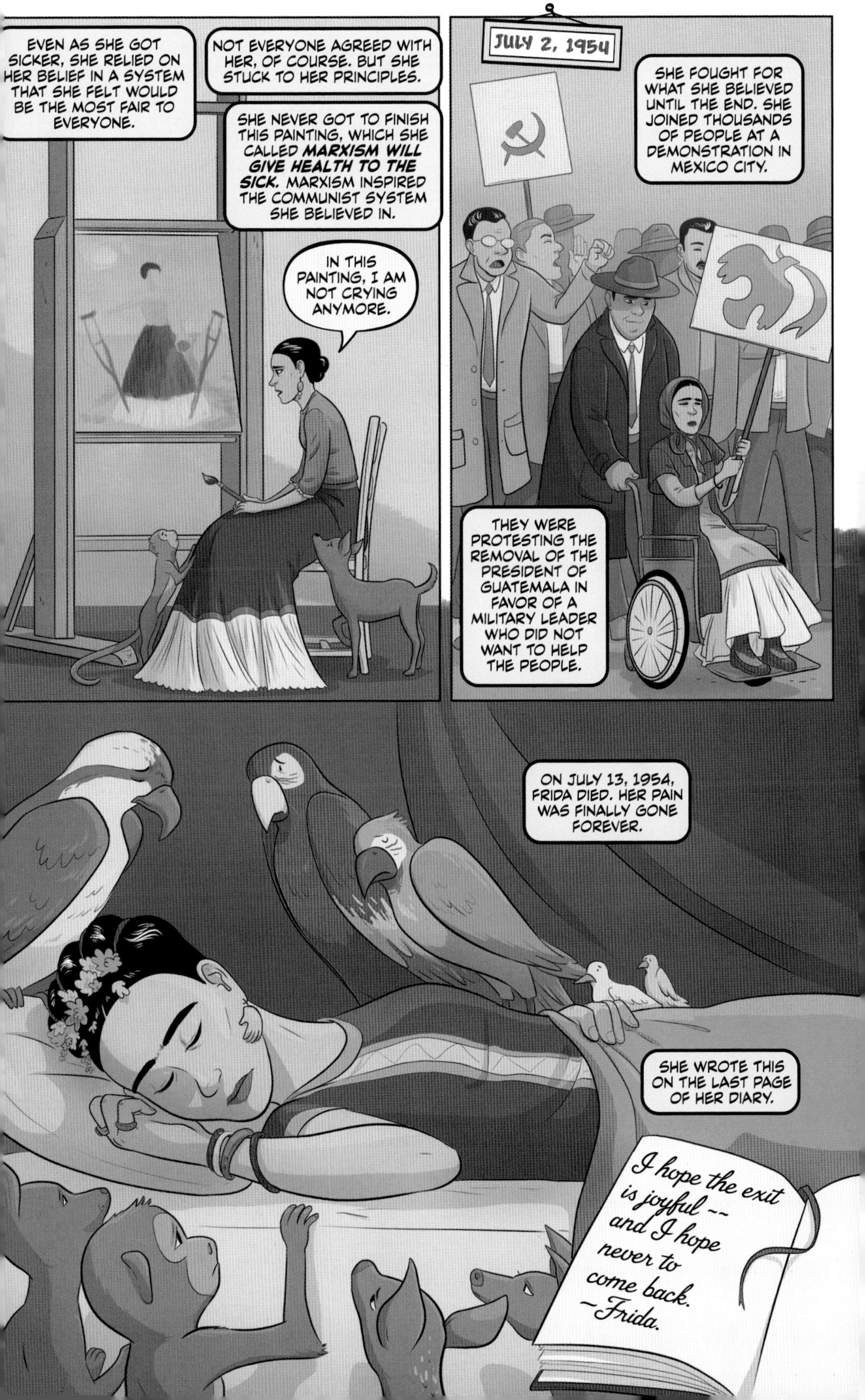
EVEN AS SHE GOT SICKER, SHE RELIED ON HER BELIEF IN A SYSTEM THAT SHE FELT WOULD BE THE MOST FAIR TO EVERYONE.
NOT EVERYONE AGREED WITH HER, OF COURSE. BUT SHE STUCK TO HER PRINCIPLES.
SHE NEVER GOT TO FINISH THIS PAINTING, WHICH SHE CALLED ***MARXISM WILL GIVE HEALTH TO THE SICK.*** MARXISM INSPIRED THE COMMUNIST SYSTEM SHE BELIEVED IN.
IN THIS PAINTING, I AM NOT CRYING ANYMORE.
JULY 2, 1954
SHE FOUGHT FOR WHAT SHE BELIEVED UNTIL THE END. SHE JOINED THOUSANDS OF PEOPLE AT A DEMONSTRATION IN MEXICO CITY.
THEY WERE PROTESTING THE REMOVAL OF THE PRESIDENT OF GUATEMALA IN FAVOR OF A MILITARY LEADER WHO DID NOT WANT TO HELP THE PEOPLE.
ON JULY 13, 1954, FRIDA DIED. HER PAIN WAS FINALLY GONE FOREVER.
SHE WROTE THIS ON THE LAST PAGE OF HER DIARY.
I hope the exit is joyful -- and I hope never to come back. ~Frida.

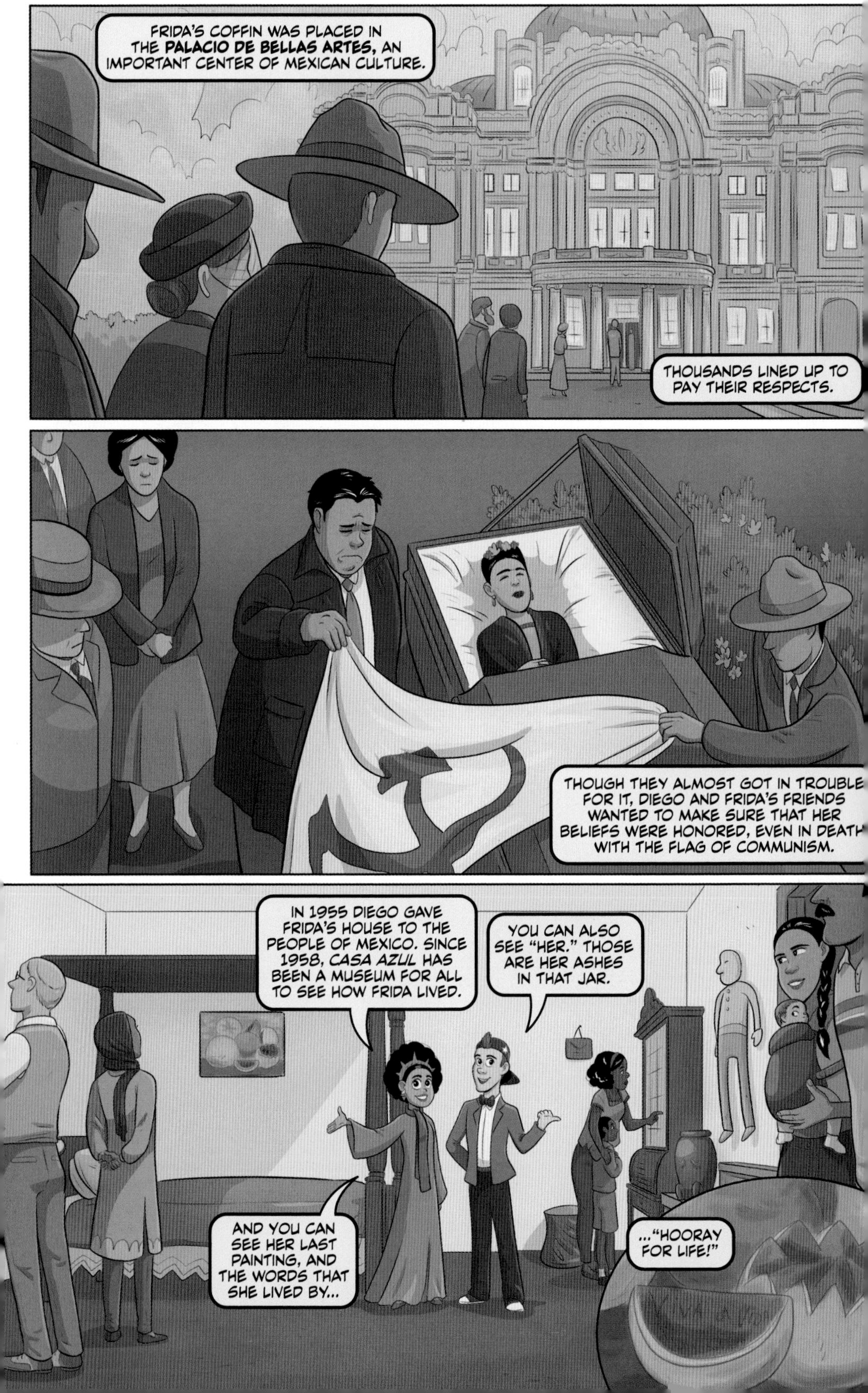
FRIDA'S COFFIN WAS PLACED IN THE **PALACIO DE BELLAS ARTES,** AN IMPORTANT CENTER OF MEXICAN CULTURE.
THOUSANDS LINED UP TO PAY THEIR RESPECTS.
THOUGH THEY ALMOST GOT IN TROUBLE FOR IT, DIEGO AND FRIDA'S FRIENDS WANTED TO MAKE SURE THAT HER BELIEFS WERE HONORED, EVEN IN DEATH WITH THE FLAG OF COMMUNISM.
IN 1955 DIEGO GAVE FRIDA'S HOUSE TO THE PEOPLE OF MEXICO. SINCE 1958, *CASA AZUL* HAS BEEN A MUSEUM FOR ALL TO SEE HOW FRIDA LIVED.
YOU CAN ALSO SEE "HER." THOSE ARE HER ASHES IN THAT JAR.
AND YOU CAN SEE HER LAST PAINTING, AND THE WORDS THAT SHE LIVED BY...
..."HOORAY FOR LIFE!"

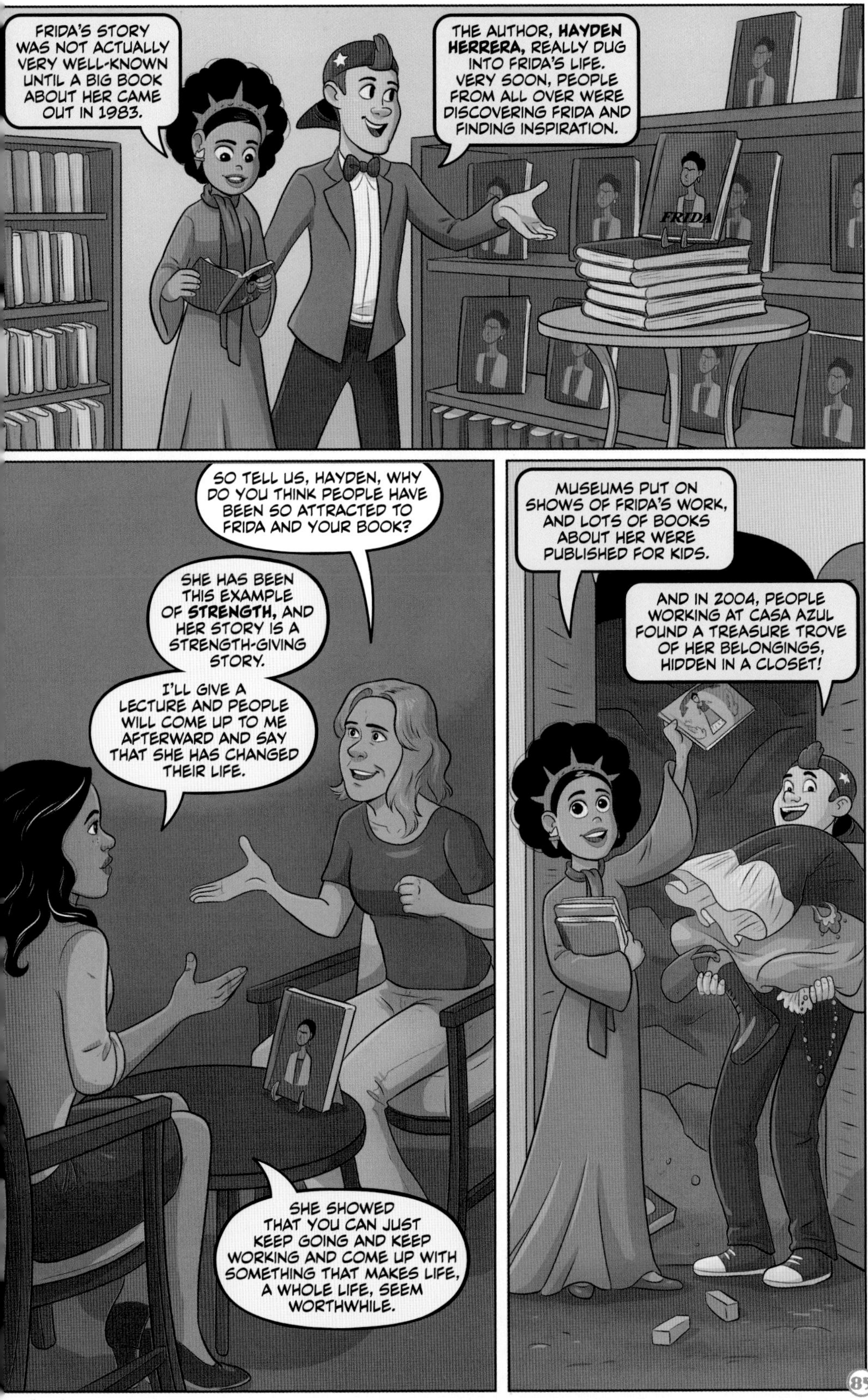
FRIDA'S STORY WAS NOT ACTUALLY VERY WELL-KNOWN UNTIL A BIG BOOK ABOUT HER CAME OUT IN 1983.
THE AUTHOR, **HAYDEN HERRERA,** REALLY DUG INTO FRIDA'S LIFE. VERY SOON, PEOPLE FROM ALL OVER WERE DISCOVERING FRIDA AND FINDING INSPIRATION.
FRIDA
SO TELL US, HAYDEN, WHY DO YOU THINK PEOPLE HAVE BEEN SO ATTRACTED TO FRIDA AND YOUR BOOK?
SHE HAS BEEN THIS EXAMPLE OF **STRENGTH,** AND HER STORY IS A STRENGTH-GIVING STORY.
I'LL GIVE A LECTURE AND PEOPLE WILL COME UP TO ME AFTERWARD AND SAY THAT SHE HAS CHANGED THEIR LIFE.
SHE SHOWED THAT YOU CAN JUST KEEP GOING AND KEEP WORKING AND COME UP WITH SOMETHING THAT MAKES LIFE, A WHOLE LIFE, SEEM WORTHWHILE.
MUSEUMS PUT ON SHOWS OF FRIDA'S WORK, AND LOTS OF BOOKS ABOUT HER WERE PUBLISHED FOR KIDS.
AND IN 2004, PEOPLE WORKING AT CASA AZUL FOUND A TREASURE TROVE OF HER BELONGINGS, HIDDEN IN A CLOSET!

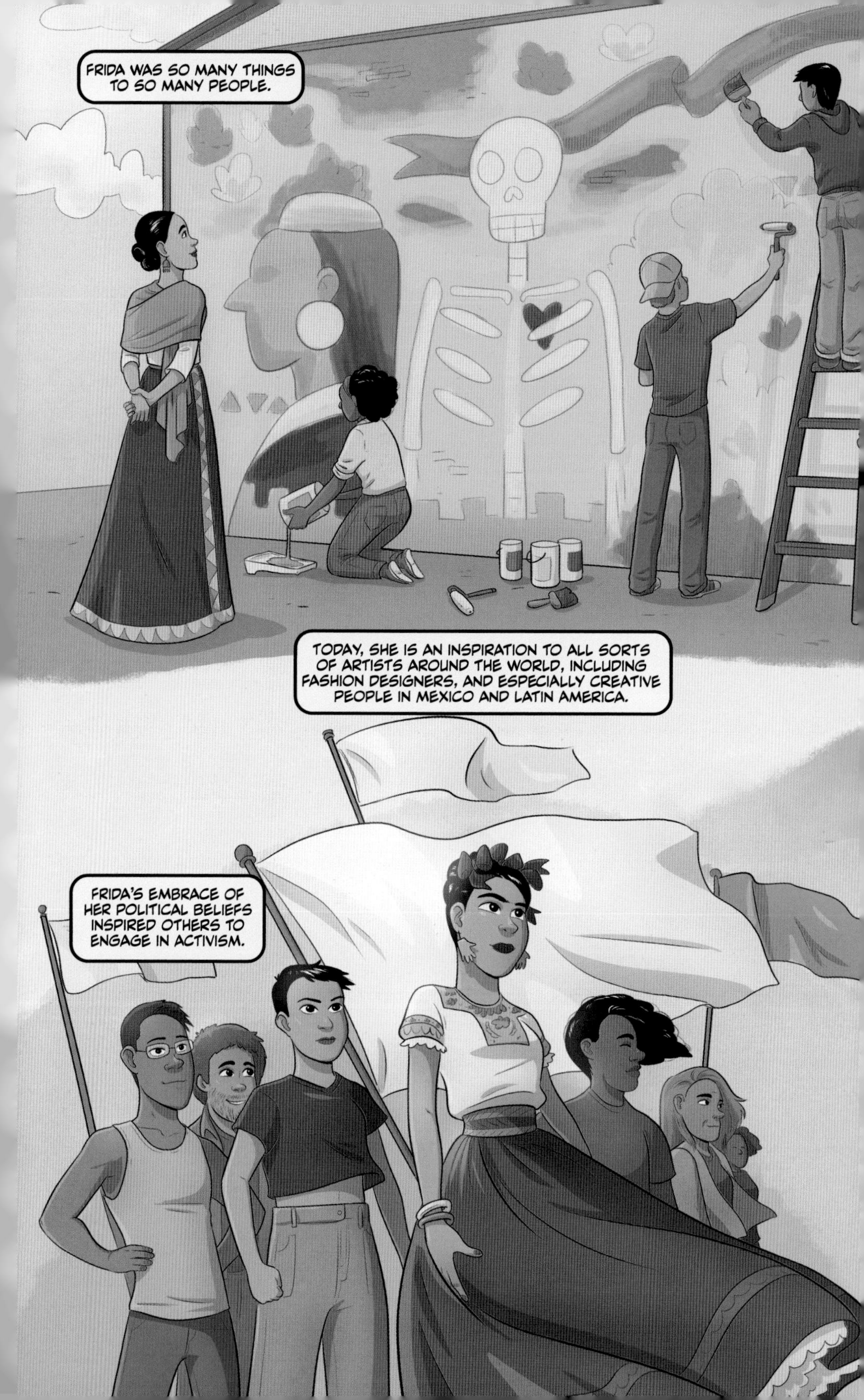
FRIDA WAS SO MANY THINGS TO SO MANY PEOPLE.
TODAY, SHE IS AN INSPIRATION TO ALL SORTS OF ARTISTS AROUND THE WORLD, INCLUDING FASHION DESIGNERS, AND ESPECIALLY CREATIVE PEOPLE IN MEXICO AND LATIN AMERICA.
FRIDA'S EMBRACE OF HER POLITICAL BELIEFS INSPIRED OTHERS TO ENGAGE IN ACTIVISM.

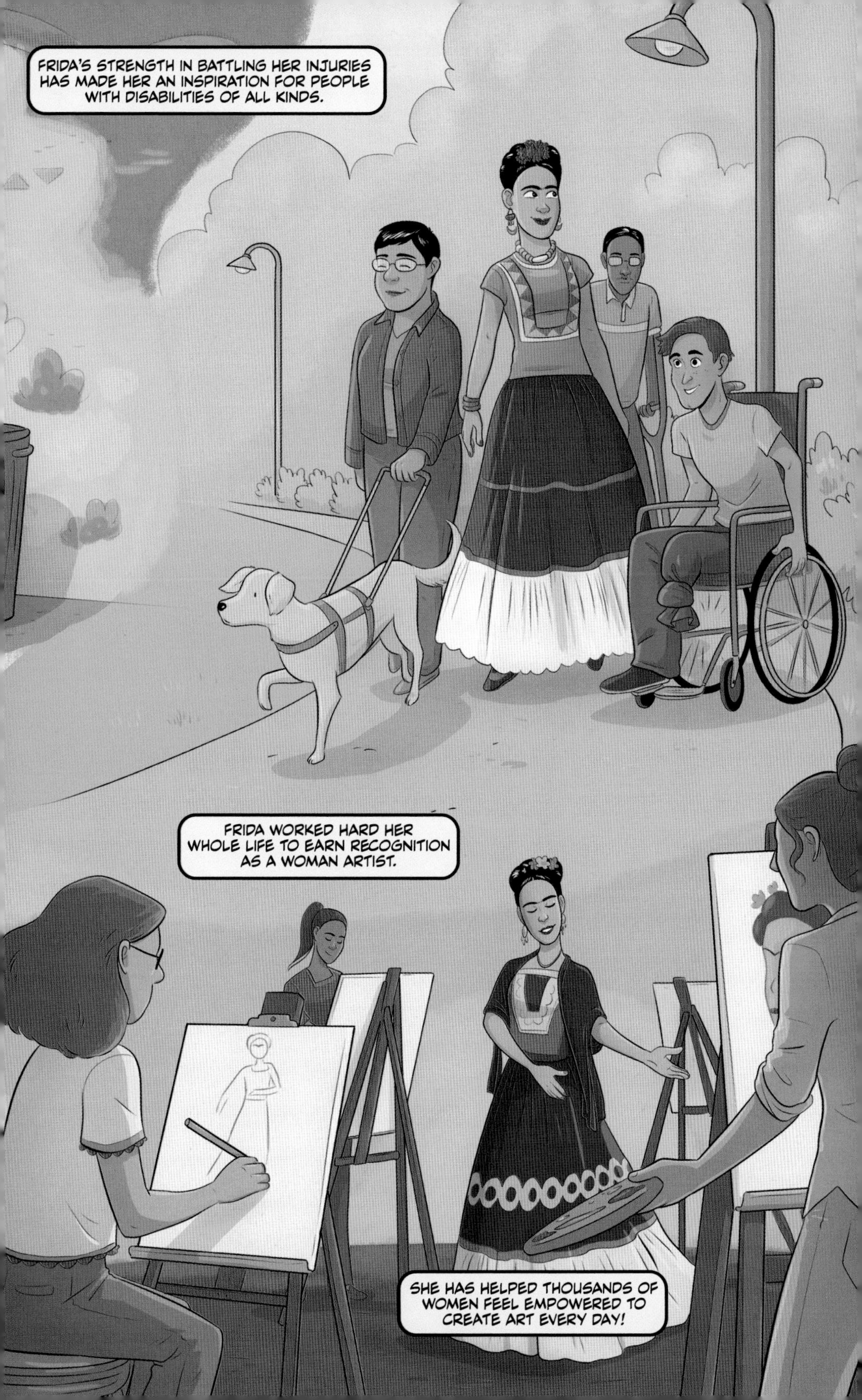
FRIDA'S STRENGTH IN BATTLING HER INJURIES HAS MADE HER AN INSPIRATION FOR PEOPLE WITH DISABILITIES OF ALL KINDS.
FRIDA WORKED HARD HER WHOLE LIFE TO EARN RECOGNITION AS A WOMAN ARTIST.
SHE HAS HELPED THOUSANDS OF WOMEN FEEL EMPOWERED TO CREATE ART EVERY DAY!

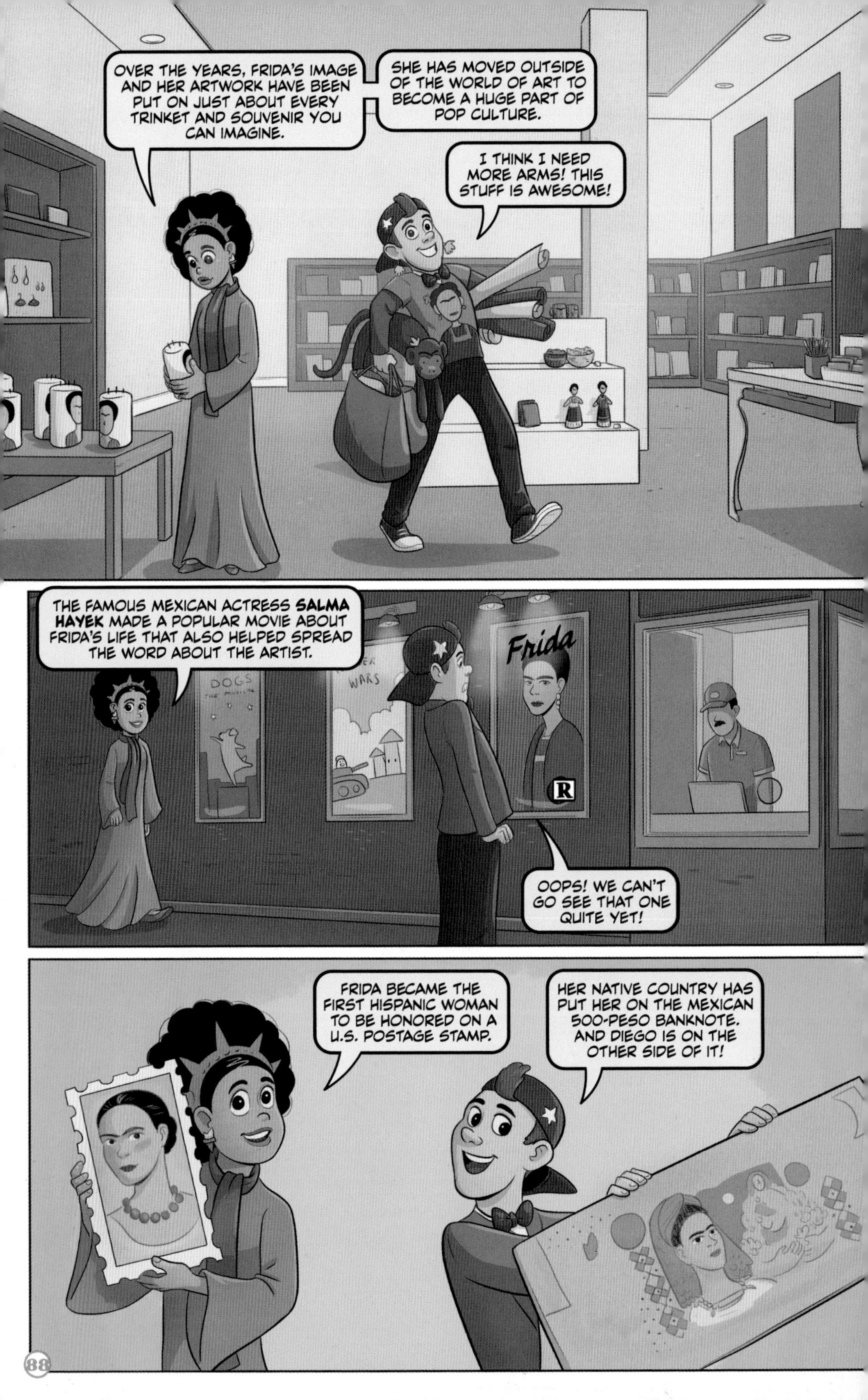
OVER THE YEARS, FRIDA'S IMAGE AND HER ARTWORK HAVE BEEN PUT ON JUST ABOUT EVERY TRINKET AND SOUVENIR YOU CAN IMAGINE.
SHE HAS MOVED OUTSIDE OF THE WORLD OF ART TO BECOME A HUGE PART OF POP CULTURE.
I THINK I NEED MORE ARMS! THIS STUFF IS AWESOME!
THE FAMOUS MEXICAN ACTRESS **SALMA HAYEK** MADE A POPULAR MOVIE ABOUT FRIDA'S LIFE THAT ALSO HELPED SPREAD THE WORD ABOUT THE ARTIST.
DOGS
WARS
Frida
R
OOPS! WE CAN'T GO SEE THAT ONE QUITE YET!
FRIDA BECAME THE FIRST HISPANIC WOMAN TO BE HONORED ON A U.S. POSTAGE STAMP.
HER NATIVE COUNTRY HAS PUT HER ON THE MEXICAN 500-PESO BANKNOTE. AND DIEGO IS ON THE OTHER SIDE OF IT!

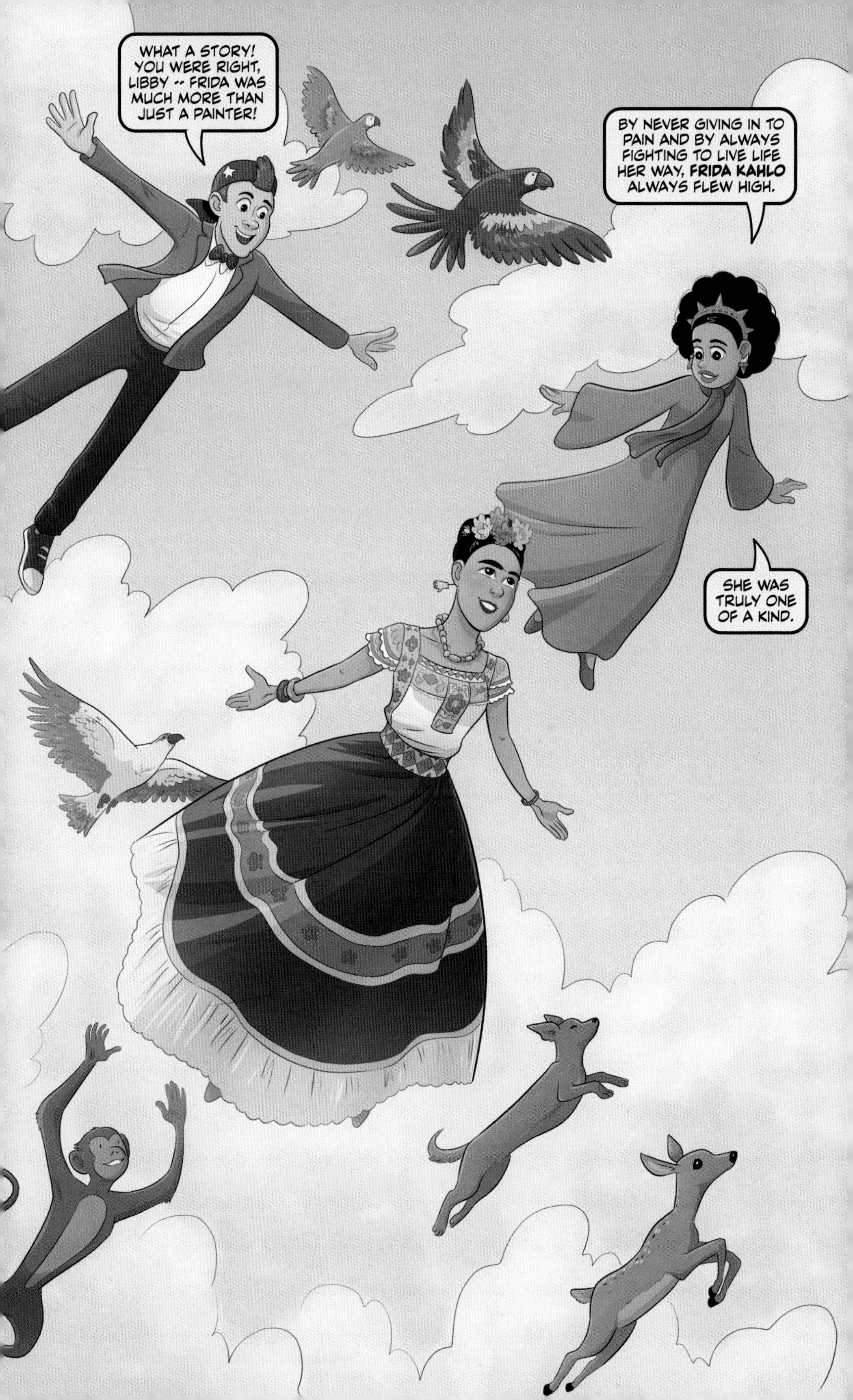
WHAT A STORY! YOU WERE RIGHT, LIBBY -- FRIDA WAS MUCH MORE THAN JUST A PAINTER!
BY NEVER GIVING IN TO PAIN AND BY ALWAYS FIGHTING TO LIVE LIFE HER WAY, **FRIDA KAHLO** ALWAYS FLEW HIGH.
SHE WAS TRULY ONE OF A KIND.

OTHER IMPORTANT FEMALE ARTISTS

RUTH ASAWA (1926-2013) created intricate sculptures using wire; they often were meant to hang and move. Her work was featured on a set of U.S. postage stamps in 2020.

LOUISE BOURGEOIS (1911-2010) was born in Paris, but lived most of her life in America. She used sculpture, painting, and printmaking to create abstract forms and designs.

MARY CASSATT (1844-1926) was part of the Impressionist movement. An American, she lived and worked in France alongside other well-known masters.

JUDY CHICAGO (1939-) creates what are called installations, which can be as big as rooms and include sculpture and found objects.

GEORGIA O'KEEFE (1887-1986) became known for her paintings of the American southwest and of beautiful flowers such as irises.

Photo collages with large, thought-provoking captions have made the work of American **BARBARA KRUGER (1945-)** recognizable around the art world.

Action and bright color are part of the work of **FAITH RINGGOLD (1930-)**, who creates tapestries, quilts, and fabric sculpture.

The sculptor **AUGUSTA SAVAGE (1892-1962)** was part of the Harlem Renaissance and made large works that often showed Black people; she also worked to create opportunities for other Black artists.

KARA WALKER (1969-) uses cut paper and silhouettes and shapes that can seem quite pleasant, but often reveal deeper and darker themes.

FRIDA KAHLO TIMELINE

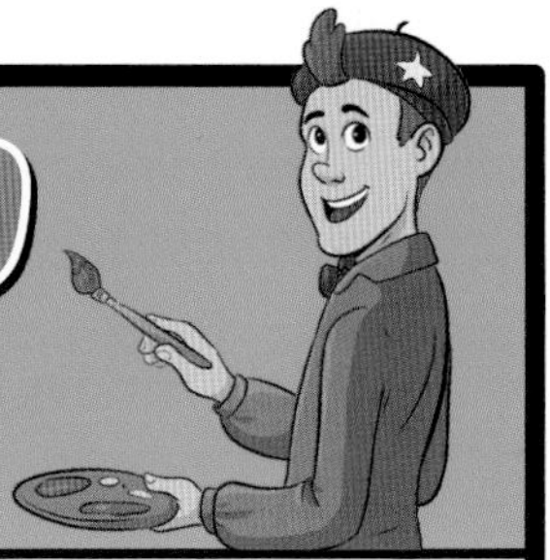

1907 Magdalena Carmen Frida Kahlo y Calderón is born on July 6 in Coyocoán, a suburb of Mexico City.

1913 Frida gets sick with polio.

1922 Frida is accepted at the important National Preparatory High School, one of only 35 girls in a class of 2,000.

1925 A terrible accident in which her bus collided with a trolley leaves Frida with terrible injuries that will affect her for the rest of her life.

1928 Frida joins the Mexican Communist Party, starting a lifetime of commitment to that cause.

1929 Frida marries famous artist Diego Rivera, whom she has known off and on since 1922.

1930-1933 Frida and Diego work and live in San Francisco, Detroit, and New York City.

1938 The Julien Levy Gallery in New York City gives Frida and her paintings her first solo show.

1939 Frida visits France; later in the year, she divorces Diego.

1940 Frida and Diego get married again (with conditions!).

1943 Frida becomes a teacher at a new art school in Mexico City.

1953 For the first time, Frida gets a major solo show in her home city; she is so sick that she has to attend the opening in her four-poster bed!

1954 Frida passes away at the age of 47.

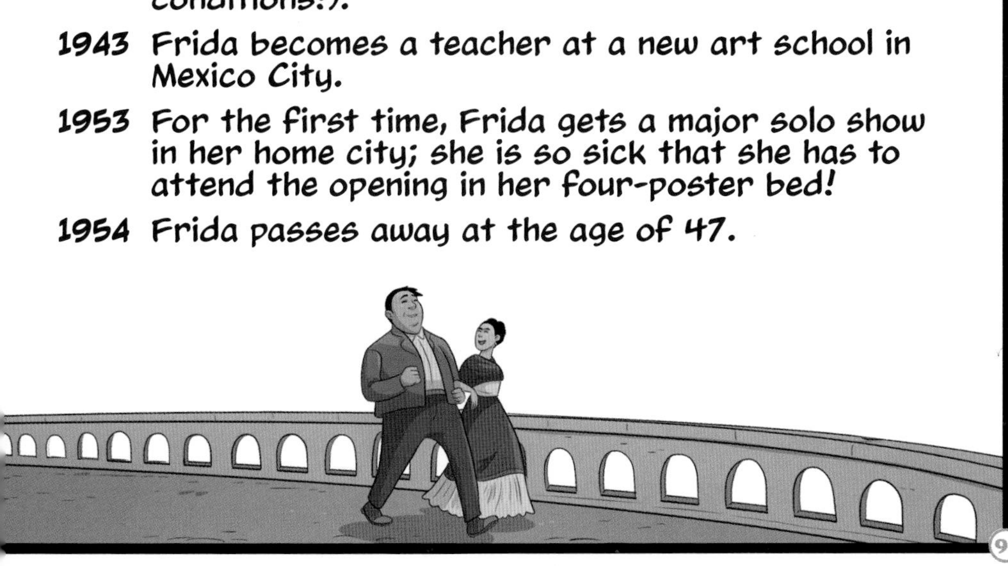

AMPUTATE: Remove by surgery.

CONTEMPORARY: In the art world, the period of the present.

FINANCIAL: Having to do with money and the economy.

GRINGOS: A not-very-nice Spanish-language nickname for white people.

ICON: An important person with lasting influence.

INDIGENOUS: Native to a place.

POLIO: A disease of the spinal cord caused by a virus.

REPUGNANT: Something very unpleasant or awful.

TREASON: Working to harm your own country.

SPANISH TO ENGLISH

BUENOS DIAS: good morning
¡CARAMBA!: an exclamation that means, essentially, "Yikes!"
CASA AZUL: Blue House
CEPILLOS: brushes
¡ESTO EL MUY DISTINGUIDO PINTOR!: You are a very distinguished painter!
LO SIENTO: I'm sorry
MAGNIFICO: great, magnificent
MI AMIGA/MI AMIGO: my friend (female/male)
MI HIJA: my daughter (also shortened to "mija")
MUCHO GUSTO: my pleasure (a traditional greeting)
MUY BONITA: very beautiful
PATEARME: kick me
PINTURAS: paints
POR FAVOR: please
QUESO: cheese
SEÑOR: Mr.
SEÑORA: Mrs.
SEÑORITA: Miss
SÍ: yes

BONUS! GERMAN WORDS!
ACH DU LIEBER: "OH MY GOSH!"
GUTEN TAG: GOOD MORNING
LIEBCHEN: SWEETHEART

FIND OUT MORE

BOOKS

Fabiny, Sarah. *Who Was Frida Kahlo?* Who Was series. New York: Penguin Workshop, 2013.

Herrera, Hayden. *Frida: A Biography of Frida Kahlo.* New York: Harper Perennial, 1983.

Reef, Catherine. *Frida & Diego: Art, Love, Life.* New York: Clarion Books, 2014.

Wilcox, Claire. *Frida Kahlo: Making Herself Up.* London: Victoria & Albert Museum, 2018.

WEBSITES

Museo Frida Kahlo (The Blue House)
https://www.museofridakahlo.org.mx/en/the-blue-house/

VIDEOS

The Life and Times of Frida Kahlo. New York: PBS, 2005.

SHOW ME HISTORY!

COLLECT EVERY BOOK IN THE SERIES AND FIND THE STORY IN HISTORY!

ABRAHAM LINCOLN
DEFENDER OF THE UNION!

ALBERT EINSTEIN
GENIUS OF SPACE AND TIME!

ALEXANDER HAMILTON
THE FIGHTING FOUNDING FATHER!

AMELIA EARHART
PIONEER OF THE SKY!

ANNE FRANK
WITNESS TO HISTORY!

BABE RUTH
BASEBALL'S ALL-TIME BEST!

BENJAMIN FRANKLIN
INVENTOR OF THE NATION!

FRIDA KAHLO
THE REVOLUTIONARY PAINTER!

GANDHI
THE PEACEFUL PROTESTER!

GEORGE WASHINGTON
SOLDIER AND STATESMAN!

HARRIET TUBMAN
FIGHTER FOR FREEDOM!

HELEN KELLER
INSPIRATION TO EVERYONE!

JESUS
MESSENGER OF PEACE!

MARTIN LUTHER KING JR.
VOICE FOR EQUALITY!

MUHAMMAD ALI
THE GREATEST OF ALL TIME!

NEIL ARMSTRONG
FIRST MAN ON THE MOON!

SACAGAWEA
COURAGEOUS TRAILBLAZER!

SUSAN B. ANTHONY
CHAMPION FOR VOTING RIGHTS!

WALT DISNEY
THE MAGICAL INNOVATOR!

PARENTS AND TEACHERS: VISIT OUR WEBSITE FOR MORE *SHOW ME HISTORY!* FUN...

SHOWMEHISTORY.COM

... WHERE YOU CAN LEARN MORE ABOUT THE AUTHORS, SIGN UP FOR OUR EMAIL NEWSLETTER, AND DOWNLOAD OUR READING GUIDES!

ALSO FOLLOW US ON *SOCIAL MEDIA!*

 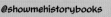

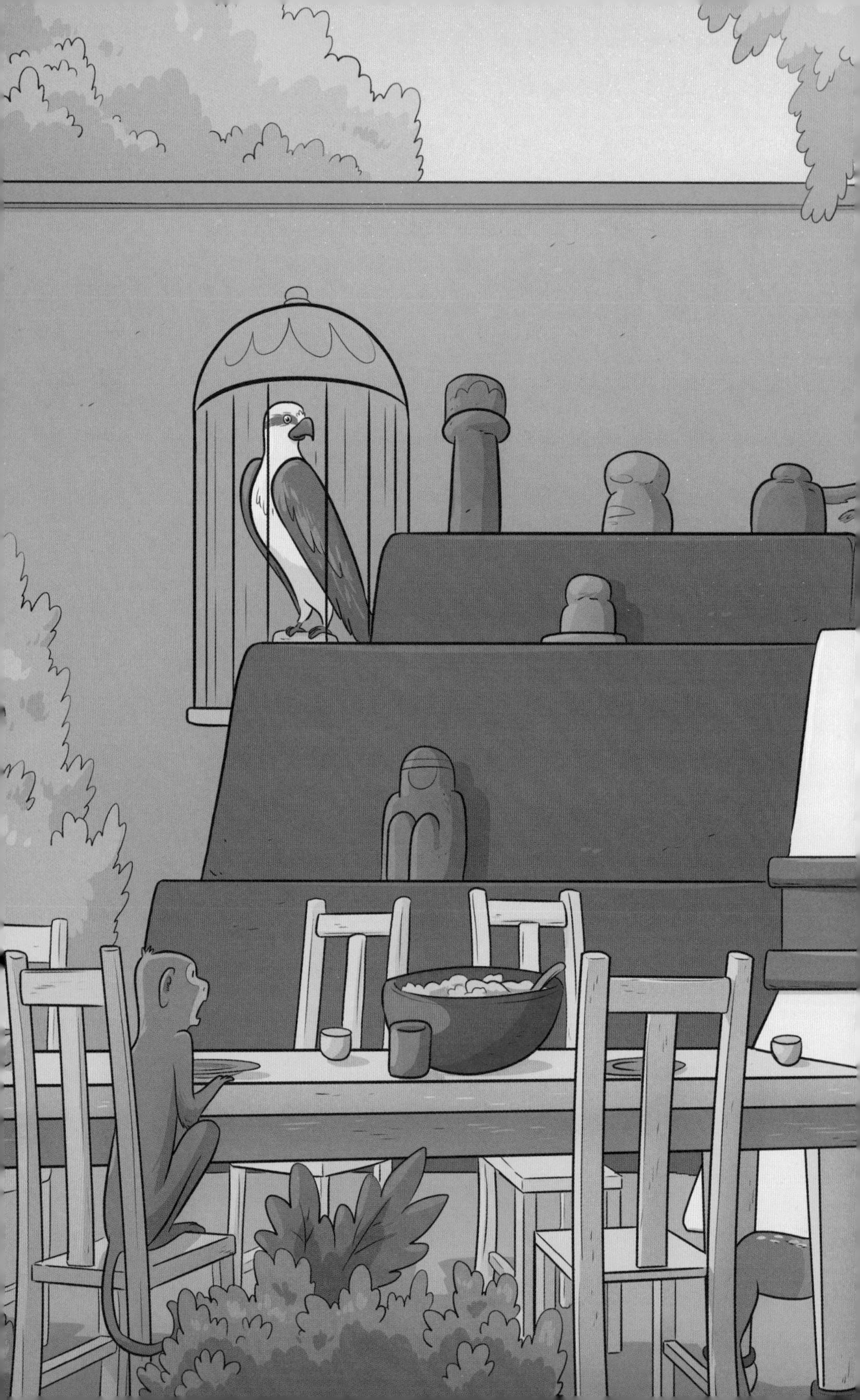